P9-BZK-493

Praise for *John Lennon vs. The USA*

"A fascinating book about an historic case by the great lawyer who won it. This compelling account of the John Lennon case shows why Leon and Michael Wildes are my go-to guys when it comes to immigration law."

> —Alan Dershowitz, Harvard law professor
> and author of *Taking the Stand: My Life
> in the Law*

John Lennon vs. The USA is a great read! I appreciate Leon Wildes and his son Michael Wildes from when they handled my friend John Lennon's green card, right up to Michael's handling of my very own visa. This wonderful book tells the story and their legend as champions of international immigration."

> —Pelé, soccer legend/icon

John Lennon vs. The USA is a must-read for fans of pop culture, history buffs, and anyone who cares at all about immigration and human rights. Leon and his son Michael Wildes are great lawyers. Love the history and their advice."

> —Boy George, musician/performer

"Leon Wildes and the Lennon case are legendary. Perhaps as important is that today, many years later, Leon and his son Michael Wildes are still the 'best' immigration lawyers in the United States. Period!"

> —Ben Brafman, criminal defense lawyer

JOHN LENNON vs. THE USA

JOHN LENNON vs. THE USA

The Inside Story of the Most Bitterly Contested and
Influential Deportation Case in United States History

LEON WILDES

FOREWORD BY MICHAEL WILDES

Cover design by Andrew Alcala/ABA Publishing.
Interior design by Betsy Kulak/ABA Publishing.

The materials contained herein represent the opinions of the authors and/or the editors, and should not be construed to be the views or opinions of the law firms or companies with whom such persons are in partnership with, associated with, or employed by, nor of the American Bar Association unless adopted pursuant to the bylaws of the Association.

Printed in the United States of America.

20 19 18 17 16   5 4 3 2 1

Library of Congress Cataloging-in-Publication Data

Names: Wildes, Leon, author.
Title: John Lennon vs. the U.S.A. : the inside story of the most bitterly contested
    and influential deportation case in United States history / Leon Wildes.
Description: Chicago : American Bar Assocociation, 2016. | Includes index.
Identifiers: LCCN 2016019623 (print) | LCCN 2016019716 (ebook) |
    ISBN 9781634253864 (casebound : alk. paper) | ISBN 9781634253871 ()
Subjects: LCSH: Lennon, John, 1940-1980—Trials, litigation, etc. |
    Deportation—United States. | Emigration and immigration law—
    United States. | Aliens—United States.
Classification: LCC KF228.L47 W55 2016 (print) | LCC KF228.L47 (ebook) |
    DDC 342.7308/2—dc23
LC record available at https://lccn.loc.gov/2016019623

Discounts are available for books ordered in bulk. Special consideration is given to state bars, CLE programs, and other bar-related organizations. Inquire at Book Publishing, ABA Publishing, American Bar Association, 321 N. Clark Street, Chicago, Illinois 60654-7598.

www.ShopABA.org

In memory of John Lennon and
my late wife Ruth Wildes.

Those who cannot remember the past are condemned to repeat it.

—George Santayana

Contents

Foreword

Michael Wildes

"You can have your father back now." I remember former Beatle John Lennon's warm words at the final immigration hearing as if it was yesterday. It was my brother Mark's ninth birthday, and the music legend was sporting a smile, a new suit and a fresh green card grasped in his hand after a long, bravely fought legal battle. The surreal scene remains etched in my mind. Even as a twelve-year-old boy, I knew at this moment that John Lennon was the focus of what seemed like the entire world's attention as we stood outside the Immigration and Naturalization Service's (INS) Manhattan office. Years later, looking back, I would realize that childhood perception was true. Cameras and eyes were all focused on Lennon, his wife Yoko Ono, and my father, Leon Wildes, Lennon's immigration attorney—the man I literally, both then and now, as a grown man and his law partner, look up to for his brilliance, fairness, temperament, and strength.

Because their notoriety limited the Lennons' ability to move with ease, my father would normally meet with them at their home in the Dakota after regular practice hours. But years before the Lennons came into our lives, I was a son who adored his father and clamored to spend time with him at his office at 515 Madison Avenue in Manhattan, the same place in which our practice continues today.

After the Sabbath was over, I often joined my father on a Sunday morning at his office just to cut scrap paper and eat sandwiches prepared and wrapped in tin foil by my mother at the waterfall park half a block away. It's the same lunch spot that my children like to frequent when they visit me at the office decades later. When I was a boy, my father would give me a few law books for my bookshelf at home. Later I would realize those books were my father's way of introducing me to the practice of immigration law by choice, his subtle way of strengthening the foundation of the firm.

To date, my father remains the most remarkable man I have ever known. He is my biggest source of inspiration: my role model, teacher, mentor, and, yes, my hero. Those feelings for my father encouraged me to want to follow him into his profession. Since he was a lawyer, I knew I would become a lawyer too. It was that simple. Wherever my father was, that's where I wanted to be. And thanks to God's grace, I have been able to work by my father's side for my entire professional career.

Leon Wildes was born in 1933 and raised in a small coal-mining town in Pennsylvania. Olyphant had a population of no more than 10,000 in its heyday, mainly Polish and Ukrainian immigrants and their families. My father, the only Jew in his class, was raised in a Sabbath-observant home. His father, Harry Wildes, was a merchant who prided himself on also being a peddler, taking his wares door-to-door in the more remote, even smaller towns that surrounded Olyphant. He was not afraid of hard work. Regaled as "Harry the Honest Jew," my grandfather walked miles to return a customer's change on occasion.

Harry was an "American by choice," comparing himself to others who were born in this country and were "Americans by chance." He cherished his adopted country and inculcated all that it stood for in his home. In a world where Franklin D. Roosevelt was a virtual deity, and the United States government could do no wrong, my father worked in the family dry goods store under a portrait of FDR, which was held in a place of honor. Every day for twelve years in Olyphant's public schools, my father took to heart his pledge of allegiance to the flag that stood for his family values as well as his country's principles.

Harry saw a bright future for his two sons, encouraging my father to explore better opportunities. Harry believed in the great American adventure and its system of justice. He urged his older son, Jerome, to attend medical school and my father to become a lawyer when Leon was considering the rabbinate. After completing a sociology degree at Yeshiva University, my father was honored with a scholarship to attend New York University Law School. Upon completion of an LL.M degree, he accepted employment with HIAS, the Hebrew Immigrant Aid Society. He knew the organization not only helped people to migrate, but also taught these newcomers the American way.

Immigration law was not a popular field in the 1960s and 1970s for new lawyers to go into, and my father became one of the early pioneers of what has now become a robust and very important field of law in our nation. Dad penned many early scholarly works on immigration, refugee, and nationality law issues. When he managed to save enough funds to start his own law office, the articles he authored resulted in a good number of referrals from attorneys who gave him their "impossible cases." Assisting a person to regularize his or her immigration status and get started on life in a new country was—and remains—his most rewarding task.

Through the years, Dad developed an extraordinary reputation for diligent work and successful outcomes for his clients. In 1970 he was elected national president of the American Immigration Lawyers Association, the national bar association in our field. In fact, it was shortly after completing his term in office that he got the call to consult with John Lennon and Yoko Ono about their immigration problem.

In 1980, he happily accepted the invitation of Yeshiva University's Benjamin N. Cardozo School of Law to lecture on immigration law, before there was even a textbook on the subject, a position he held for thirty-three years. It was in his class that I met my wife, Amy. I now have taught that class for five years, and the two eldest of my four children, Raquel and Joshua, are enrolled to attend Cardozo Law next semester.

To understand who my father is, and why I have always held him in such high regard, you have to understand his core beliefs, integrity, and strong work ethic. I remember my father's eulogy at Harry's funeral. He compared my *zeidi* (grandfather) to a compass that capably steered millions of tonnage on a ship in a stated direction.

My father ingrained in me two values through my childhood and young adult life: scholarship and ethics. Scholarship meant keeping up-to-date with the most current knowledge available in your career field. More important was abiding by a proper code of ethics. Both my parents were genuinely observant Jews who taught their children the importance of good *midos*—character traits. My father studied Torah in college and lived the notion of *tikkun olam*, literally "fixing the world." Honesty, integrity, transparency, responsibility, and kindness were central to his ethical code. It is this very moral compass Dad spoke of at his father's funeral.

These values were particularly important as he stood by my side in the practice of law and even in politics when I served as a city councilman and mayor in the sometimes-murky world of New Jersey politics. There was no greater tool as we worked together on cases for high-profile clients and for private individuals and families, who sometimes couldn't afford to pay us for our time and efforts. Today my brother, now a rabbi and founder of the Manhattan Jewish Experience, and I pay it forward by imbuing these values in our children, students, and mentees.

Dad's collegiality and respect earned its way into the government's halls. His reputation was built by taking courageous, yet credible, positions for our clients. When I served as a special assistant US attorney (1989-1993, EDNY), colleagues and judges followed the firm's latest cases and Dad's efforts to see that America remained a safe haven for refugees and those in jeopardy. Keeping the government on track was often accomplished by first earning their trust.

A steady "hand at the helm" in a world deemed by many to be upside-down is just as important to a client. Dad always took my brother's and my calls, no matter who he was with or what he was doing. Protocol would have the receptionist call out "Ruth in a booth" when our mother would call in from an outside telephone booth. When my father was on the telephone, you couldn't tell if he was speaking with one of the world's most famous rock stars or a housekeeper. Each client was equally the focus of his attention, and was treated with dignity and respect in the same manner.

The Sabbath was sacrosanct time with his family. Even John Lennon would call our home at its conclusion, respectfully asking if "it was okay" to talk to our father. When the FBI started recording his conversations, John would often disguise his voice as that of a woman. My father would make life difficult for those listening to his telephone conversations by summarizing the Lennon case's developments in Yiddish when he spoke to Harry (with the hope that the FBI would then have to hire a Yiddish speaking translator to boot).

Family was a value that we share with the Lennons. My mother, Ruth, and Yoko were dear friends. Over the years, Yoko confided that she stayed the course of the case in great measure due to the friendship they developed. No birthday would pass, nor a single holiday, without best wishes or gifts being exchanged. Yoko and Sean, John and Yoko's son, bought us a beautiful silver cup for our Sabbath table with a personal note inscribed to us when our first child, Raquel, was born.

Friendships were forged in my father's treatment of John Lennon. He would show up early to pick up his famous clients before hearings, and would help John choose the right suit. The clothing advice went full circle when my father bought his first pair of "dungarees" (as he still calls them), and insisted that my brother and I take piano lessons. On a recent breakfast excursion to the Dakota, my father smiled with pride when he looked at the white piano in the corner. He remembered fondly sitting by that very piano with John playing out a tune he too was trying to master. John's creative wit and humor, coupled with Yoko's insight into the case, built a strong team. Our families reveled in our professional and personal triumphs, and faced challenges with a deep personal commitment and concern. I recall John apologizing to me on the telephone that he couldn't attend my Bar Mitzvah celebration because Sean had an "earache."

John Lennon and Yoko Ono were remarkable people. They were immediately understanding and accepting of who my father was. For instance, my father was not familiar with popular music of the era and didn't know who John was when they first met, something that would have put off a more ego-driven public figure. There was not an ounce of hubris to be found in John or Yoko. When John told my Dad he had been convicted for possession of cannabis resin (hashish) in England, my Dad asked whether cannabis resin was marijuana. "Oh no," John replied, "it's much better."

John's murder in 1980 had a profound effect on our family. My parents were in Aruba at the time, and I'll never forget the personal loss and sadness that permeated our household. The week before he was killed John and Yoko sent us a beautiful basket of kosher fish and an elegantly handwritten card wishing us well in the new decade. Today, we maintain Yoko's love and we are privileged to work on matters graciously referred through her. When my mother Ruth Wildes passed away in 1995, Yoko immediately sent condolences and flowers. In the many years that followed, Yoko has always gracefully honored her memory and friendship.

In November 2014, my father and I appeared on MSNBC's Lawrence O'Donnell's "The Last Word." O'Donnell and scores of others credited President Barak Obama's Deferred Action proposal on the scholarship and jurisprudence derived from the John Lennon immigration case. As a result, the Department of Homeland Security (which replaced the INS) makes use of its prosecutorial discretion today to consider deferred action cases. It recognizes that like all law enforcement agencies, it has finite resources and it is not possible to investigate and prosecute every immigration violation. In its efforts to use its limited resources wisely, it is able to benefit deserving individuals. Lennon's contribution to the development of this program of prosecutorial discretion should be recognized as a legacy of immense value that he bequeathed to his adopted homeland.

My father always felt that his career pretty well fit the "big dream of an all-American success story for a kid from Olyphant." With this case, though, he found himself defending not just John and Yoko's personal dreams, but the foundation of the American dream itself. Clients today still ask about the case and how my father admirably strategized and managed to keep John in the United States despite the best efforts of the Nixon administration to get him out. I'm sure my children will pass down the same story to their own children as only Zeidi Harry from Olyphant would envision that his meaningful legacy be told. In the interim I work daily to further my father's legacy, as my children will after me.

Michael Wildes
New York City, New York
June 2016

Leon and Michael Wildes

Acknowledgments

We would like to thank the American Bar Association for recognizing the message this story holds for those attending law school or contemplating a career in the law. Indeed, one man can change the world through one case. We would like to thank our law partner Steven Weinberg and the staff of Wildes & Weinberg, P.C. whose talent and stewardship have helped not only with this case but has insured the safety and approval of thousands of immigration matters, at our offices in New York City, New Jersey, Miami, and Los Angeles (see www.wildeslaw.com). A special note of thanks is extended to the families of two dear friends who passed away, Vincent Schiano, the INS's lead prosecutor, and former New York City mayor Ed Koch for their thoughtful support and perspective.

We also express our heartfelt appreciation to Harvard law professor Alan Dershowitz for his steadfast friendship and scholarship. Professor Dershowitz prepared a masterful brief and legal analysis of the criminal law issues in the Lennon case. We gratefully acknowledge our dear friend Nathan Lewin, a legal scholar, for his critical guidance on the appellate work. I thank them and others who fought to safeguard the constitutional underpinnings of our immigration system.

This work was created by my father over the last four decades. He would venture away with a portable dictaphone and spend his vacations adding new chapters. No doubt our mother, Ruth Wildes, though sorely missed, added her own touch to this journey and would be proud of her eight grandchildren and the love and admiration they have for their grandfather.

Finally, we would like to thank Yoko Ono Lennon for her kindness in reading the book and authorizing its publication. Thank you to Bob Gruen for his extraordinary photographic talents; our agent, John Willig; and Jon Malysiak at Ankerwycke Books, who worked faithfully to see that this important story was told.

Thousands of fans signed petitions in the 1970s to keep John Lennon on American soil. As we face new challenges let us be reminded of his dedication to our nation and the love and peace he sought for us all.

Compiled by Michael Wildes

Planning the book with New York City's late great mayor Ed Koch over dinner in New York City.

Introduction

With the publication of this book, I at last make good on a promise nearly forty years old. Back in the 1970s, when I was exhausting my best efforts but not making much headway against the Nixon administration's attempts to kick John Lennon out of this country, I promised John that I would share my research and data so that others, less financially able to litigate, might have a better chance of prevailing in court. That much I've succeeded in doing, in a series of five law review articles and innumerable telephone conversations discussing cases with other immigration lawyers.

But I was never able to follow up on the other project that John urged on me at the end of the case—that I write a history of what we went through, how we managed to fight a government hell-bent on deporting John and his wife, Yoko. John suggested it, and Yoko said it would be an important historical document. It's not that I ignored their requests—perhaps I put too much work into it, as decades' worth of abortive attempts to tell the tale have resulted in brief essays on almost every facet of the case. So what led me at last to clean up my act—not to mention all those literary fragments—and create this account?

Maybe it's because, as a working immigration lawyer, I find that the current controversy in my field directly relates to John Lennon's battle against deportation all those years ago.

In 1972, I found myself fighting a long and bitter campaign whose outcome continues to affect the practice of immigration law even in the present. And just as the 1970s marked a watershed for this nation of ours, the years I spent on the Lennon case profoundly altered my view of the law—and of our government.

Today people are used to the most bitter partisan politics and the easy resort to violent imagery and even physical brutality. That's the dark legacy of the 1960s. For most people who came of age when Dwight Eisenhower was president, the late sixties and early seventies were a profoundly disturbing time. Growing up in the small town of Olyphant, Pennsylvania, the world was as black and white as the hats on the cowboys in the western movies I loved to watch. The good guys were the G-men—the government men. But the sixties shook those simple views. People were killed because of the beliefs they espoused—John F. Kennedy, his brother Bobby, Martin Luther King. Destructive riots broke out in American cities, and a popular movement emerged, not only willing to challenge government policies and the people in power, but more and more willing to confront them physically.

By the time Richard Nixon squeaked into office, I can appreciate why he and his circle had an almost apocalyptic view of the world. I can appreciate that, but I can't and won't approve of what he did, because the Nixon world-view intersected with the high point of what historian Arthur Schlesinger called the "Imperial Presidency."

Ever since Franklin D. Roosevelt was elected, the size and power of the executive branch of our government expanded tremendously. Under Richard M. Nixon, however, this power began to be abused for minor political or personal reasons. A case in point comes from a set of the infamous White House tapes finally released in 1997. Among other things, they reveal Richard Nixon ordering Attorney General John Mitchell to stage a raid on the offices of the *Los Angeles Times* in search of illegal aliens. The date was October 7, 1971.

The reason for such high-level action? On the previous day, the newspaper ran a story about the INS arresting thirty-six suspected illegals working for Nixon's nominee for US treasurer. In retaliation, the president specifically ordered his attorney general and his secretary of the treasury to investigate and harass the family who owned the *Times*.

Nixon didn't care about legality or government administration, as he made clear on tape in the crudest possible way: "The fellow out there in the Immigration Service. . . . is a kike by the name of Rosenberg. He is to be out. Transfer him to some other place out of Los Angeles. I don't give a goddamn what the story is. There is one thing that I want done, and I do not want any argument about it. I want you to direct the most trusted person you have in the Immigration Service that they are to look over all of the activities of the *Los Angeles Times*. And they are to send their team in to see whether they are violating the wetback thing." He continued, "Now let me explain, 'cause as a Californian I know. Everybody in California hires them."

Considering Nixon's attitudes on inconvenient laws and aliens, you can easily imagine the rage he felt at a non-citizen in this country impudently speaking out against Nixon's handling of the war in Vietnam, against Nixon's drug policies—against his very presidency, suggesting that people "Dump Nixon." These were John Lennon's "crimes," especially threatening because Lennon enjoyed huge popularity with young people between the ages of eighteen and twenty-one . . . people who had recently gotten the vote. And, just as in the case of the attack on the *Los Angeles Times*, in 1972 Nixon's administration set out to use the INS to deal with a political enemy.

The sad fact of the matter, however, is simple. When the government proceeded against John, they had no case, and despite later claims to the contrary, the deportation proceedings against the Lennons were anything but routine. John and Yoko were in the United States in a totally legal status. While John had a British marijuana conviction, he had a complete waiver that allowed him to visit the United States, having given full disclosure of his legal trouble.

Moreover, the purpose that brought John and Yoko to this country was perhaps one of the strongest reasons imaginable, namely, to seek the custody of Yoko's child, Kyoko, by a prior marriage. In many years of immigration practice, I never heard so strong a reason for a proper visit to the United States.

So why were they suddenly threatened with deportation? It was not the result of any violation of law nor any legal misstep committed by John or Yoko. After granting a routine prolongation of their permission to visit and with no warning, the government sent a notice canceling the time already given and scheduling them to appear in deportation proceedings. In essence, the government set up the Lennons for deportability as "overstays" by revoking the stay it had already permitted them.

From that point on, the Nixon administration made life intolerable for John Lennon and Yoko Ono. I had been practicing immigration law and representing aliens in deportation proceedings for fifteen years before the Lennons retained me, and I had never seen the government so determined to remove anyone from the United States. Every effort I made was thwarted in a relentless process to deport them as quickly as possible.

While I fought the INS bureaucracy on the deportation, the government failed to produce the files and the replies that I had requested in trying to make a case. At the same time, officials attempted to scuttle any consideration of the Lennons' applications for residence. In fact, those applications might never have seen the light of day, except for my filing a federal lawsuit demanding their adjudication.

The government opposed every request for any legally available benefit that I attempted for my clients, as though I was representing international criminals or terrorists. I not only had to defend them in deportation court but also had to initiate a series of suits in federal court, including the first filing under the Freedom of Information Act in a deportation case, before I could finally get to the bottom of what was going on.

What I discovered shook me to the core, because I found that my case, derided by many as a mere celebrity deportation, involved one of the most vital issues in our constitutional democracy. Our constitution commits vast power to the president and his executive branch of government, but it also attempts to curb this power with a system of checks and balances. Occasionally, however, a bold administration can circumvent these limits on its power and actually use the agencies of government as instruments to punish its political opponents. This is what happened in Watergate. The Nixon White House took great pride in "getting" its "enemies" through improper use of US government agencies, such as IRS tax audits and FBI investigations.

The sole reason for deporting the Lennons was President Nixon's desire to remove John and Yoko from the country before the 1972 election and a new, much younger electorate getting the vote. To ensure his grip on power, any "dirty tricks," including the abusive misuse of the immigration process, were acceptable.

History records the final result of all this abuse of power. President Nixon was forced to resign in 1974 rather than undergo an impeachment trial before the Senate. His attorney general, John Mitchell, who had been his law partner and the head of his reelection campaign, was indicted, convicted, and sentenced to jail for a string of illegal acts, as were a number of other co-conspirators. Like the operation of a self-cleaning stove, the governmental system cleansed itself of what Nixon's White House counsel, John Dean, referred to as a "cancer in the White House."

In the forty years since, the Watergate scandal has pretty much disappeared from the national consciousness, although we have made some progress since the early 1970s. Some important federal agencies are more difficult for a president to manipulate today than they were previously. Congressional oversight of executive power has been expanded. But the post-Watergate era has not brought a solution to many of our government's problems, such as the influence of money in politics and the ability of an administration to pervert the purpose of its agencies to follow its lead in the cause of "national security."

Unfortunately, what happened to Lennon would continue to afflict many other non-citizens in the United States who are unable to mount the defenses that Lennon was able to support, both with financial and human resources. The abuses of the immigration process that take place to this day are every bit as serious as those recounted in these pages.

In today's immigration atmosphere, accusing a non-citizen of being a security risk can still result in years of often hopeless efforts at defense. Non-citizens are now subjected to warrantless searches and seizures as much in violation of the Fourth Amendment as the attempted silencing of Lennon violated his First Amendment rights. And in the background, the government pursues an illegal policy of monitoring our telephone conversations without recourse to the court that was established to rule on such searches, holding non-citizens indefinitely without charge or trial, and actually torturing detainees if it is considered necessary.

Efforts to ameliorate these actions fall on deaf ears as Congress fails to enact reasonable legislation to benefit non-citizens. While the current president has managed to implement some hopeful, modest reforms, merely raising the topic of immigration seems more likely to result in political controversy and posturing. And beneath it all, like a snake in the grass, lies the uncomfortable, intractable fact— the immigration system is still as subject to abuse by any incumbent administration today as it was in 1972.

Now we face revelations of the Justice Department seizing phone records of reporters, an action that has actually been described as "Nixonian." The last thing this country needs is to go back to those days.

That is why this story needs to be told.

1

Battle Lines Forming

If we are to have respect for law in America, we must have laws that deserve respect.

—Richard M. Nixon, accepting the
1968 presidential nomination

On July 5, 1971, President Richard Nixon certified the Twenty-Sixth Amendment to the US Constitution, lowering the voting age to eighteen. The president expressed all sorts of misgivings but didn't mention his main objection—this new constituency threatened his reelection prospects in 1972.

Who could imagine that the emergence of the youth vote would lead to one of the strangest and most bitter, politically motivated government prosecutions in history—aimed at a figure who couldn't even vote in American elections? But the Nixon administration feared John Lennon—feared that he could galvanize the more than ten million new American voters under the age of twenty-one, so they set the machinery in motion to deport Lennon and his wife, Yoko Ono.

Nixon's concern about young voters was understandable. Supporters of the amendment had framed the argument bluntly. "Old enough to fight, old enough to vote." America was in the middle of the Vietnam War, and opposition to the conflict, especially from young people, kept growing louder. Antiwar protests rocked the 1968 Democratic National Convention in Chicago. Street fighting resulted in criminal convictions for Jerry Rubin, Bobby Seale, David Dellinger, Rennie Davis, Tom Hayden, Lee Weiner, and Abbie Hoffman—the infamous "Chicago Seven." After that debacle, Democratic candidate Hubert Humphrey never regained his footing as he campaigned against Nixon. That summer also saw the assassinations both of presidential candidate Bobby Kennedy and civil rights leader Martin Luther King, Jr. Riots in cities nationwide after King's death added to the feeling of national upheaval.

Nixon campaigned on the themes of law and order and claimed to have a "secret plan" to end the war. He carried the election, but by an extremely narrow margin. In the popular vote, he won by 500,000 votes—approximately one percent of the total votes cast. In three key electoral states, he won by only three percent of the vote—200,000 votes in California, 140,000 in Illinois, and 90,000 in Ohio. The effect of the youth vote on such thin majorities made for difficult political calculations, especially since Nixon's "secret plan" turned out to be a mere continuation of fighting in Vietnam.

College campuses became hotbeds of antiwar activism, with protests often leading to police overreactions. At Kent State University in Ohio, demonstrators were actually fired on by National Guard troops, resulting in deaths. On May 1, 1971, a May Day march took place in Washington, DC—the largest example of civil disobedience in American history. Demonstrators pressed the Nixon administration to stop the war, which at this point had cost billions of dollars and the lives of nearly 50,000 American troops. Vietnamese casualties had swelled to almost three million deaths.

Nixon faced further embarrassment with the disclosure of the Pentagon Papers, a series of CIA reports confirming that the war in Vietnam was simply not winnable. A group of secret operatives working for the president's reelection effort got the job of finding the leak—and the nickname of "plumbers."

On a more formal basis, the 1972 campaign became the responsibility of Nixon's former law partner, John Mitchell, who was also the attorney general. With an estimated cash slush fund of fifty million dollars and the services of the plumbers, not to mention the legal machinery of the US government, Mitchell and C.R.E.E.P. (the Committee to Reelect the President) could exert pressure in many directions.

John Lennon brought himself to the administration's attention in December of 1971, about a month before I met him, by participating in a rally and concert at the University of Michigan campus in Ann Arbor to support radical writer and musician John Sinclair. Sinclair at that point had served two years of a harsh ten-year prison sentence for selling two marijuana cigarettes to an undercover policeman. The sale charge had to be dropped because of apparent entrapment. But the possession charge had stood, even though it was based on the same evidence. A jury had convicted Sinclair, and Judge Colombo had passed a maximum sentence.

Publicized as "Ten for Two," the Free John Sinclair Concert culminated a week of rallies, bringing out countercultural figures like Allen Ginsberg, Jerry Rubin, Rennie Davis, and Bobby Seale, all vocal critics of the Nixon administration and the Vietnam War.

Jerry Rubin promised a series of rallies like the one for Sinclair, to culminate at the Republican convention in San Diego, all with the aim of defeating Nixon's attempt for another term. Dave Dellinger, also a "Chicago Seven" alumnus, spoke of a "people's convention at San Diego next summer."

Besides the political rhetoric, there were bands like Commander Cody and His Lost Planet Airmen, entertainers like Stevie Wonder and Phil Ochs . . . and John Lennon, making his first concert appearance in five years and his first performance since the Beatles had broken up. Fifteen thousand people were on hand, a packed house, as he and Yoko Ono appeared onstage around 3:00 A.M. Lennon had written a song, "John Sinclair," for the occasion. His song decried the outrageously severe sentence imposed by Judge Columbo for so minor an offense and demanded that Sinclair be set free.

If that wasn't clear enough, Lennon told the crowd, "We came here not only to help John and spotlight what is going on, but also to show and say to all of you that apathy is not it, and that we can do something. Oh, so flower power didn't work, so what, we start again!"

Within fifty-five hours after John and Yoko left the stage, a board of Michigan appellate judges released John Sinclair on bond. It was a recognition of reality. The Michigan House of Representatives had already passed a bill limiting the maximum sentence for possessing marijuana to ninety days.

But John Sinclair attributed his release to John and Yoko's appearance. So did Jerry Rubin, calling the release "an incredible tribute to the power of the people. . . . We won!" He also called for "two, three, four, many more Ann Arbors!"

However, the undercover FBI agents in the audience took a different message from all the speeches. As Rubin said from the concert stage, "Right now we can really unite music and revolutionary politics and really build the movement all across the country."

Perhaps the agents were correct to consider the matter serious. The 1968 demonstrations at the Chicago convention brought out about 20,000 people. The following year, 250,000 appeared for the Vietnam Moratorium in Washington, DC. And in the summer of 1969, 500,000 assembled for the rock concert in Woodstock. Richard Nixon and others in his administration might well worry about what a volatile mixture rock music and politics could become. And, unfortunately for him, John Lennon had been one of the first to present himself on a stage with people such as Jerry Rubin and others of the New Left movement.

The initial FBI response was a twenty-six-page memo on the events in Ann Arbor, the beginning of an inches-thick file on John Lennon. But the initial report became a "Letterhead Memorandum," a fairly significant document in the government's eyes, with copies forwarded to FBI field offices in New York, Boston, Chicago, Milwaukee, San Francisco, and Washington, DC—likely locations for similar rallies in the future.

The audience for these and other memoranda on the "New Left" reached the highest echelons. They were to and from the director of the FBI, J. Edgar Hoover himself.

Although none of the documents bears the signature of Richard Nixon himself, his chief of staff, H.R. Haldeman, was kept informed by Hoover of the progress of the FBI's campaign to "neutralize" Lennon.

At the same time, a Senate Subcommittee was getting a darker view of John Sinclair than perhaps John Lennon and Yoko Ono were aware of. Although most Americans believed that the Senate Judiciary Committee's Subcommittee to Investigate the Administration of the Internal Security Act and Other Internal Security Laws had ceased to exist after the Red Scare of the 1950s, these descendants of Joe McCarthy apparently survived and found a new purpose— delving into the "New Left" and its possibly subversive efforts against the Vietnam War and the government in general.

On March 16, 1971, a pair of officers from the Michigan State Police Intelligence Unit testified before an executive session of the subcommittee on their investigations into subversive activities as defined under Michigan state law. Detective Sergeant Clifford Murray and Detective Richard Shave described a variety of radical projects in the state, including people organizing illegal trips to communist Cuba.

One of the people they discussed in their testimony was John Sinclair. He had initially established a group called Trans-Love Energies, devoted to the creation, promotion, and distribution of creative arts, poetry, and music. The group created a commune, but grew increasingly more radical. Sinclair created a new group, the White Panther Party, emulating the Black Panthers. They distributed radical literature, ran rock concerts to recruit new members, and organized a revolutionary media conference in Ann Arbor.

Using funds generated by Sinclair's management of a popular rock group, the MC-5, the White Panthers engaged in increasingly dangerous activities, obtaining guns and dynamite, blowing up the CIA office in Ann Arbor, and laying plans for guerrilla actions in northern Michigan.

In addition, the White Panthers ran a campaign to make marijuana legal in Michigan, and Sinclair was arrested numerous times for violating state narcotics laws. When Sinclair was incarcerated, elements of the group advocated following the example of the Tupamaro rebels in South America—kidnapping elected officials to obtain the release of persons they considered to be political prisoners.

Michigan congressmen could be traded for prisoners such as Sinclair, while more national figures such as Congressman Gerald Ford and Michigan Senator Robert P. Griffin might be exchanged for Black Panther leaders such as Huey Newton and Bobby Seale. With a prominent hostage such as Vice President Spiro Agnew, a radical could "write his own ticket."

Senator Griffin, who presided over the session, was not amused.

As Detective Murray concluded, "Gentlemen, based on the information that we have obtained through other normal police functions, we would have to consider the White Panther Party an organization bent on total destruction of the present government of the United States and detrimental to the welfare of this country."

Ultra-conservative Strom Thurmond, the senator from South Carolina and another member of the committee, drafted a memo on the testimony about the rally in support of John Sinclair. Thurmond underscored the friendship between Lennon and New Left figures such as Jerry Rubin, pointing out that members of the Chicago Seven had now "devised a plan to hold rock concerts in various primary election states . . . to recruit persons to come to San Diego during the Republican National Convention in August 1972" and that they "intend to use John Lennon as a drawing card to promote their success. . . . If Lennon's visa is terminated it would be a strategic countermeasure."

Senator Thurmond knew exactly the line of command that his letter would climb. As attorney general, John Mitchell headed the entire Immigration and Naturalization Service, the agency that decides who to deport, when, and how. Mitchell didn't miss a beat, forwarding Thurmond's letter and memo to the attention of his deputy Richard Kleindienst.

United States Senate
COMMITTEE ON ARMED SERVICES
WASHINGTON, D.C. 20510

February 4, 1972

PERSONAL AND CONFIDENTIAL

Honorable John N. Mitchell
Attorney General
Department of Justice
Washington, D. C.

Dear John:

Find attached a memorandum to me from the staff of the
Internal Security Subcommittee of the Judiciary Committee.
I am a member of the subcommittee as well as the full
Judiciary Committee.

This appears to me to be an important matter, and I think
it would be well for it to be considered at the highest
level.

As I can see, many headaches might be avoided if appropriate action be taken in time.

With kindest regards and best wishes,

Very truly,

Strom Thurmond

ST:x

Enclosure

-8-

In turn, Kleindienst passed the memo on to the commissioner of immigration, Raymond Farrell, who within days had Sol Marks, district director for New York, revoke John's visa status and begin deportation proceedings.

JOHN LENNON

John Lennon, presently visiting in the United States, is a British citizen. He was a member of the former musical group known as "The Beatles." He has claimed a date of birth of September 10, 1940, and he is presently married to a Japanese citizen, one Yoko Ono.

The December 12, 1971, issue of the New York Times shows that Lennon and his wife appeared for about 10 minutes at about 3:00 a.m. on December 11, 1971, at a rally held in Ann Arbor, Michigan, to protest the continuing imprisonment of John Sinclair, a radical poet.

Radical New Left leaders Rennie Davis, Jerry Rubin, Leslie Bacon, Stu Albert, Jay Craven, and others have recently gone to the New York City area. This group has been strong advocates of the program to "dump Nixon." They have devised a plan to hold rock concerts in various primary election states for the following purposes: to obtain access to college campuses; to stimulate 18-year old registration; to press for legislation legalizing marihuana; to finance their activities; and to recruit persons to come to San Diego during the Republican National Convention in August 1972. These individuals are the same persons who were instrumental in disrupting the Democratic National Convention in Chicago in 1968.

According to a confidential source, whose information has proved reliable in the past, the activities of Davis and his group will follow the pattern of the rally mentioned above with reference to John Sinclair. David Sinclair, the brother of John, will be the road manager for these rock festivals.

Davis and his cohorts intend to use John Lennon as a drawing card to promote the success of the rock festivals and rallies. The source feels that this will pour tremendous amounts of money into the coffers of the New Left and can only inevitably lead to a clash between a controlled mob organized by this group and law enforcement officials in San Diego.

The source felt that if Lennon's visa is terminated it would be a strategy counter-measure. The source also noted the caution which must be taken with regard to the possible alienation of the so-called 18-year old vote if Lennon is expelled from the country.

EXHIBIT A

-10-

In coming to the defense of John Sinclair, John Lennon and Yoko Ono had made some very dangerous political enemies. These were people I'd never tangled with in all the years I'd spent practicing immigration law, people I'd never even imagine as adversaries. Like it or not, though, my political naivete was about to come to an end.

2

I Get Recruited

We can use the available political machinery to screw our political enemies.

—John Dean, counsel to President
Nixon, in an August 1971 memo

The telephone call that introduced me to the John Lennon case came on the afternoon of January 14, 1972.

"Leon, I have a possible new client for you to meet," a former law school classmate, Alan Kahn, told me. "Real heavyweights. I wonder whether you could find time to come along to meet them later this afternoon."

"Certainly, Alan," I replied, a little puzzled. "But what do you mean 'come along'?"

"These are really heavyweights, Leon, and they don't come to lawyers' offices. I'm talking about John Lennon and Yoko Ono. I can't assure you that you'll be retained, but they are looking for special immigration counsel, and I have recommended you."

"I'd be pleased. When and where shall we meet?"

"Why don't you come to my office at 5:45? I'm at 1700 Broadway. You may not know it, but I'm no longer in private practice. I'm now counsel to Apple Records and Allen Klein, who managed the Beatles." His voice just about radiated pride as he made this announcement.

Today I'm embarrassed to admit that none of the names Alan mentioned rang a bell. I had never heard of John Lennon, much less Yoko Ono. While I was vaguely aware of the Beatles, I certainly couldn't name any of the band members. Neither Allen Klein nor Apple Records struck a familiar note, but my old friend Alan had never misled me before. We had occupied offices in the same building on Madison Avenue and worked on a number of cases together.

Promptly at 5:45 I arrived at the large and ultra-modern offices of Apple Records, just a four-block walk along 53rd Street. The building was a classic office tower with a prime location and a collection of tenants boasting top-flight show business enterprises. As I entered, the whole place reeked of success. Snappily dressed elevator attendants guided me aboard a fast elevator the moment I mentioned Apple Records. When I arrived upstairs, an attractive blonde receptionist ushered me down a long corridor gleaming with framed gold records to Kahn's office. Alan welcomed me with a broad smile as he showed off his new digs, especially the glass wall with a broad view of midtown Manhattan. Pride and excitement mixed in his voice as he spoke about his new work and the important show business people he counseled.

"Leon, you were one of the first people I thought of. Most immigration lawyers would give their eyeteeth just to meet John and Yoko. Let me brief you before you meet Allen Klein, my boss."

"Before you tell me about their legal problem, Alan, I must tell you that I have no idea who these people are. I take it they're some kind of musicians?"

Alan seemed dumbfounded by my admission. He stared at me for a moment, open-mouthed. "I can't believe it, Leon. You really never heard of them?"

I shrugged sheepishly. "Never."

"I wouldn't advertise that, Leon," he said, lowering his voice. "They have enormous egos, like most of the people I meet in this industry. John Lennon is probably the greatest musician who ever lived. Yoko is his wife. She is some kind of artist, who nobody understands, but everyone has heard of them."

He broke off as Allen Klein came into the office. A short, husky man in his forties, Klein had a shock of brown hair and a shirt open to where his tie might have reached, if he'd been wearing one. He might not dress like an executive, but he changed the atmosphere of the room by his very presence, shaking my hand as Alan and I were speaking, interrupting loudly.

"You the immigration lawyer? Alan told me about you. Let's get moving." He turned on his heel, acknowledging neither of us completely, but definitely confirming that he was in charge of the operation.

"Let's get going, Leon," Alan said quietly. "I'll fill you in on the case in the car." The car, a black Cadillac, was chauffeur-driven, of course.

It took about a half hour to reach the Lennon digs in Greenwich Village through the late afternoon traffic. I used the time to acquaint myself with the nature of the problem they'd called me in to discuss.

Alan explained, with a peppering of interruptions by Allen Klein, that the Lennons were in the United States on a temporary visa that permitted them to do business here. Obtaining Lennon's visa always involved a hassle at the London US consulate because of a 1968 British drug conviction, which rendered Lennon inadmissible in any visa category to the United States. He always had to apply for a waiver of his inadmissibility, and invariably the papers had to find their way to Washington before the American consul in London could do the honors. Now John and Yoko's visas were soon to expire, and they were more than concerned that a further extension might never be granted. Alan showed me the record of the conviction, for "criminally possessing cannabis resin without authorization."

Then Alan explained what had brought them to the United States. "Yoko has a child by a prior marriage, called Kyoko. She is about nine years old and has been the subject of a custody squabble between Yoko and her former husband, Tony Cox." Alan gave the facts quickly, but my friend's voice grew softer as he mentioned the child. "To make a long story short, Leon, Cox absconded with the child, and we began a custody proceeding in St. Thomas, the US Virgin Islands, where Yoko's divorce had been granted in 1969. We appeared there and won a temporary custody order for Yoko. Cox absconded with the child again, directly violating the court's order. The judge held him in contempt and entered an order requiring him to be fined and brought before the court, but he disappeared completely."

With one eye on his impatient boss, Alan rushed to finish the story. "Then Cox turned up in Texas, commencing another custody action in Harris County, for some reason or other. John and Yoko appeared there with me and a local lawyer, and we believe we will be successful again. But Tony Cox still has the child, although we have brought his past behavior to the attention of the court in Texas. Yoko needs time to try to get physical custody of the child. It is really heartrending."

The car turned into Bank Street in Greenwich Village and passed a neat row of homes, obviously inhabited by artist-types.

Allen Klein led the way to one of them and proceeded to bully his way past the door. "I am Allen Klein, and I'm here to see John Lennon," he announced, bulldozing his way past the young man peering through the peephole on the other side of the door.

The apartment was several steps below street level, and we entered a space obviously intended to be a living room but used as an office. We passed a copying machine and walked through a corridor of filing cabinets, storage boxes, and work desks as we were taken to the kitchen area of the apartment.

We sat at a kitchenette table where Alan Kahn started unpacking his briefcase, showing me documents that immediately placed me in the picture of their present immigration status. Alan had copies of the visas and John's waiver. John and Yoko had been admitted on August 13, 1971, about five months earlier, in the immigration status of visitors. They were authorized to stay only until January 31, 1972, barely three weeks away.

I had no more than a moment or two to glance at the documents when the door to a backroom opened. A slight woman entered, dressed entirely in black, with Asian features, long black hair, and large, expressive eyes. She extended her hand to me with some grace, smiled warmly to Alan Kahn, and almost failed to acknowledge Allen Klein. In return, Klein didn't seem to notice her. Given my own brusque introduction to the manager, I wasn't sure whether this indicated conflict between them, or if Klein was annoyed at being summoned to his client's apartment. Whatever the case, he clearly didn't trust this matter to Alan Kahn's judgment. Lennon was Klein's client, and he wasn't about to allow Alan to make major decisions, like engaging private counsel, without his personal approval.

"John will be out in a moment, Mr. Wildes," Yoko said. "Let me fill you in on some details. John has an immigration problem, a drug conviction. His business dealings have brought him to the United States every so often to conclude deals, record contracts, royalties, you know. We have a child, Kyoko, from my former marriage, whom I have been trying for some time to locate. Her father, Tony Cox, is really paranoid about it all. He is convinced that the powerful John and Yoko will disappear with his little daughter, and she will never be heard from again—there is no convincing him otherwise. He probably lives in some kind of commune and managed to elude us for a long time. We actually chased him halfway through Europe." She studied me carefully as we spoke, as though trying to asses my sympathy for her situation.

"Of course, as an American, he thought he could convince an American court that he was a more suitable parent for our child than the Japanese dragon lady, but with Alan's help and the local lawyers, we won Kyoko's custody. That didn't do us much good, because Tony got paranoid again and disappeared with her." She smiled at Alan Kahn as she spoke.

"We had all kinds of private detectives helping us to locate her, but nothing worked. Until he showed up in Texas and filed another lawsuit, thinking he would do better there. I'm glad that he showed up anywhere, as maybe there is a chance now for us to actually see Kyoko and take care of her." Yoko became more animated as she discussed the efforts to trace Kyoko, almost seeming to snuggle an imaginary child in her arms as she spoke.

"I never wanted her to become a 'famous child'," Yoko went on. "I'm not anxious for any publicity which might scare Tony off again. I just want to be here long enough to get the matter resolved and see whether we can convince Tony that the dragon lady won't overwhelm his little girl."

Yoko then proceeded to ask a number of questions that seemed more than intelligent to me. She was apparently well informed about legal matters relating to her husband's immigration situation and shared her concerns.

"We have been critical of US government policies, especially the Vietnam fiasco, and the administration probably thinks we're too vocal. Lots of ordinary people agree with our criticism, but the immigration people are all, like, super patriots. I'm afraid that they will deny future extensions to us." Yoko leaned forward, holding out open hands as if to plead for more time. I saw Alan nod in sympathy. "If immigration decides to deny our extension, they might use my appearance at the Philharmonic as a pretext. I'm a conceptual artist, you know, and I perform my art in a somewhat unconventional manner. While attending a performance of Earth Symphony at the Philharmonic, I stood at my seat and conducted the orchestra. Although I wasn't paid, and most people wouldn't regard it as a performance, I could never deny that it was, given my special brand of art."

She seemed intent on making it known to me that she was not just John Lennon's wife but an accomplished artist in her own right. Allen Klein looked bored, fidgeting impatiently and still not actually looking at her. He seemed to take her talk about her art form less than seriously. John Lennon was his client, and it was obviously Lennon he was there to please. My friend Alan Kahn was the perfect gentleman, smiling as he encouraged Yoko to explain her problem. She smiled in return, appreciating that he shared her concerns.

Yoko obviously wanted to explain her situation and Kyoko's before John appeared. I thought her words were significant to the situation.

The rear door opened again, and in walked a lean, lanky young man whose stylishly long brown hair dropped almost to his shoulders. By no means an imposing person, his outgoing nature shone through immediately. He smiled naturally, with no sense of self-importance.

While Alan and Klein both acknowledged him, he headed directly to me and extended his hand.

"So you're the hotshot immigration lawyer. How d'you do?" Like a housewife angry that her husband had served nothing to their guests, he said "Can I brew ya some tea?" Everyone agreed that he could, and he proceeded to the kitchen, still talking, to heat the kettle. Then he joined us at the kitchen table, turning directly to me. "Do you think you can keep us here so we can find Kyoko, Leon? Yoko thinks the FBI won't allow it. What do you think?" His questions tumbled out quickly, impetuously.

Allen Klein spoke up, explaining that he'd represented John on his previous trips to the United States, lining up Congressional help to secure a waiver of John's marijuana conviction. As the manager spoke, Yoko's expression seemed to grow more tense. She looked as if she regretted not having more of a chance to explain her side of things. Clearly, Klein concentrated more on the interests of John, the heavyweight icon, than on her hopes of regaining her precious child.

I asked for permission to ask a few questions before offering any opinion. They were quick to oblige. Alan gave me the conviction document.

"The conviction seems to be your main problem with visiting and staying in the United States; was it the result of a contested trial?"

"Not at all," he responded promptly. "My lawyer told me that I'd best plead guilty."

"Were you guilty?" I had no idea what prompted me to ask such a foolish question. Past experience had shown me that it never elicited a truthful response. Here, though, it brought a surprise.

"Actually, I was completely innocent." Seeing my real interest in the proceeding, John took pride in relating the full story of how he'd gotten arrested. "Now mind you, I do not deny having used hash, or a lot of other junk. But at the time, we were tipped off that there would be a police raid. The drug squad at Scotland Yard was out to get rock musicians, and I was on their list. They had already bagged Mick (Jagger, as I later discovered) and George (Harrison)."

John's face grew serious as he continued the story. "Yoko and I had taken over this apartment from some musicians. We weren't on drugs at all at the time. Actually, we were on a macrobiotic diet, and drugs just didn't go. To make sure, we cleaned the apartment top to bottom."

I leaned forward, focusing on what seemed like a critical fact. "And your lawyers still recommended that you plead guilty?" I couldn't understand what he'd just told me. "Sounds like you had a complete defense."

"Well, there were lots of reasons. Yoko was an alien enemy," he crinkled his nose and grinned in mockery of the officialdom of the United Kingdom—a pretty advanced attitude for 1971, when anger over Pearl Harbor and World War II still ran high. "And the lawyers said it wouldn't make any difference anyway."

It didn't make sense that a lawyer worth his salt (and Lennon could obviously afford the saltiest) would let the prosecution get away with planted evidence. I tucked the information away for future reference.

"Besides," John continued, "I had no criminal record, and they told me that only a nominal fine would be imposed, so I pled guilty, and followed the lawyers' advice. Lawyers don't make mistakes, do they?" Again, the crinkled nose and the playful grin. Alan and I both enjoyed his charming humor.

"What was the substance you were convicted of possessing?" I asked as I inspected the conviction documents. "Was it marijuana?"

He shrugged. "No, it was hash."

"Forgive my ignorance. First, I must apologize for not really knowing who you are. I understand that you and Yoko (I was careful to add Yoko to the formulation) are both distinguished artists, but I am totally unfamiliar with your art. I must also admit that I haven't the slightest idea about the difference between marijuana and hashish. Is hash the same as marijuana?"

"Hash is much better than marijuana!" John replied impishly, suddenly mimicking a teacher at an imaginary blackboard. "Let me enlighten you. Hash and grass—that's marijuana—actually come from the same plant, but the hash is much more powerful. A lot of people are trying to legalize grass, but it would be unlikely that hash would get the same treatment in most places. Hash is definitely the more serious drug."

"Would you and Yoko like to remain here permanently?" I asked.

Their shoulders sagged, and an air of hopelessness descended upon them both, but John answered. "That's not possible—but then again, you should know that." It was clear to me that I was not the first lawyer who'd consulted with the couple.

"Well actually, Leon," John said, "Everything in our world— we're artists, you know—now comes up in the USA It's like the time of the Impressionist artists, when everything took place in Paris, or in early Rome. It's all here now. This is where it's at, and we'd love to be here. We just understand that it can't be arranged."

"I don't think there would be a problem in my getting permanent immigration status here," Yoko interjected. "But we understand that John's conviction can never be waived on a permanent basis. The waiver is only given for temporary visits and won't be given again if we appear to abuse the privilege."

I wasn't about to offer any advice or comment until I had all the information. Once again, Yoko had confirmed my initial sense that she wanted me to know that she was a person too, the one with the most personal problem, being separated from her child, and not necessarily included in every statement about her illustrious husband.

"Well, counselor, what sage advice can you give us two starving artists?" asked the impish Lennon.

I fought back an instant inclination to give my advice in the form of a biblical homily. As an avid Bible student, I might have done so in more familiar company. Each of my prospective clients had a dream. Yoko dreamed of being reunited with her daughter. Her husband dreamed of being in the United States legally, free of hassle. I was tempted to quote the biblical Joseph who could interpret dreams, saying, "The two dreams are one." But this was no time for sermons.

They were both quiet as they waited for my advice. I couldn't help noticing the obvious strong relationship between these two dreamers. They seemed to think alike. As one spoke, the other would interrupt to complete the sentence. Though obviously of unlike natures—John fast, witty, result-oriented, Yoko more thoughtful and deliberative—they were, nevertheless, a team, notwithstanding the cultural and temperamental differences.

Yoko settled comfortably into her chair, raising her shoeless feet onto another chair to lean back thoughtfully. John seemed impatient, his body inclined toward me as he sat.

"If all you'd like is a couple of months' time to look for your daughter, with her custody case in active litigation, I think you'll have no difficulty obtaining that result," I told them. "I have never heard a stronger reason for requesting an extension of a visitor's stay. Nor do I think there will be any problem in extending the waiver of John's conviction which must accompany the extension of stay. The reason for the extension is one which is of high humanitarian concern, and that is precisely one of the statutory grounds for granting this type of waiver. I also think that if a few months' time will satisfy your needs, Alan here is more than competent to secure that time. I have just looked at the papers he prepared for your last extension, and they are as good as anything I could do."

John and Yoko remained silent at a point where they might easily have concluded our discussion. They plainly were hoping for more, and I believed that I had something to add that might offer a better outlook.

"On the other hand, if you would like to stay permanently or more than the few months that I think Alan can obtain for you, I have some suggestions."

I had brought along a copy of the immigration statute and opened it to the section of law which was involved. Then I read it aloud:

> People are excludable from the United States "who have been convicted of any law or regulation relating to the illicit possession of . . . narcotic drugs or marijuana."

I looked up from the pages. "Every word in the statute must be taken seriously. For example, a former version of the statute did not include the words 'or marijuana'. The words were added as a result of the claims in two California cases where the persons involved claimed that their convictions involved marijuana and that marijuana was not a 'narcotic drug'. The courts had to agree, as apparently marijuana is a hallucinogen rather than a narcotic."

From their reaction, neither of the two had ever seen the actual immigration law in black and white before. Yoko drew closer, leaning together with John to follow my words. "To close up the loophole, Congress amended the statute, adding the words 'or marijuana.' The statute does not mention hashish. It only mentions 'marijuana.' My impression is that a court might have some doubt as to whether hashish is properly included within the legal meaning of the term 'marijuana' in this statute. In other words, it is quite possible that a conviction for possessing hash might not be the kind of conviction which should keep a person permanently out of the United States. I understand that there are other drugs which are neither 'narcotics' nor 'marijuana,' like LSD, for instance. It is therefore quite possible, although no one can say for certain, that a court might hold that John never even needed a waiver of excludability for his visits to the United States, and that there is no barrier to his application to remain here permanently." Now Allen Klein and Alan Kahn leaned toward me. It seemed my lecture on marijuana was also new to them.

"There is another issue which interests me. From your explanation, John, I cannot understand why a competent criminal lawyer advised a client to plead guilty, in the face of evidence of his client's innocence. It may be that John's lawyers in England know something about the British law there which might be useful to us here. Perhaps the conviction is one which would not be considered a proper 'conviction' in our system. In any event, there is lots of authority for the proposition that each word in a statute such as this should be carefully examined to determine whether it is being properly interpreted. That is what the courts are for. While I would have to do a good deal of research to test my theories, and perhaps come up with some different ones, I think there may be some glimmer of hope here."

"How would we go about raising these questions?" Yoko hunched forward, her face intent. "Suppose we are refused an extension of stay at some point? How do we get a court to rule on such questions?"

I was building up a serious appreciation for Yoko's intelligence. She had placed her finger on the essence of the legal problem—when and how to proceed.

"It's a little like a game of chess," I answered, "and there are a number of moves we'd have to make. First, you'd need to apply for permanent residence status. For this, you need a preference on the immigrant visa waiting list. Otherwise, the question couldn't even be raised. I have some ideas on this question, as well. Aside from the preference categories for relatives of American citizens and permanent residents, the only way to get on a waiting list is to be sponsored for a professional preference. The statute"—at this point I turned a few pages to find the section I wanted—"covers persons who are outstanding in the arts and sciences."

Yoko seemed to tighten up. As she did, a strategic move occurred to me, and I continued, "What is interesting about the statute is that it provides for visas for persons"—and again I quoted from the text—"'who because of their exceptional ability in the sciences or the arts will substantially benefit prospectively the . . . cultural interests . . . of the United States.'

"Normally, when a couple applies for residency together, only one petition need be approved, so that the beneficiary of that petition qualifies both persons for eligibility for the preference. In your particular case, I would be inclined to file two separate applications and ask the government to rule that each of you is an artist of exceptional ability. That's because a dependent spouse's application could be defeated if the primary applicant were technically not eligible for residence because of a conviction. If we filed separate applications for each of you, you could each apply separately for permanent residence. The result of a denial of residence in one case and the grant in the other would be contrary to one of the main purposes of our immigration law, the reunion of families. And the government wouldn't look very good, permitting one outstanding artist to remain and deporting the other."

Yoko quickly grasped my explanation and the opening it described. Her expression changed instantly. John, too, realized that I was describing a new possibility here, something that none of them had considered before. I had a very attentive audience as I continued. "There's also a policy of allowing outstanding artists to remain while waiting on the 'availability of visa numbers under the quota.' This policy might be useful in your case. In any event, it would be nice to have the attorney general confirm that, in the words of the statute, each of you qualifies as an individual whose presence was 'prospectively beneficial to the . . . national culture' and then explain to your fans why he gave only one of you residence and insisted that the other leave."

As my strategy unfolded, Yoko's apprehension began to disappear. John sank deeper into his seat and drained his teacup. They were both obviously pleased with the prospects that my strategy offered. Apparently, none of their previous advisers had told them there was actually some chance of their staying permanently in the United States. I sensed that for Yoko it was also an opportunity for equal time for her dream—equal treatment with her famous husband. It also afforded her greater hope that eventually she could be reunited with her child.

"On the other hand, if your original interest still stands, Alan can do as well as I in getting the necessary extension for a few months. In those circumstances, you really don't need me."

Yoko and John looked at each other without uttering a word. Then they both turned to me, and Yoko said, "We need you. Can we have your home telephone number?"

●●

The taxi ride from Greenwich Village to my home in Forest Hills, Queens, gave me time to think through our long discussion. How would I proceed to obtain residence? John and Yoko didn't have the close US citizen family required for the higher preference categories. The only approach would be the one I described to them—obtaining a preference as outstanding artists.

I felt good about the idea of filing two separate petitions. But this strategy relied upon our also obtaining such classification for Yoko. I had no notion of what her art was, much less her acceptance in her field. Suppose the government rejected her as an artist? Allen Klein had snickered when we discussed her achievements.

In any event, as the cab approached 67th Road I certainly had something to tell my wife Ruth about.

"So who were the 'heavyweights' you had to leave your office and go to see?" she asked as I walked into our bedroom exhausted from the long meeting.

"Well, let's see," I started to answer, the long evening of dealing with personalities and strategies swirling around in my head. "I think it was Jack Lemmon and Yoko Moto."

My dear wife gave me a long, hard look. "Wait a minute, Leon. Do you mean John Lennon and Yoko Ono?"

"Uh, yeah," I had managed to mangle their names completely.

"Oh my God, Leon! Where have you been all of these years?" Ruth asked, "You really had no idea, did you? John Lennon and Yoko Ono. I can't even think of two people more famous than they are."

Obviously, I had a lot to learn about my clients. If someone told me what else I would find out during this case, maybe I wouldn't have been so gung ho. I considered myself a seasoned legal practitioner, pretty much ready for anything. Little did I know I was about to get schooled with some pretty hard knocks.

3

Into the Minefield

Listen, if anything happens to Yoko and me, it was not an accident.

—John Lennon, in a 1972 conversation
with humorist Paul Krassner

Well, it looked as if I would be representing John Lennon and Yoko Ono. That meant I'd have to educate them on some of the quirks—which is a nice way of saying special challenges—involved with my branch of the legal profession.

A client who is an alien, legal or otherwise, doesn't have the rights in an immigration proceeding that people know from so many courtroom dramas. A person accused of a crime has the right that the government prove a case against him (or her) beyond a reasonable doubt. Evidence may not be submitted against him in a criminal trial if it was obtained illegally. He can only be charged once and cannot be twice punished for the same offense.

An alien, on the other hand, does not stand in the same position under the US Constitution as does a citizen. In a deportation proceeding, a case may be proven against the alien defendant with evidence that is doubtful. Illegally obtained evidence can be used to prove a ground to deport him, and then he can be removed for the very same offense.

No wonder an immigration lawyer looms large in the perspective of his client. Who else can protect him against the vagaries of the law and the immense power of the government to remove him?

The immigration law is also noted for its unfathomable subtlety. Like a giant iceberg, much of the danger in an alien's situation often lies beneath the surface, revealed only through the skill and talent of a lawyer experienced in such matters.

The facts I'd discussed with John and Yoko were, on the surface, quite routine. A mother was visiting the United States, trying to get custody of her child. A highly acclaimed musician accompanied her—however, he was ineligible for a visitor's visa because of a minor drug conviction in England. This bar to his entry was temporarily waived so that he could accompany his wife and also conduct business here. Their authorized time was soon coming to an end, but they needed additional time to accomplish their original purpose.

Given the apparent situation, an application for extension of their temporary stay seemed to be a complete solution.

But Yoko saw beneath the surface, and John trusted her intuition.

She had a sense, almost a premonition, that the government wouldn't permit their continued stay in this country, and her reasoned approach to life would not allow her to face such an eventuality unprepared. Something unspoken had passed between us in our first conversation—she seemed to sense that I was a kindred soul, given to anticipating problems early. Yoko had probably consulted with other attorneys and found their strategy lacking. Given her thoughtful nature, she wouldn't go with the first option offered. She'd want to consider her choices.

Yoko anticipated that the government might deny their request for an extension of stay.

If that happened, they faced very limited choices. There was no appeal of a denial of an extension of stay. While a motion might be made to reconsider the decision, it could be given short shrift. In fact, the government could reject it outright, with little hope that future trips would be authorized.

Should the Lennons refuse to leave, they would be placed in deportation proceedings as aliens who had overstayed their allotted time. And deportation proceedings were very dangerous, since the government had an ironclad case. The immigration judge hearing such a deportation proceeding cannot even reconsider the denial of their request for an extension of their temporary stay. He must accept the action of the Immigration Service as being final.

If they were placed in deportation proceedings, the Lennons had only two options available. They could request permission to "depart voluntarily," a discretionary remedy available to most aliens, or they could be removed forcibly. The first choice could gain them some time—typically the government offered thirty days to leave voluntarily after a deportation proceeding. But an offer of that grace period would be coupled with a further order automatically ordering deportation if they did not leave within those thirty days. John and Yoko would then be in the government's hands completely.

In ordinary cases, where an alien subject to deportation has a basis to seek status as a lawful permanent resident, he would use the proceeding to file such an application, even requesting a waiver to overcome any problems with his case.

Unfortunately, convictions involving narcotic drugs or marijuana were not permanently waivable. The waiver that John had received for a temporary visit was the maximum benefit allowed by law. Moreover, the Immigration Service in those days was heartless in its treatment of even the most minor drug offender. That generation of officialdom neither understood nor wanted to understand the problem of drugs. We had enough "druggies" of our own and didn't need to import foreign ones.

Was there any chance then for the Lennons, should the government decide to remove them? I saw a faint glimmer of hope in John's description of his criminal offense. He was never aware of the fact that he had an illegal substance in his possession. As such, he should never have been convicted and had no reason to plead guilty. Indeed, he pled guilty on the advice of counsel. Perhaps the proceedings in England could be reopened to make this claim now. Or maybe the availability of new witnesses who knew the apartment had been thoroughly cleaned before the police arrived might be useful.

However, I believed my best chance lay in exploring whether there was something unusual about the British law under which Lennon had been convicted. Maybe it could be used in his defense here. After all, the immigration statute required a "conviction," and although the US government seldom delved behind foreign legal proceedings, there were certain principles that had to be met before a foreign conviction could be recognized. Research into John's drug case might be fruitful.

Another point that Lennon had mentioned also stood out in my mind. Immigration law punished the possession of narcotic drugs or marijuana. I knew that the specific words "or marijuana" had been added to the statute after the courts had ruled that marijuana was not a narcotic drug. There might be some wiggle room because hash was not specifically mentioned. However, John had mentioned that hash was the more serious of the two drugs. If there were different criminal penalties involved in other US statutes, what effect might that have on our case?

I still felt that the best way to challenge the government involved securing approvals for two separate third preference alien applications for John and Yoko. That would place the government in the uncomfortable public position of attempting to deport two extraordinary aliens whose presence in this country would be beneficial to the national culture. Nor would it look good to declare that Yoko could remain here to join her child, but John must leave or be deported. I could see myself urging Yoko to proclaim publicly that she was being forced to choose between her child and her husband!

First, however, I decided to request an extension of the Lennons' temporary stay. Since this would also require the extension of John's temporary waiver of his drug conviction, I would make the application directly to Sol Marks, the district director of the New York district of the Immigration and Naturalization Service.

A good part of routine business in immigration law is knowing which application to make—and to whom. One year, when I'd taken a summer rental in Long Beach, New York, I spent many mornings commuting on the same train with Sol. We often accomplished a lot of business before we even reached our respective offices. A career immigration officer with well over thirty years of experience on the job, he had risen through the ranks and acquired a legal education, attending law school at night. When he sought the top position he currently held, I was the national president of the American Immigration Lawyers Association. Sol had asked for my recommendation back in 1970.

Though I was pleased to give it, I told him that I couldn't use the letterhead of the organization I headed. I'd be happy to write a recommendation on my personal office letterhead. Sol appreciated that, even though he was limited to securing only one reference letter from a member of the immigration bar.

While Sol was the top official exercising immigration authority in the important New York district, I'd never consider asking a favor of him. He was a straitlaced government worker who'd resent such behavior. Still, I regarded him as more of a colleague than an adversary when I made an appointment to see him on the twelfth floor of the INS building at 20 West Broadway.

A burly man who worked to stay in shape, Sol gave me a vigorous handshake and greeted me warmly. "What brings you in to see me?" he asked.

"I've been consulted by an important couple, John Lennon and his wife, Yoko Ono. They're in the midst of a contested custody proceeding."

Since an extension of stay for visitors in New York was completely in Sol's discretion, I explained in detail how Yoko and John had devoted years to searching for Kyoko and their pending cases in the Virgin Islands and in Texas. "The Lennons are now litigating for custody of the child in both proceedings and need an extension of their temporary stay for a number of months, hopefully, to arrange for joint custody of the child and appropriate visitation. I can think of no more compelling reason for an extension of stay."

Sol's expression turned grim. He turned to a steno pad on his desk and scribbled a few words as though he needed a reminder for future action. "I didn't know they were within my jurisdiction at this time," Sol said, as though it was customary for every foreign visitor to report to him personally.

"Since Lennon has a marijuana conviction, the central office in Washington issued a temporary waiver of his excludability, which will also need to be extended," I went on. "For that reason, I thought it best to come directly to you, Sol. Would it be okay for me to draft an extension application requesting a six-month extension under these circumstances?"

"I'll check it out and let you know, Leon," Sol answered. I figured his notation was probably a reminder to call the commissioner of immigration's office in Washington. That didn't surprise me. I knew he had to contact his superiors, because they had to extend the waiver of Lennon's excludability as part of the process.

The office where we sat was a familiar place. I had appeared there at numerous meetings, both with Sol and his predecessor, Peter Esperdy, during liaison meetings conducted with the immigration bar. From his desk chair, Sol had a view of the Statue of Liberty out in New York harbor, and I recall remarking to him once that whoever sat in his chair needed to be a person of vision.

Certainly, Sol enforced the law in one of the biggest entry ports in the country with confident authority. He was a career civil servant who could be relied upon to carry out any policies set by the commissioner of immigration. Of course, the commissioner's job was a purely political appointment.

"Sol," I added, "I had an interesting talk with the Lennons. While they are basically interested in getting as much time as they can to handle their custody and visitation proceedings and leave, they have been speaking with other attorneys about what further, if anything, could be done for them. They consulted with Joe Califano, of the office of Edward Bennett Williams, who seems to have recommended federal court litigation under the First Amendment. They actually thought that was rather severe, and asked me what I thought.

"Apparently, Mrs. Lennon has no ineligibility problems," I went on. "As for Mr. Lennon, it appears that a constable from Scotland Yard made a practice of planting drugs on rock musicians in London. I told John that the British proceedings might be reopened to accept such a defense, in which case he would have no conviction at all to deal with. Under those circumstances he could apply through the third preference as an outstanding artist and get residence for himself and his wife. That would allow him to remain here indefinitely and help with this child-custody problem." Although I was showing a lot of my cards, I purposely didn't mention the possibility of presenting two third preference petitions.

Sol smiled in appreciation of my advice to John and Yoko. He always enjoyed the imaginative approach I took when it came to immigration problems. Though he expressed no opinion, his expression showed that he considered my plan more appropriate than a brash First Amendment litigation.

"Suppose I check this out and get back to you tomorrow," he said. "Just remember, there's a long waiting list of third preference applicants ahead of them filing for permanent residence."

"I know," I replied. "If the quota waiting list for third preference is over-subscribed, there is a policy which is applied to those cases where aliens of extraordinary ability are concerned. Generally they are allowed to remain until visa numbers become available under that preference category." I smiled. Sol rolled his eyes.

With a wry smile, he said, "Leave it to you to come up with something like that, Leon. I doubt whether a person who isn't even eligible for residence would be entitled to use that theory, but I can look into that as well."

"Sol, you understood that the Lennons' time is to expire on January 31st, less than a week away. I know that you'll need to consult with Sam Bernsen." Bernsen was the associate commissioner for adjudications, one of the least politically motivated people in the upper echelons of the INS and a man whose legal expertise I respected.

I smiled, thinking of Yoko's premonition that the government was trying to get them out of the country. This would be the real test—there would have to be some very strong reason to convince Bernsen if this particular extension was to be denied. While I knew that the commissioner and his other associates were more likely to react to political factors, Bernsen was a real scholar, who would deal with the law. After all, he had signed John's original waiver.

I thanked Sol Marks for his time, and he promised to call me in a day or two. But before leaving the immigration building, I stopped in to see Ben Perlitch, the senior adjudicator in the applications unit of third preference petitions. He had heard of John Lennon but not of Yoko Ono. We sat in his office, reviewing the process for filing individual and joint applications and discussing how to invoke the special practice I'd discovered to allow John and Yoko to remain here until quota visa numbers became available.

Early the next day, I received a telephone call from Marks. Not only had he spoken to Sam Bernsen and been told that Sam would need to consult with others in the INS central office, but Sam had already gotten back to him in record time. "Leon, Mr. Bernsen told me that the climate in Washington isn't good for granting permission to the beneficiaries of third preference applications to remain on in a case like Lennon's . . . because of his drug conviction." Marks then went on to tell me that the climate was good only for consideration of an extension application in the Lennon case for a period of one month—that meant until February 29, 1972. Sol said that if I filed such an application, that would be approved, provided that it was supported by evidence relating to status of the custody proceedings.

Sol's voice over the phone sounded downright ominous. His whole tone had changed since our conversation the day before, but he tried to act as if this were mere routine. "Leon, because it's you, your clients will get a one-month extension," he went on in a firm voice. "Don't ask me any questions. These people will never get another extension."

Then he hit me hard: "And, Leon, tell them to get out!"

In spite of his "no questions" remark, I had plenty to ask. "Why this negative response, Sol?"

But Marks only replied, "I'm not at liberty to say."

Setting the phone down, I sat dumbfounded by Sol's decision and by his bold language. As entertained as he'd seemed to be by the theories I'd spun earlier, Marks obviously wasn't letting personal feelings get in the way. He delivered the hardball decision of the INS central office without any kind of embellishment.

Then I called Alan Kahn and told him of the shocking response from the INS.

Alan wasn't happy. "I thought you said this Bernsen wasn't a political guy."

"He isn't," I responded. "But obviously the political atmosphere in Washington is seriously against the Lennons, and Bernsen is going along with it."

"Well, I'm glad you're the one handling the case," Alan sighed. "What can I do?"

He quickly agreed to obtain a letter from the Texas attorney representing John and Yoko in the custody proceedings there. And when I discussed the documentary requirements for filing third preference petitions, he said, "We can secure any number of references from top-notch people in the music and arts community."

Alan paused for a second. "Yoko was right, wasn't she?" His voice showed reluctant admiration for the way Yoko had predicted the government's reaction.

"She seems to have a sixth sense about what's going on." I admitted. "Maybe I should be asking for her opinion more often from now on."

Technically, the most recent extension of their stay was in a professional working visa category, which allowed the Lennons to make various appearances. Earlier, they'd spent a week co-hosting the Mike Douglas program, five episodes in which they had introduced several of their new friends, including Jerry Rubin, to the TV audience.

The working visa category also covered their Michigan appearance when they performed at the rally for John Sinclair about a month earlier.

But no one had told me about that appearance yet. I may have taken some first steps on this case, but to a great extent, I was walking in the dark.

4

Dirty Tactics

*The Department of Justice is a law enforcement
agency. It is not the place to carry on a program aimed
at curing the ills of society.*

—John N. Mitchell

Yoko's premonitions about political interference against her and John
seemed correct. Certainly, District Director Marks chose to handle
their case in a very unusual way. I had been involved in many deportation cases before this one, but never with one which commanded the
personal attention of the district director himself at each juncture.

Years later, both through investigation and use of the Freedom
of Information Act, I managed to get a look at the INS file on the
Lennon proceedings. It made for some interesting reading.

For instance, after Marks agreed to a one-month extension of
stay, I filed the request for the Lennons on January 31, 1972. The
file shows how Sol Marks forwarded the papers to the applications
unit with a note: "Mr. Spivack—in re: Mr. & Mrs. John Lennon,

discussed cases with Assistant Commissioner Bernsen. Okay to grant change of status and extend stay to 2/29/72 for both aliens. Sol Marks 1-31-72."

Reading on in the file, just two days later, a memo went out from the central office to all INS regional and district offices regarding Lennon, stating that as to "any further applications for extension of stay, adjustment of status or other services" it was required that all officers "defer action and contact the central office." John Lennon had become a marked man.

Had I been aware of all this behind-the-scenes activity, I might not have been surprised when on March 3 I received a copy of a letter written to my clients and signed by Marks. In this communication he advised them that their temporary stay as visitors expired on February 29 and that "it is expected that you will effect your departure from the United States on or before March 15, 1972. Failure to do so will result in the institution of deportation proceedings." Sol had warned me to tell John and Yoko to "get out." Now he was obviously working to make that happen. John and Yoko thought that the two-week authorization showed some consideration, but that feeling didn't last long.

The same morning, I received a call from Marks personally advising me to disregard that letter. This wasn't good news, however. Sol told me that another letter of the same date was being sent to my clients and me. This letter contained the same information but also included an additional paragraph, instructing us to "please notify this Service, of the date, place and manner of your departure at least two days in advance of your leaving by calling Mr. Orville R. Conley at 264-5896."

Marks was crossing his T's and dotting his I's as though someone was looking over his shoulder every step of the way.

We had another surprise in store. Two INS investigation officers, fellows I knew from previous cases, appeared at my office to serve papers on me. They indicated that they had already served my clients with the same papers. In all of my prior and later years of practice in the immigration field, this had never taken place!

The papers consisted of copies of a letter to my clients stating:

"Your temporary stay in the United States as visitors expired on February 29, 1972.

"On March 1, 1972, we advised you in writing that you were expected to effect your departure from the United States on or before March 15, 1972. It is now understood that you have no intention of effecting your departure by that date. We are therefore revoking the privilege of voluntary departure as provided by existing regulations."

Attached to the letter were two "Orders to Show Cause," the charging documents which commence deportation proceedings, dated March 6. The charge consisted of allegations that John and Yoko were citizens of Great Britain and Japan and that they had overstayed their stay in the United States. It was claimed that as a matter of law each had "remained in the United States for a longer period than permitted." That was pretty much routine. What shocked me was the fact that the deportation hearing was scheduled for March 16, 1972. Why did Marks find it necessary to rush through the usual short grace period for voluntary removal, instead of having a hearing at the expiration of that time? Why did he not simply wait until March 15 and *then* start the deportation process, the customary approach? The way these papers were drafted might well provide me with a defense: that my clients were authorized until March 15 to stay, not February 29. Although this would still permit the government to issue new papers charging that they stayed beyond March 15, it left the "overstay" charge subject to challenge.

The whole situation seemed more than a little strange. John had gotten the okay to enter the country with his wife for child custody proceedings that still hadn't been resolved. To allow John entry, the government had waived the drug conviction that made him technically ineligible. Now, suddenly, the government was shocked, *shocked*, to find that John had been convicted in England and decided that he had to leave forthwith! And, if he dared to hang around and argue his case, he was labeled an overstay and again would be deported. The INS seemed to be going out of its way to manufacture new charges.

I didn't get much time to consider the oddness of the government's posture. On the next day, March 7, the same two INS officers appeared at my office and served me with copies of "superseding"

Orders to Show Cause against my clients. The two men looked a little sheepish, obviously feeling like "Keystone Kops," serving new papers whenever someone at the INS decided that the prior ones were not serious enough. Though trying to sound professional, the INS officers seemed embarrassed as they confirmed that they had just served the Lennons with the same "superseding" papers. They too must have realized that this kind of personal service was highly unusual.

These papers were dated March 7 and still required a deportation hearing on March 16. However, they contained additional allegations, correcting the earlier error. The new papers alleged that my clients were "granted the privilege of departing the United States voluntarily on or before March 15, 1972." They also alleged that the Lennons had abandoned their intention to depart from the United States by March 15, 1972, that on March 6 the "privilege of voluntary departure to March 15, 1972 was revoked." Further, the papers alleged that the Lennons "remained in the United States after February 29, 1972 without authority." Also, an additional legal charge had been added. Instead of simply alleging that my clients were overstays, this document also alleged that they "failed to comply with the conditions" of their temporary status. Now I was really stumped. Was there some additional way that John and Yoko had violated their visitor status other than by remaining on American soil?

The correctness of Yoko's intuition that higher authorities in Washington were behind the INS's haste to remove them was becoming clearer and clearer to me. Plainly, the INS was not approaching this case in a normal, routine way. In no other case that I knew of had aliens been served personally with Orders to Show Cause at their home address. And in no other case had I ever been served personally with copies of such papers at my office. While I had received "superseding" Orders to Show Cause in other cases, they were generally served at the hearing when it became clear that the original charging papers were defective. Somebody was guiding these proceedings, someone who had the authority to tell Marks that they did not like his original papers. Why was it necessary to revoke the permission to remain until March 15, which had been authorized, and have the hearing on the very next day? What was so holy about the March 16 date?

these materials in Schiano's locked desk drawer. The next morning, although only Schiano, DeVito, Schiano's chief clerk, and the security officer knew the combination to the drawer lock, seven of twelve of the files were missing.

Schiano complained that this was "not the first time" that had happened. When DeVito reported the disappearance of the reports to Sol Marks, who seemed unaffected by the incident, DeVito is quoted as having screamed at Marks, "You're a Jew, don't you care?"

As if the Lennon case didn't tax Schiano enough, his investigation of Ryan brought more problems. Even the meager sums to be paid by the INS to the elderly, poor witnesses who had come to testify against Ryan never materialized. Several of the witnesses received threatening calls, as did DeVito's German wife at the time.

DeVito had married a young German woman years earlier when he served in the US Army. He had actually visited Majdanek a few days after its liberation by Russian forces. Schiano and DeVito were said to have taken up a collection to reimburse some of the witnesses' travel expenses.

Because of stories like these about his efforts to persuade his reluctant INS superiors to prosecute former Nazis, I considered Vinny Schiano a worthy opponent. Despite the fact that he was my antagonist in the courtroom, I trusted him. And I admired him. No matter what Cold War reasons might have brought these people to the United States, Schiano felt there was no excuse for allowing Nazis who perpetrated war crimes to remain here after lying their way into this country.

Even when evidence came from Soviet sources, which, given the politics of the era, were considered biased and less reliable, Vinny Schiano didn't hesitate to prosecute. He was a man of principle. This gave me a great deal of respect for his handling of the Lennon case.

5

A Question of Conviction

*Mr. Lennon is ineligible for a visa and admission into the
United States because of a conviction of possessing
cannabis resin.*

—INS form letter to people requesting
information on the Lennon case

I can never read the heading above this chapter without getting
annoyed. For all the harping on John's possession arrest, this simply
wasn't a relevant point. Thanks to a waiver of this famous drug conviction, John Lennon *had already received a visa and had been admitted*
into the United States. He had a legitimate reason to ask for an extension of his stay. Yet in thousands of letters responding to questions
and complaints about the deportation proceedings, the INS slipped
in this little disclaimer.

Whether it was for publicity or political reasons, I can't say.
Certainly, the official reason for declaring John Lennon ineligible

to stay in America was his drug conviction back in 1968. But did that conviction automatically bar his application to remain in the United States permanently? For the government, it certainly seemed sufficient. That belief emboldened them to take the drastic step of attempting to deport John and Yoko. Whether voluntarily or by force, the Nixon administration and the INS figured that the Lennons would soon cease to cause trouble—they would be gone.

Precedent decisions, of which I was painfully aware, stood practically unanimous in the government's favor. Congress had a clear intention to exclude those with even the most minor of drug-related convictions. Waivers of such convictions were available only for purely temporary trips to the United States, and then only grudgingly granted. Oddly enough, the law allowed waivers for immigration by persons convicted of burglary or even serious or violent offenses like rape and murder. But by law, conviction for an offense involving marijuana or a narcotic drug allowed for no mercy, even for those with otherwise unblemished records, like Lennon.

So, without precedent to help me, I plunged into researching John's legal troubles back in Britain. The first thing I discovered was the media circus that had swirled around his trial. In 1968, the Beatles were at the top of their game. Since they first came to prominence, John Lennon, now twenty-eight and one of the eldest of the group, had been regarded as the dominant member. Together with Paul McCartney, he had composed most of their successful songs. In 1968, they debuted their huge hit, *The White Album*, which sold thirty million copies. Most people didn't even have a clue that the Beatles would break up in a year.

As I read the coverage, I imagined that the Marylebone Magistrate Court must have presented a strange sight back on the morning of November 28, 1968. Young men in leather and fur and young women in purple and pink spoke excitedly as a huge crowd gathered. When they tried to enter the building, they were told that the court would not open for another hour. One of the policemen on duty accused the crowd of being "hooligans." But they were only Beatles fans, anxious to see John Lennon and his friend, Yoko Ono Cox, as they faced charges after their arrest by Scotland Yard's Drug Squad for possessing drugs. Detective Sergeant Norman Pilcher, who headed the squad, seemed to make a career out of busting famous British rock musicians on drug charges.

The gathered fans were in for a disappointment. When John and Yoko arrived in their Ford Executive, they were smuggled into court through a side entrance. Still, they were supportive. "Get 'em John!" shouted one well-wisher.

Lennon wore a black corduroy suit, white shirt, and white tie. Yoko—who was charged in her full name as Mrs. Yoko Ono Cox—was in black flared slacks and a white bell-sleeve blouse. They stood in the dock side-by-side with their solicitor, Martin Polden. In another blow to the fans, only nineteen people got permission to observe the proceedings, filling the public area of the gallery. Most were teenaged girls.

The clerk of the court told Lennon and Yoko they would be dealt with by the magistrate, or they could be tried elsewhere. Lennon replied briefly: "Here." The charges were then read to them, and they were permitted to make their pleas.

Roger Frisby, the prosecuting attorney, said that Lennon had accepted full responsibility for the drugs found when police raided a flat where the couple lived in Montagu Square, Marylebone, on the morning of October 18. By taking this step, John implied that Yoko had nothing to do with the drugs.

"There is no evidence that she did, and in the circumstances, I think it right to accept the plea," stated the prosecutor. He then moved on to the second charge, obstruction of justice. This was based upon the police report that seven or eight minutes passed before the doors were opened to the arresting officers. Lennon's lawyer explained that the cause of the delay was the need for the couple to get dressed, and the fact that they had called Lennon's solicitor.

Frisby acknowledged that there appeared to be reasons for the delay that were totally unconnected with the drugs, and that "there is no suggestion that the two defendants took advantage of this delay of seven or eight minutes before the officers were admitted to dispose of drugs."

At this point, Magistrate J. C. Phipps looked at Yoko and said: "There is no evidence on either of the charges against you, and in the circumstances, both charges will be dismissed."

The magistrate then told Lennon that there was no evidence against him to hint that he had in any way obstructed the police and that the obstruction charge would also be dismissed.

Frisby said that when the police told Lennon they had a search warrant, he replied: "All right, I have already rung my solicitor." The police reported that when asked whether he had any drugs in his possession, Lennon replied: "Yes, I have some prescription 'Black Bombers' for slimming." He shook his head when asked if he had any other drugs. Frisby confirmed that the flat was searched with the help of police dogs and traces of cannabis resin were located in several places, including a binocular case on the mantlepiece.

Lennon was quoted as having asked the police: "Can I just ask a question? If this stuff is all mine, it will be me only that's involved?" Detective Sergeant Pilcher told him, "That would be for the court to decide."

The prosecutor then stated that at the police precinct, when being charged, Lennon declined to make any statement about the drugs.

Mr. Polden, Lennon's solicitor, explained to the magistrate that John and Yoko had occupied the flat for about three months before the police searched it. They moved there following Lennon's matrimonial difficulties, first bringing very few belongings with them. They were on a macrobiotic diet and had used no drugs, nor did they have any in their possession. Later on, Lennon arranged for a number of items to come from his Weybridge home, but these were largely undisturbed and not really unpacked. Lennon really believed at the time of the police search that he was "clean" of drugs.

He further pointed out that Yoko had been in the hospital for several weeks, hoping to save her unborn child, but unfortunately had suffered a miscarriage. The circumstances were, therefore very emotional, and the publicity attendant to the matter had not been welcome. Lennon acknowledged prior experience with drugs but was not on drugs when the apartment was searched, Polden continued, implying that any drugs located in the search had been delivered with still unpacked items from his other residence.

"I hope you will accept that he has made efforts to cleanse himself," Polden said. "He is an artist of note and integrity, he has brought some pleasure to millions, and has stood by his views. He is entitled to some compassion from the court." The attorney also mentioned a current government report on drugs, which was being studied by the British Home Secretary, suggesting less severe penalties for people smoking cannabis.

The magistrate responded by asking Mr. Polden: "Has anyone suggested that £250 is too much for any cannabis offense?"

When Polden responded "No," the court imposed a fine of £150, plus costs.

That was the story as reported in the media. However, as John and Yoko told me, there was considerably more going on. The Drug Squad had gotten quite a reputation not only for finding drugs on rock stars they raided, but for planting them as well. Yoko intimated that she and John had gotten tipped off about the prospective raid. Their macrobiotic diet required them to strictly avoid any drugs at all, but since the apartment had been used by some other musicians, they took no chances and had it thoroughly cleaned.

Sergeant Pilcher had come with his police, his dogs, and his drugs. Lennon was charged with possession of cannabis resin and obstructing justice. He explained to me that obstructing justice in his case involved "trying to get your trousers on and get to the door before they broke it down."

Apparently these celebrity raids were all part of a master plan by Detective Sergeant Pilcher to rid England of what he considered to be the source of the drug problem among British youth.

In preparing to go before the magistrate, John's major consideration had been Yoko. She was, after all, not a British subject, and a conviction might have gotten her deported from the country. John's solicitor advised John that his plea of guilty would solve the problem and that he would probably be punished by a fine, with no jail time. Martin Polden also believed that this plea, taking responsibility for the drugs, would permit the magistrate to dismiss the charges against Yoko. The fine he could easily afford, and it was highly unlikely that a minor conviction for possessing cannabis resin in England would ever cause him difficulty in the future.

Four years later, this proved unfortunately not to be true.

However, after contacting Martin Polden, I became convinced of the man's legal talents. If such a capable lawyer knew that the drugs were planted by Sergeant Pilcher, he would not have pleaded John guilty if there was a way of demonstrating his innocence of the charges.

I resolved to study the British law carefully on my own and asked Polden to furnish me with the necessary materials. In addition, I was interested in determining whether Lennon could reopen his drug case at this point. Four years had passed since the conviction was entered. The British legal system required Polden, a solicitor, to obtain an opinion from a barrister by issuing "instructions" requesting such an opinion.

I told Polden that the formidable US immigration law required a complete expungement of the conviction, which would leave the accused in the position as though he were never charged with a crime at all. Reopening the case in a way that only affected the punishment or "penal consequences" of the crime was insufficient. Even a foreign pardon would not have the necessary effect, nor would an act of the British Parliament, which is not a court but a legislature. A court would have to accept an appeal, quash the conviction, and direct a judgment or verdict of acquittal.

Polden promised that he would get me some proof that these questions were being researched and that a proceeding of this nature might be brought. He made no assurances of the ultimate outcome, which he warned me was at the least highly speculative. The process would require the British Court of Sessions to first permit the filing of a late appeal, and then for the House of Lords, acting in its judicial rather than its legislative capacity, to rule on the subject.

Still worse, even if we succeeded in filing a late appeal, Lennon would need to be physically in the United Kingdom for the proceedings, which would immediately defeat our proceedings here. He would likely never be admitted to the United States again.

We also had to deal with the question of the charge against Yoko, dismissed when John chose to plead guilty. Perhaps that would need to be revisited as well. This was hardly a matter that I wanted her to deal with at this critical time in her search for Kyoko. The fact that the American repercussions of the British conviction were greater than they were in England itself was not a positive factor to be considered by the British Home Office. Polden did not hold out much hope.

However, the solicitor reported to me that certain members of the Drug Squad, who were involved in Lennon's arrest, had "since come under scrutiny themselves by police higher authority," and that "indeed one detective sergeant is now having his past activities inquired into, and the nature of the inquiries are such as to lend support to the assertions of Mr. Lennon."

At this point, it seemed to me that the best likelihood for gaining a reversal of Lennon's case was to await the outcome of the investigation of Detective Sergeant Pilcher's activities on the Drug Squad. I asked Polden to have someone assigned to watch that investigation carefully. He promised to report regularly.

Considering the worry and mental anguish Detective Sergeant Norman Clement Pilcher brought upon the Lennons with his planted drugs, it seems only just to note that Pilcher himself was charged with a similar offense . . . and subsequently faced deportation.

Pilcher's arrest grew out of the Sands Case in London in June of 1972. The trial, which lasted for over a month, resulted in the conviction of four men and a woman for conspiring to import or acquire possession of twenty-four pounds of cannabis. A more critical result however, was the light it shed on a bitter dispute between the Scotland Yard Drug Squad and the London Customs Branch. Both British agencies were involved in enforcing the drug laws, much as the FBI and the Drug Enforcement Agency had similar responsibilities.

Pilcher's chief, Victor Kelaher, a decorated and successful officer, had a very close relationship with US drug agents, which caused British Customs to become more than jealous. In his unusually close cooperation with the Americans, Kelaher violated British law by allowing the export of drugs to the USA where federal agents arrested the drug smugglers. British Customs obtained a court order to tape one of Kelaher's informants. They learned that Kelaher was cooperating with him and dealing in drugs. After overcoming bureaucratic hurdles, British Customs succeeded in charging Kelaher, together with Pilcher and others in the Scotland Yard Drug Squad, with "perverting the course of justice" and perjury.

Now-former sergeant Pilcher had resigned his position with the Drug Squad and left to reside in Australia, where he was arrested on board a liner as he arrived with his family. Extradition proceedings commenced.

I immediately requested Lennon's permission to have someone in London contact Pilcher or his attorney to see whether we could do anything about John's old conviction.

As for the other officers facing charges, including Detective Chief Inspector Kelaher, they were suspended from their Scotland Yard duties. The case in which they conspired resulted in a dismissal, and a mother and daughter charged with drug offenses walked free from the Old Bailey. The court found that "the only right and proper course would be for the Crown to offer no evidence against these two defendants."

At this point, however, we had no assurance that we could prove similar misconduct took place in our case, nor could we be certain that the court would permit the reopening of a judgment entered four years earlier.

However, I developed several good theories on how my client might qualify for lawful permanent residence status even if he didn't get his conviction expunged. I believed we had a good chance of proving that the British legal system at the time would not have required the prosecution to prove its case against Lennon beyond a reasonable doubt. Specifically, if British law did not require the government to prove that Lennon had *mens rea*, guilty knowledge of a crime, then a conviction could be entered in England even if he never knew he had drugs in his possession. In the United States, however, such a conviction would be considered to deprive him of due process. It might be a real conviction in Britain, but it shouldn't be used against him in this country. And even in England, my research turned up a new twist. Some time after John's conviction, the British Parliament amended the Dangerous Drug Act, adding the word "knowing" to the description of the type of possession required for a conviction under the statute.

The INS thought they had a strong conviction to use against the Lennons. I, however, had a strong conviction that we might surprise them when we finally got to court.

6

Off to Court

The District Director of the US Immigration and Naturalization Service announced that former Beatle John Lennon and his wife, Yoko Ono, have been asked to appear at a hearing later today to show cause why they should not be deported.

—Reuters News Service, March 16, 1972

A deportation proceeding is divided into two separate parts. First, the government must establish the ground of deportation, in this case, the fact that the Lennons had overstayed their permission to remain since February 29. Then came the application portion, where the Lennons had to prove they were entitled to the privilege of permanent residence.

With respect to the first part, the Lennons didn't have to testify—why help to make the government's case? On the other hand, based on what I'd learned of their drug case, I expected a large media presence in the courtroom, and I wanted John and Yoko to appear to be fully cooperative as innocent parties in the situation. Accordingly, even though I could have insisted that the government prove every allegation of the charge, I decided to allow my clients to testify, but to indicate simply that they had not made up their minds as to whether or not they would depart by March 15. Of course, they could not have departed after March 15, because from the moment they were served with papers for a deportation hearing on March 16, they had no choice but to stay and appear. How could they leave?

This case promised to be different from other cases I had handled. I'd have to concern myself about the media and how my clients would appear to the general public. That didn't always make for good lawyering.

I knew that the Lennons, though they'd both worked professionally onstage, would be nervous witnesses. Like most people placed in deportation proceedings, they were very anxious and upset. As March 16 and the dreaded hearing came nearer, they fired questions at me about what deportation court would be like. In their prior brush with the law, both had appeared in the Marylebone Police Precinct and then before a magistrate. When John pleaded guilty, Yoko was not required to participate—the case against her was dismissed.

I assured them that although the proceeding was very serious, and the government was intent on removing them from the United States, I knew the people involved. I had the highest respect for Chief Trial Attorney Vincent Schiano. He was a decent man—and a Beatles fan. I had also appeared before Judge Ira Fieldsteel, an elegant gentleman and a fine, respected scholar in the immigration field.

To put my clients at ease, I made a special arrangement through Vinny Schiano to have us enter the INS building at 20 West Broadway an hour early. That way we could avoid crowds and meet privately in Schiano's office, where John and Yoko might relax for a while before entering the courtroom. Vinny was thrilled to have them in his office. His son Ray, also an avid Beatles fan, joined us, and my clients were immediately at ease with his informal, friendly manner. Schiano was much more familiar with the Beatles' music than I, and the conversation, which lasted quite a while, was very pleasant. Vinny's usually ruddy face had even higher color than usual.

When it was time to appear before Judge Fieldsteel, Schiano took me aside and whispered, "I don't think they realize that I'm the prosecuting attorney. Perhaps you should talk to them."

I turned to John and Yoko and said, "It's time to go into the courtroom now. I hope that you're more at ease, knowing that Vinny, here, is the INS prosecuting attorney."

Lennon jumped to his feet, whipped out a handkerchief from his pocket, bent down, and started polishing Schiano's shoes! He looked up with a grin and asked, "Is there anything else I could do for you, Mr. Schiano?"

By the time we were escorted into the hearing room, my clients were calm. As we entered, I noticed two tall men in suits seated at the front of the room. Lennon's driver, a former police officer, later advised me that they were New York City police officers assigned to the drug unit. (This was not the last occasion that I noticed these two in the INS court room. In fact, their faces appear near Lennon's on videotapes as he left the INS building after hearings. For policemen who should have been out of sight, they invariably ended up closer to my clients than I did.) After seeing them, I warned my clients that night. This development might mean that the INS had enlisted the New York police to bolster their case with a drug arrest.

Looking further, I saw quite a few members of the press, their notebooks at the ready. I also spotted another client of mine, Peter Bendry, who worked as the Lennons' assistant. He had a lavender-scented handkerchief, whose aroma seemed to fill the courtroom. The assembled observers buzzed about the fact that it smelled like marijuana. Judge Fieldsteel called the hearing to order and asked someone to open the window.

Once the scent of lavender dissipated, John and Yoko were sworn in as witnesses and Fieldsteel got to the case in a hurry: "Your name is John Winston Lennon?"

"Yes sir," John replied. "I did add Ono to my name in England legally—I don't know what that means here . . . I tried to drop Winston, but they made me keep Winston as well." The judge corrected the name of one of the respondents in the case to "John Winston Ono Lennon." I'm still not certain why, but that made me feel good.

The judge entered the charging papers into evidence. These called upon us to show cause why each of the parties should not be deported. However, when Fieldsteel asked us to respond to the allegations of the Orders to Show Cause, I indicated that I was not prepared to do so at that time and requested an adjournment of the proceedings. The judge allowed me to make a presentation supporting my request. I told him that I had requested Sol Marks, the district director of INS, to cancel the charges for being "improvidently issued" under the regulations. If we started the proceedings at this time, Marks would no longer have jurisdiction to rule on that request.

As a second basis for an adjournment, I pointed out that "third preference petitions as outstanding artists have been filed on March 3, 1972, with the district director and have not yet been adjudicated," adding that "it is the practice of the Immigration Service . . . to accord to the beneficiaries of third preference approved cases or those likely to be approved the privilege of remaining here to await the availability of visa numbers while they prepare applications for adjustment of status. . . ." Thus, I explained, Marks might decide to allow the Lennons to remain while he considered their third preference cases and further proceedings might be considered. District Director Marks granted an extension until February 29; he then ruled that John and Yoko might depart by March 15, but when he received our third preference petitions, he revoked that permission and issued charging papers with an order to appear in court on March 16 to show cause why the Lennons should not be deported. I admitted some puzzlement—why did the district director feel it necessary to revoke the short two-week period of time given to my clients to remain? Was there some emergency?

I explained that my clients were taken by surprise by the unusual urgency to rush them out of the country—they couldn't conceivably prepare a defense to these proceedings in the few days we had been given. I also drew attention to the fact that my clients also faced serious and emotionally taxing child custody proceedings in two out-of-state American courts, which took up a good deal of their time and emotional energy.

As I finished my arguments, I watched Judge Fieldsteel for some clue on how the hearing would proceed. Frankly, he disappointed my hopes, trying to short-circuit my adjournment request. The judge indicated that he could deal with the same request that I had filed with Marks, that is, to terminate the deportation case, as well as the district director could. I knew, however, that would put us in a bad tactical position. If I agreed to proceed, the judge could simply say that he would reserve his decision as to whether or not to terminate the proceedings until after he heard all the testimony. That would never have served my purpose. I needed more time.

Judge Fieldsteel also stated that he understood that my clients planned to apply for permanent residence status, because the third preference petitions were a first step in that direction. If so, the pendency of a residence case might prevent my clients from any necessary travel out of the United States, so he thought we should proceed to get the application for residence over with as soon as possible. I didn't appreciate Fieldsteel's cooperation with the district director's plan. Unfortunately, I couldn't show any such feelings to the judge.

I thanked Judge Fieldsteel for his concern but indicated that we also had ongoing dealings with the Lennons' British attorneys to find whether we could approach the British court and obtain an expungement of his conviction. That expungement, if granted, could potentially make him eligible for residence in the United States. "I have been advised as late as yesterday by counsel in England that in a period of two months he will have sufficient information either to provide us with an expungement or an opinion that it can or cannot be obtained in the courts of England." Until then, I was not in a position to determine whether or not we would be applying for lawful permanent residence and on what basis.

While the immigration judge responded, I looked around the room, especially at the representatives of the media. With them in mind, I hastened to point out to the judge that we would need to submit the testimony of a number of important personalities, and that arranging for the presence of such witnesses could not be done on such short notice.

I knew that I could get an adjournment of the trial. It was the practice to grant at least one adjournment to allow time for an attorney to prepare a defense to a deportation case. No way was I going to budge from my request.

I couldn't help feeling suspicious, though, about the way that everyone seemed to be talking about John's conviction—especially since there was no evidence in the immigration court record that such a conviction existed at all. The Lennons' official immigration file was in the hands of the INS trial attorney, Mr. Schiano. In such proceedings, the immigration judge has no file at all, except for any documents handed to him and admitted in evidence and the testimony he hears from witnesses. All Judge Fieldsteel had were the Orders to Show Cause. Of course, since the matter had been covered in all the local newspapers, I assumed that the judge had read about it. If he had discussed the case with Sol Marks, or with his attorney, Mr. Schiano, outside my presence, it would have been grounds for challenge. Certainly, unless he was furnished with a copy of the conviction in open court, Judge Fieldsteel had no way to rule on its effect in this deportation case.

I had decided to request an eight-week adjournment of the trial. When I stated that, Schiano predictably opposed the idea, stating that the case should be tried and an order of deportation entered. If we succeeded in obtaining an expungement of the British conviction, he asserted, the case could then be reopened to consider any applications for residence. Of course, that was not truly an option. Once the judge entered a deportation order, John and Yoko would be removed from the country, immediately!

I pointed out to Judge Fieldsteel that this was the first time the case was on the calendar and that a two-month adjournment was quite routine in this kind of case.

Schiano could not very well oppose an adjournment completely. So he argued that two weeks was "more than enough" to prepare a defense. As a compromise, the judge granted an adjournment of one month, to April 18, 1972.

It was now clear to me that my third preference petitions were the critical key to the future handling of the case. Without an approval on them, I could not apply for permanent residence for my clients at all, and the judge could simply order them removed.

When Judge Fieldsteel granted a one-month adjournment, I knew that my work was cut out for me. And, going by the attitude of the immigration judge and the prosecuting attorney, I wouldn't get much time to do what was needed.

7

Another Day in Court

*The attorney commented that his client felt he
was being deported due to his outspoken remarks
concerning US policy in S.E. Asia.*

—Urgent, coded teletype to FBI Director
J. Edgar Hoover, April 18, 1972

The case certainly kept me busy, checking with overseas attorneys, researching the British law, and examining American case law to find a way around the statute that seemed to bar John's chances of staying here permanently.

In addition, almost two months had passed since we'd filed our third preference petitions. We hadn't seen any activity, not even an acknowledgment, from the government in that time. Since the procedure required the INS to contact the Department of Labor for an opinion regarding the petitions, I checked with friends at Labor. No one had seen or heard anything connected with the Lennons. Word would have spread like wildfire through that small department if applications for such a celebrity couple had come to them from the INS.

With all this on my plate, on April 17 I received a telephone call from Vinny Schiano.

Vinny told me that the government would be opposing all my requests. It would challenge John's eligibility for permanent residence based upon the statute. If instead he applied for permission to depart the United States without a deportation order (as he was required to do to avoid being deported) the INS would oppose that, too. Vinny confirmed that Sol Marks was about to deny the preliminary motions I had filed with him regarding both John and Yoko, and that Schiano was under instructions to seek a prompt and final order of deportation in both cases.

Vinny then made a "helpful" suggestion, that I consider separating the two cases, so that Yoko's case might have a chance on its own. He offered this recommendation because his client instructed him to oppose any application that Yoko might make as well, if she was in the same proceeding with John.

Besides, Yoko's case was a simpler matter. Assuming approval of her third preference request, it came down to determining whether she was entitled to apply for residence since she had no conviction.

John's case, on the other hand, even assuming the approval of the third preference application, would face the government's opposition because of his drug conviction. My alternative in John's case would involve applying for the privilege of "voluntary departure." This is permission to depart the United States without the entry of a deportation order. Then John could apply to come as a visitor again, if he qualified to do so. In a deportation case, one must apply for any benefit to which one is entitled. If the application is not made, it is considered forfeited. Vinny put it plainly—since the issues were completely different, it would be best to separate them.

I respected Vinny as a man of integrity. But I also suspected him as a courtroom tactician. I often saw him with his arm around the shoulder of his opponent in a case, walking down the long corridor in deep conversation. He'd seem very agreeable, offering his opposing counsel generous time to work out some hoped-for resolution in a case. Actually Vinny was maneuvering for an airtight stipulation on the record in a deportation proceeding. To get that time, the opposing lawyer had to consent to the removal of his client if he couldn't accomplish what was needed by a given date—no ifs, ands, buts, or appeals allowed. One had to look carefully at any gifts from this gentleman.

Vinny was sharp. He knew that having both John and Yoko appear in the same proceeding was dangerous for the government. In the event that the hearing granted Yoko permanent residence but denied it to John, she would face a heartbreaking choice in the full glare of the public media. Splitting up the cases would defuse this high-tension situation. Even if the same immigration judge were to preside in both cases, it wouldn't be the same. We were better off in one proceeding.

I told Vinny that I appreciated the call and that I would have to consult with my clients to see which way they'd prefer to proceed. Privately, it was good to know that the government was concerned about its public image. Vinny's call left me convinced that my strategy of keeping John and Yoko together in one case was on point.

We were proceeding to what might be a final hearing in the case, and I still didn't have any word about the pending third preference petitions. If those petitions were not approved before the date of our hearing, I had very little room to maneuver. The government wouldn't need to deny John and Yoko's residence cases, because we couldn't even file them! And if we applied for voluntary departure, that could be denied, with the Lennons forcibly deported from the country. The situation was treacherous. I realized that I had to act quickly, yet very carefully.

In what would become a ritual throughout the case, I visited the Lennons so we could all go to court together. This morning, they were puzzled about what one wore to one's deportation hearing. Bearing in mind Vinny Schiano's continuing attempts to separate their cases, I saw a wonderful opportunity.

"What clothes do you have that are exactly the same?" I asked. "I want you to dress exactly alike. You should appear like a matched set, a couple who no compassionate judge would want to separate."

That broke the tension. After a good deal of banter and some shuffling behind closet doors, it appeared that both John and Yoko had black suits, white shirts and black ties. John looked as if he had dressed to go to high school; Yoko looked quite smart in her black-and-white outfit. They really appeared like a matched set! What's more, they seemed to enjoy the look.

I hadn't finished, though. I told them they should sit together to my left in the hearing room, hold hands, and never separate. If anyone suggested that their cases be tried separately, they were to make the saddest faces possible. Sticking together, both physically and legally, was crucial to the success of their case.

As we entered the building that housed the INS at 20 West Broadway, a battery of TV cameras greeted us. John handled the reporters masterfully, as usual. After we got in the elevator with INS guards, he turned to me with a grin. "You're never going to be quoted in the papers, Leon, if you keep talking in sentences of over five words."

Once in the courtroom, John and Yoko took their assigned places, and, indeed, looked like a well-matched pair. In black and white, holding hands, they made a beautiful picture of a truly devoted couple. Yoko also carried a bright red apple, an allusion, no doubt, to their business corporation, known as "Apple Corps."

As I turned to observe the courtroom that day, I spotted the same two plainclothes narcotics officers John and Yoko's driver had previously pointed out to me. Since cameras and TV equipment were not allowed in the room, the small courtroom was filled with media representatives, complete with pencils and pads. Several additional INS investigators stood at the doors, controlling who could enter.

Immigration Judge Fieldsteel opened the hearing, asking John and Yoko whether I was still their attorney. The judge then turned to me and asked whether I had any applications to make in the proceeding.

Of course, I did. "When we last appeared here, I had made a motion to the government, to the district director, to terminate these proceedings . . . yesterday afternoon by telephone the district director informed me that he would be denying our motion." I gestured to the judge. "I therefore respectfully renew these motions before you today."

The grounds for my motions, I explained, were both technical and humanitarian. "Mrs. Lennon has absolutely no legal impediment whatsoever in her application," I said. Starting a deportation proceeding against her was "certainly improvident and possibly a severe abuse of discretion." Once again, I raised the fact that when third preference petitions were filed, historically petitioners could remain until their applications were adjudicated and their residence applications processed. "This is the uniform practice of the Immigration Service," I said, "and it was departed from in this case."

As for John, my reading of the statute did "not in my opinion disqualify Mr. Lennon for applying for residence." Moreover, the case law that I had reviewed offered one situation where a California defendant, arrested while under the influence of marijuana, was not deported under the provisions of the law. I quoted from part of the decision: ". . . while Congress undoubtedly intended to close every possible loophole where a person had been convicted of a crime related to the possession of narcotics, the legislative history indicated that the committee's aim was to eliminate *traffic* in narcotics as distinguished from *use*."

I then moved to the humanitarian ground in my request to terminate the proceedings. One aim of the Immigration Act was the reunion of families. Now, John and Yoko were both technically the parents of an American citizen, Yoko's daughter Kyoko. Both court orders in the ongoing custody case required that Kyoko be raised by John and Yoko *in the United States*, but the US government was attempting to deport them, certainly not in Kyoko's best interests. "Will it be then," I asked, "that the father simply intends to wait out his time until they are removed from the United States in order that he can continue his illegal custody of the child?"

Considering the time and effort the Lennons had expended trying to locate Kyoko's whereabouts in order to care for her in this country, I felt justified in arguing "that the proceedings here are not in the public interest and constitute a severe hardship to these respondents and should be terminated."

I then turned to how the Lennons had spent their time in the United States, focusing on the great public benefit from their presence here. "As recently as two or three days ago, they were appointed by an executive assistant to the president to participate in a national antidrug media effort."

(That comment sparked a great deal of excitement for the FBI, which was monitoring the proceedings. They wanted to know how this could have happened, in view of the Nixon administration's opposition to the Lennons. I'm afraid in the flow of my oratory, I slightly overstated the case. They were actually appointed by an executive assistant to the president of the American Bar Association, not President Nixon.)

The Lennons had also recently arranged a concert to help poor children in Bangladesh, a country wracked both by a war of independence and a terrible tidal wave. As I explained, their efforts raised funds that "exceeded in value the contribution of the United States government to the United Nations for that purpose."

Carried away with the drama of the request, I declaimed, "I have the impression that we stand on the threshold of repeating our error in the Charlie Chaplin case. Whether deportation proceedings are instituted, continued, or prosecuted, or whether they are terminated is completely discretionary, and that discretion is to be exercised in the public interest. It is well-known that every day the immigration authorities in this building exercise their authority to terminate and withhold deportation proceedings on humanitarian grounds, in the cases of minor children, persons seriously ill, in cases where third preference petitions are pending, and in a host of other areas . . . that normal, everyday approach to a case has not been followed in this case."

I turned to the media people as I continued. "The very institution of the proceedings against the Lennons is in our opinion solely for the purpose of restraining protected First Amendment rights. The Lennons have expressed their views publicly in the United States with respect to United States policies—particularly with respect to our involvement in Vietnam. These proceedings are deliberately an effort to silence the expression of serious, dispassionate, and seri-ously-held opinions that happen to differ with those of some of the officials of our government. . . . the American citizenry has a First Amendment right to hear, which is a constitutionally protected right. Nothing is more pernicious or destructive of our entire system of law than when the public has a feeling that the law is a tool whereby those in power can harass those who threaten or oppose them with otherwise lawful means. . . . the unfair application of the law is just as serious an offense as the passage of a law which is discriminatory on its face. There was no reason in the world requiring the govern-ment to commence deportation proceedings or to refuse to grant additional time to the parents of this child whose custody they have sought and whose whereabouts are still unknown to them. It is, in our opinion, a cruel misapplication of the law to permit to stand pro-ceedings to deport the parents of a child under these circumstances. In our opinion, what exists here is a frivolous, discriminatory action which appears to be punishment meted out to still two courageous voices of sincere dissent."

Vinny Schiano looked annoyed with my passionate plea. As the prosecuting attorney, he objected strenuously to my argument. The immigration judge, on the other hand, was more interested in know-ing whether Yoko would continue to apply for permanent residence if John's application were denied. It seemed to me that before he even heard any testimony, he knew what course he intended to follow. I let him have it.

"That is a question," I responded, "on which I would have to consult with them and discuss very carefully, in view of the fact such a situation would probably place her in a position of having to choose between her child and her husband."

The judge felt that it wasn't necessary for both of my clients to have permanent residence in order to look after the child. He noted that John had been given permission to visit the United States on prior occasions. I quickly pointed out that we'd been told that would no longer be possible. As I had anticipated, the judge then denied my application to terminate the proceedings. He stated that the proceedings were properly before him, and that if the charge was not sustained, then he could terminate the proceeding. Moreover, there was, as yet, no application placed before him. I then told the judge that I was not prepared to file the applications for residence yet. This would take at least an additional two weeks. I also intended to call a number of witnesses. These were important people both within and outside the United States, and we'd have to make arrangements for them to participate. The courtroom reporters got busy taking notes.

The immigration judge was anxious to know which people I intended to call as a witness. I explained that one was a member of Parliament in England, perhaps another was a member of the US Congress, and there were some renowned artists who knew the Lennons through the years and could testify as to their good character.

Schiano objected once again. He argued that Lennon's conviction prevented him from filing an approvable application—that disposed of the need to call witnesses in John's case.

Then he got into *his* issue—separating Yoko's application from John's. "There has been again, no motion to sever the cases, and if he wants that to be considered at this time, then we can consider the problem of witnesses." Luckily, the immigration judge passed over the issue of severing the proceedings and turned to the deportation charge. He asked whether we were prepared to plead to the various allegations of the Order to Show Cause. I responded that we were not—we needed an additional period of at least two weeks to proceed further.

The judge ruled that we should appear again in two weeks and be prepared to respond to the Order to Show Cause as well as to file the applications for adjustment of status to permanent residence. He assured us that if witnesses became relevant, he would authorize a further adjournment to give us time to arrange for their appearance.

On one hand, I was glad that the judge had kept John and Yoko together—maybe he enjoyed having both celebrities in his courtroom with the attendant media attention. However, I had to consider the possibility that Judge Fieldsteel simply planned to deny John's application based upon his conviction and rule that therefore we had no need for witnesses at all.

At least I had succeeded in obtaining another short adjournment, something I found very important. It gave us time for mounting a serious effort to get the third preference approvals by the new hearing date. I had to be ready by May 2, 1972. That wasn't just a tight deadline. It turned out to be more of a struggle than even I anticipated.

8

Lennon vs. Marks

*Mr. Greene advised Mr. Marks that it was the
Commissioner's position that we should not approve
any third preference visa petitions on behalf of the
male subject.*

—Carl G. Burrows, INS assistant commissioner for
investigations in a 1972 memo classified "Confidential"

Today, hearing the title of this court case makes some people laugh—
while it horrifies old-line Socialists. Now I can chuckle, but at the
time I brought the action, I considered this serious business indeed.

By the time we finished the legal skirmishing in the second
deportation hearing, I knew that John and Yoko's third preference
applications for permanent residence status loomed as crucial elements in our case.

The INS lists a variety of preference levels that an alien can use
to attain residency in the United States. At the time we're looking
at, if you won an Olympic gold medal, an Oscar, or maybe a Pulitzer
Prize, or were a famous researcher, you might apply under the third

preference. If you had an advanced degree, exceptional ability, or knowledge that might be in the national interest, another preference might work for you. A lower preference category involved skilled workers, professionals, and "other workers," where the restrictions were less stringent, but you faced a longer backlog of cases waiting for visa quota openings.

However, back in the early 1970s, third preference was the classification sought by extraordinary aliens in the arts or sciences. It was available to groups, as well as individuals. From the moment I decided to apply for permanent residency, my office staff had worked on the formal library research on John and Yoko's background. I had decided that it was very important to get separate, individual third preference petitions approved for both John and Yoko. She could not use the approval of John's petition as an outstanding alien to get residence for herself, unless his residence application was approved. Since the government seemed likely to deny John's residence, Yoko would be left without a basis for her own application for residence.

I felt it was crucial that I achieve permanent residence for Yoko, especially if John's case was delayed by appeals. Then I could show the hardship that their separation would cause.

I found no shortage of staff at my office willing to work on a draft of John's application to prove that he was an outstanding artist whose presence in the United States was prospectively beneficial to the national culture. No one volunteered to work on Yoko's paperwork, as clearly they were less familiar with her work. My own impression of Yoko was that she was highly intelligent and blessed with an analytical mind. I was also impressed that she had a special gift, an apparent sixth sense, figuring out why things happened. So I undertook that part of the research myself.

Yoko's career did not follow the usual pattern of most artists, whose work was limited to a specific area or field. She had achieved international notoriety and professional acclaim in a variety of artistic endeavors, particularly in the avant garde scene as a media artist, an artist whose work involved the participation of the viewer in the various media. Her message, which complemented John's, was about seeking peace, brotherhood, and the use of human resources to achieve an uplifting state of love and peace; her work combined various media as an expression of a completely new and imaginative art form.

But Yoko also showed her grasp of the practicalities when she sent over a pile of documents for me to review, including the names of some "friends" in the art and music world who would be happy to write reference letters for the Lennons. I quickly realized that John and Yoko had an excellent chance of proving they were both outstanding figures in the arts, with a little help from their friends.

In the area of film, Yoko was confident that she could get reference letters from Elia Kazan, a producer and director of note, as well as Stanley Kubrick and Roman Polansky. I received a series of excellent reviews of Yoko's films as well as John's.

With respect to John's talent as a composer, they mentioned such names as Leonard Bernstein and John Cage, Ringo Starr, George Harrison, Chuck Berry, Bob Dylan, and Phil Spector. For an evaluation of artistic talent, we could approach Salvador Dali, Jasper Johns, Andy Warhol, and the artistic curator of the Metropolitan Museum, Henry Geltzehler.

Other people willing to write references included Dick Cavett, on whose TV talk show John and Yoko had appeared, and who was also the performing arts program director of the Asia Society; the Associate Curator of the Whitney Museum of American Art, James K. Monte; and Professor Lawrence Alloway of the State University of New York at Stony Brook. From the media, we could contact Virgil Thompson, the *New York Times* critic, John Gruen, the cultural reporter for the *Times*, and Alan Rich, the music critic and arts editor of *New York Magazine*. Performer friends included (believe it or not) Jack Lemmon, Fred Astaire, Gloria Swanson, and numerous others.

With such a wealth of talent to draw on, the applications that I prepared boasted reference letters from an extraordinary array of important names in all the arts in which Lennon and Yoko were involved. Moreover, some of those we contacted also offered to testify on John and Yoko's joint behalf.

To add a commercial aspect to the application, we got a statement from the secretary of Apple Records, setting forth gross billing in the United States through September 30, 1971, in an amount over $237 million for John Lennon's records, and $4.5 million for Yoko's records covering the much shorter period since 1969 when she began her recording career.

When I first met John, I mentioned it to a young cab driver who was taking me home, asking in my ignorance if he knew who this musician was. The cabbie's response, about more people having heard Lennon's music than Beethoven's, no longer seemed an overstatement by the time I completed putting together John and Yoko's applications. I'd practiced immigration law for fifteen years at that point in my career. I believe the work I did for the Lennons represented the most impressive third preference applications I ever drafted and filed. In my own work, I paid special attention to Yoko's application because of the critical importance it would play in our strategy for handling the case.

I soon learned that the government had decided that the special (although routine) practice of allowing persons whose third preference applications were pending to remain here during the adjudication period would not apply to the Lennons. I verified that decision with Sol Marks's deputy and called Sam Bernsen myself. Thus the quality of the third preference petitions that I had prepared became all the more important.

As I worked on Yoko's application, I began to have some unsettling thoughts. Yoko had told me in no uncertain terms that she believed President Nixon was out to remove her and John from the United States. This apparently had something to do with Nixon's desire to be reelected and his feeling that anyone who opposed his reelection was a danger to the country.

I had read in the *New York Times* that Nixon had tapped his friend and former law partner John Mitchell to run his campaign. As chairman of C.R.E.E.P., the Committee to Reelect the President, Mitchell didn't trouble me. However, Mitchell's "day job" as attorney general of the United States made him the top man in the Justice Department. In those days, the Immigration and Naturalization Service fell under the jurisdiction of the Justice Department.

If Yoko was correct in her hunch, Nixon would have no difficulty in scuttling any applications I might file for the Lennons. Even worse, because of the secretive way in which the INS operated, we might never be the wiser if the attorney general instructed his minions to "misplace" or lose the applications I had filed. Suddenly, I felt that I might have placed my clients in a very vulnerable position. I immediately resolved to keep tabs on the applications, assuring that they were adjudicated and not lost in the shuffle.

If the applications received approval, I would be in a position to apply for permanent residence status for my clients, based upon my theory of their eligibility. If, on the other hand, the applications were denied, there would certainly be great public outrage that the INS did not consider Lennon an outstanding artist. But if the government took no action at all, what could I do? There was no other available basis for a permanent residence application for Yoko and John.

By now, almost two months had passed since we filed our third preference petitions with no activity, not even an acknowledgment, from the government. On April 20 I put in writing my request to read all of the many files relating to my clients that were in the government's hands. This was my clients' right and, since I had not previously represented the Lennons, I was not aware of their prior history with the INS.

I called Marks at the same time, and he agreed to permit me to inspect the various files that they had at the INS, of which there were plenty. I was of course most interested in the third preference petitions, so I asked him about the status of those applications. He told me that they were "under consideration." I knew better, because I had consulted the operating units both at INS and at Labor that dealt with such petitions. Had anyone seen an application for John Lennon and Yoko Ono in either unit, everyone would have known about the papers being there.

I arrived at the INS office and was shown a pile of files relating to Lennon's many appearances in the United States as a Beatle, his waivers of ineligibility for temporary visas, and some of Yoko's applications. Conspicuous by their absence were the petitions I had filed on March 3. That made me even more suspicious that the INS was up to something. I let my annoyance show, saying that I would not leave the INS office until I got to see those files.

As the third preference petitions were being brought to me, I overheard one clerk mention to another that the package had been "in Mr. Spivak's safe." I knew the gentleman they were referring to was the assistant district director in charge of the entire application unit. I couldn't be sure whether they were referring to my applications. However, when they arrived, I found my petitions still in the envelope I'd placed them in for delivery, still securely stapled as I had put them together myself. It looked as if they had *never been touched* by an adjudicator! Even the labor documents in the application, which should have been removed and forwarded to the Department of Labor, were still where I'd attached them.

No prior act in violation of my clients' rights affected me quite as much as seeing those applications that day, apparently tucked way by the INS in some out-of-the-way place to gather dust.

I returned to my office thoroughly upset over what I had discovered. Could the government manage to scuttle my entire case by simply failing to adjudicate the petitions I sorely needed to protect my clients' rights? It seemed to me that I needed the intervention of a court if those petitions were to be adjudicated in time!

I called an old friend, Kent Karlsson, a litigation attorney who was adept at drafting federal lawsuits and met with him concerning the case. We scheduled an appointment to meet with Sol Marks the next day, and Kent was at my side. He could look fierce when he wanted to, and I wanted to confront Sol and let him know that the gloves were coming off.

I told the district director that his earlier reply about the third preference petitions being "under consideration" was obviously inaccurate, and that I needed their adjudication immediately. We had deportation proceedings scheduled for May 2, and I had been informed that the government would oppose any further adjournment. If the petitions could not be immediately adjudicated, I would be filing a lawsuit in federal court demanding that remedy.

Kent and I returned to my office to start drafting the preliminary court papers. First and foremost, we had to obtain an injunction to prevent the INS from proceeding with the deportation hearing until the third preference petitions received adjudication. If the preliminary injunction was granted to stay the deportation case, it would make no difference to us how long the government took to adjudicate the applications. We stayed up all night drafting the court papers and filed them the next morning. *Lennon vs. Marks* appeared on the federal court docket!

The judge assigned to the case was Bernard J. Lasker. Upon hearing our presentation, he quickly determined that John and Yoko might suffer irreparable harm if the deportation proceeding went on and the petitions were still not adjudicated. On the other hand, the INS could show no special hardship if it had to adjudicate the petitions before the deportation proceeding was held. He therefore granted the injunction we requested, restraining the INS from holding a deportation hearing (scheduled for May 2, the very next day), and ordering that a hearing must first be held in federal court on our lawsuit before the INS could take up continuing the matter of deportation.

The deportation case was stayed, pending the outcome of the federal case. Instead of spending May 2 at the INS, we went to federal court for a hearing on our case. We had accomplished one thing for certain: the INS would not succeed in railroading the Lennons out of the country and, at the same time, fail to adjudicate their properly filed applications!

I could hardly wait to read the opposing papers filed by the INS. In my petition to the court, I claimed that there was a possible conspiracy within the government to remove the Lennons from the United States in violation of their constitutional rights. I argued that the immigration process was being misused by the administration for its own political purposes. I speculated and stated that I believed that the government had no intention of adjudicating the applications until after the Lennons were gone, a situation that would result in irreparable damage to John and Yoko. Therefore, I requested the classic legal remedy of "mandamus"—requiring an administrative officer to perform a duty which he is required to perform by law.

Judge Lasker warned me that he could not order the INS to approve the applications. The court could only order that they be *adjudicated*. I responded by saying that I knew how to handle a denial. What I couldn't deal with on my own was the government's complete failure to act. Indeed, if INS officials chose to deny the applications and claimed that John Lennon and Yoko Ono were not aliens who were distinguished in the arts, that was their prerogative.

On May 2 when the court convened, Judge Whitman Knapp called counsel to the bench. I approached the bench, together with Stanley Wallenstein, the special assistant US attorney who represented the INS in federal court. The judge told us Sol Marks had called Wallenstein, saying that he would adjudicate the applications. "You know I can't order him to either approve or deny," Judge Knapp said. "He still has discretion to rule on these petitions."

Since all the rules of adjudication had been violated in this instance, I had no idea how long this would take. I therefore asked the judge to maintain the injunction in force until "I see the decisions and until you, Your Honor, and I have original approvals or denials. At least with a denial, I know what my remedies are."

The judge agreed, and I got another adjournment of the deportation case.

I learned a vital lesson that day. Within their own domain, the INS was all-powerful. They could determine to grant no further adjournments, and that my clients should be deported. They could play games with papers or take whatever action they desired for whatever purpose they might have. In federal court, however, that was not the case. The playing field before a federal judge was level.

What concerned me even more was the fact that the allegations of a conspiracy I'd made in my court papers were *never denied* by the INS. They filed no opposing papers whatsoever. Was it possible that the suspicions I had outlined, based "upon information and belief," were actually true, and that the US attorney representing INS did not wish to file a false reply by denying it? Had I struck gold? Was

Yoko's intuition that President Nixon wanted her and John out of the country correct?

The next day we received the Notices of Approval of both third preference applications! Now John Lennon and Yoko Ono could apply to adjust their status to that of lawful permanent residents of the United States in their deportation hearing. The first step of my planned strategy had succeeded.

9

Preparation

I still believe in America, in American justice and the American people and I really would like to stay and look for my daughter.

—Yoko Ono, *The New York Times*, April 29, 1972

May 2nd, 1972, came and went, the third fateful day in a month and a half, anticipated, even dreaded. I was quite certain that the INS, like a hungry tiger single-mindedly stalking its prey, had awaited that day impatiently. The opposition must have felt spurned and disappointed when the deportation proceeding had to be delayed once again.

The third preference notices themselves gave black-and-white proof that the INS only grudgingly offered its approval. On Yoko's approval notice, the box was checked indicating that she was in the United States and had applied for residence. It was understood that she would now be filing that final residence application. John's approval notice, on the other hand, merely had the box checked indicating that the petition was approved, as though there was no likelihood that he would apply for residence. The message was clear.

I expected the INS would grant John's petition because of his fame—or even notoriety. But this seemed not to be the case. They were more willing to grant Yoko's petition than John's, apparently because they'd been dragged into court by his counsel and had no other alternative! How could they ever claim that he was not an outstanding artist?

Once the federal court lifted its injunction, we were notified that the deportation proceedings would continue on May 12. Now that we had both petitions approved, I could actually carry out my strategy of filing for adjustment of status to permanent residence for both John and Yoko.

A lot would happen at this next hearing. I'd present my case, bring witnesses to testify, submit the necessary documents, and ask Judge Fieldsteel to exercise his discretion in favor of John and Yoko, granting them permanent residence in the United States.

I hoped that the judge would rise above the government's apparent policy of denying every application the Lennons might file and actually approve the case. With over a week in hand, I proceeded to line up my witnesses, contacting people scheduled to testify, and obtaining all the necessary letters and affidavits. I had an impressive set of applications.

In my desire not to overlook any possible point, the night before the hearing I checked a large brown folder that Yoko had sent me earlier in the week. It arrived by courier from John's London home, full of papers that she thought might have some relevance to the case. I had reviewed them previously but had somehow missed one strikingly important document.

Among the mass of papers was an actual green card, dated September 13, 1964, bearing the name and photo of Yoko Ono Cox! Could it actually be true that Yoko was *already a lawful permanent resident of the United States?*

I knew that Yoko had spent almost half her life on American soil, coming and going, but I was never told that she'd even attempted to become a lawful permanent resident. If she was, the government's proceedings against her were totally improper. They were entirely based upon her obtaining a visitor's visa to the United States, coming as a visitor, and overstaying her authorized visit. A permanent resident may come at any time and stay as long as he or she is permitted. However, a departure for over a year could cause a permanent resident to lose that status.

Had Yoko lost her residence, or given it up? I called her immediately, and she confirmed to me that she recalled that she was once a permanent resident of the United States. She thought that she'd lost that status, believing it was based on her marriage to Tony Cox, a US citizen. Since she'd gotten a divorce from him, she assumed she was no longer a legal resident. I explained that wasn't so. Once having obtained residence, she could keep it forever, provided that she was here on an annual basis for any period of time.

I asked Yoko whether she had visited the United States each year since she obtained residence through her prior marriage, but she could not recall. Indeed, it would take a good deal of research to trace her travels in and out of the country during all those years.

It never occurred to me to ask Yoko such a simple question. She had shown me the US visitor's visa in her Japanese passport, and the proof of the fact of her admission as a visitor. At the time, that seemed to be all the documentation I needed.

After I hung up the telephone, something even more significant struck me. When I visited the INS office to inspect the files on John and Yoko, I had been shown "all" their information—or so the INS claimed. In fact, after I noticed the third preference petitions were missing, I insisted on seeing them, and they were ultimately produced.

If Yoko had become a permanent resident of the United States through marriage to an American citizen, the INS obviously had a full and complete file on her case. It would have included proof of Tony Cox's US citizenship, his petition and affidavit of support for Yoko, her application for residence, and a dozen additional documents required in such a case—things like an FBI report, a medical examination, and other investigatory materials. *Why was I never shown that file?*

How would the immigration judge deal with Yoko's green card as a new piece of evidence? It seemed clear to me that the government anxiously sought to accomplish this deportation with as little publicity as possible. Vinny Schiano, the INS trial attorney, had urged that the judge should not allow my witnesses to testify because Lennon was ineligible by statute to obtain residence in the United States. Would Vinny consent to reinstate Yoko's old residence if that would simplify the proceedings?

However, in doing so, he would fall into the trap that I had carefully laid for him. The government would be forcing Yoko to choose between continuing the search for her abducted daughter or following her husband into effective exile. I considered either outcome a public relations nightmare for the INS and the whole Nixon administration.

As for the witnesses Vinny Schiano wanted to dispose of, there was one I desperately needed—expert testimony, in fact. The main point in the government's case against John centered on his 1968 drug conviction for illegal possession of "cannabis resin." The statute specifically barred eligibility for those with drug offenses involving "narcotic drugs or marijuana."

I knew that cannabis resin was not a narcotic drug. I needed to prove that it was also not marijuana. For help on that score, I turned to the criminal bar, specifically to my attorney friend Alan Dershowitz. Besides being an esteemed colleague—we referred cases to one another all the time—Alan was indeed a friend. We discussed the case one Friday night at Grossinger's, the Catskills resort, and Alan offered his advice in the hopes of getting an autographed Lennon album. (All these years later, all I can say is, "Sorry, Alan.") Dershowitz told me that Dr. Lester Grinspoon of Harvard Medical School was one of the best doctors in the country—and a top expert on marijuana.

So I called Dr. Grinspoon and asked, "Is cannabis resin marijuana or what?"

"Oh," he replied, "cannabis resin is not marijuana. It's hashish!"

That was all I needed to hear. I told Dr. Grinspoon about the case. "Name your fee," I said, "I need your testimony."

He said, "I'm very sorry. You can cite my book, but I don't testify anymore."

This was a blow. While Dr. Grinspoon's book, *Marihuana Reconsidered*, was becoming the standard text in discussing the drug, offering nearly 500 pages of scholarly research would not have the impact of a few words from the expert himself. I was very disappointed and tried to reach some other doctors.

Then I got a call from Dr. Grinspoon. "Mr. Wildes, I haven't testified in years, but I have a special, personal situation. I have a 12-year-old son who has terminal leukemia. Since we first spoke, I found out that he idolizes John Lennon. If you can get me some things autographed by John Lennon, I will be happy to testify at my usual rates."

As soon as I put the phone down, I left my office and set out to buy as much Lennon paraphernalia as I could find. I located records, albums, poems, and posters, a whole shopping bag full. That evening, when I visited John and Yoko to prepare their testimony, I had John autograph it all.

I met Dr. Grinspoon the next evening at the Plaza Hotel with this whole pile of autographed stuff and gave it to him in anticipation of his testimony.

I was ready now. Things were going to get serious.

10

Presenting Our Case

*I don't know if there's any mercy to plead for
because this isn't a Federal court but if there is,
I'd like it, please.*

—John Lennon, *The New York Times*, May 21, 1972

We followed the same pattern we'd used for earlier hearings. The Lennons' driver picked me up at my home in Forest Hills to arrive at their apartment around 6:00 in the morning. Despite the early hour, I sensed that my presence was reassuring. They could ask about anything that troubled them.

Getting to the INS building on West Broadway meant just a short drive, but I'm a compulsively early person. I wanted to be there and make certain that John and Yoko had time to get comfortable with the proceedings. We found quite a number of people already gathered outside the building when we arrived and proceeded through the supportive crowd, heading directly to the immigration judge's courtroom.

Judge Fieldsteel first swore in John and Yoko and satisfied himself that they were still represented by me. Then he got down to business, saying rather impatiently, "Mr. Wildes, we have been proceeding now for almost two months, we still haven't gotten to the element of deportability. Are you prepared to concede deportability in these cases as charged?"

I knew full well from my practice that cases were often adjourned for years with no such pressure from the immigration judge to plead as to deportability. Two months was no time at all!

How to level the playing field? I told the judge that I was not prepared yet to plead to the allegations of the Order to Show Cause, but that I would do so today nevertheless, after making some preliminary comments. Privately, I wanted to make sure that the events of the past few weeks got into the record. "Other than those," I said, "we are prepared to proceed. We are *not* here to request any special adjournment."

The immigration judge looked a little happier at that statement. Ah, well. I knew that mood wouldn't last when he heard the rest of what I had to say.

"There is a discriminatory kind of prejudgment of every application and request made by my clients in this case," I began. I then ran through my experience of going to the immigration offices and finding the third preference applications untouched after being filed two months earlier. Despite my meetings with Sol Marks, the district director further declined to take action, so I was forced to go to federal court and request a temporary restraining order the day before the scheduled deportation proceedings. That temporary restraining order was issued and signed at 4:30 in the afternoon before the scheduled hearing. The next day, when we were scheduled to be in Judge Fieldsteel's courtroom at the INS, we were instead in federal court. The US attorney representing the INS reported that he'd received a telephone call from Marks, conceding that he would adjudicate these applications that very day.

I further explained that the normal processing of third preference petitions would have required the bulk of the application to go from INS to the Department of Labor for its recommendation, which should have taken place shortly after we'd filed the petitions with the INS. That had not taken place, and I added, "I assume that the district director telephoned the Labor Department and got their approval in that way, so that the applications could be adjudicated the very same day."

"Are you complaining, Mr. Wildes," asked the immigration judge, "that the applications were approved too quickly . . . that there wasn't the necessary degree of delay through processing? It would appear so."

"I am not at all complaining about that," I replied. What struck me as unusual, though, was how the government had acted when I went to secure the preliminary injunction. I'd made allegations in my sworn statement that, "upon information and belief," the INS was trying to remove the Lennons as quickly as possible, not for legal reasons but for political ones. I presumed this was happening on instructions from Washington that their presence in the United States was deemed to be politically dangerous to the Nixon administration. It seemed to me that the district director had been instructed to hide or deny each and every application that my clients might file. What disturbed me was the fact that the government *never responded* to these strong allegations. In fact, the district director's same-day decision to grant the petitions seemed an attempt to avoid responding to them. I could only conclude that there was a good deal of truth to the charges I'd made.

I then offered in evidence the order of the federal court enjoining the deportation proceedings pending the hearing in federal court and the notices of approval for both third preference petitions. "Yoko's approval stated that she might now apply for residence. John's petition gave the impression that he had no right whatsoever to apply for residence." To my mind, this was further proof of prejudgment.

Then I dropped my little bombshell, asking why, when I examined the INS files, none of them "pertained to the many years during which Mrs. Lennon was in this country prior to the last two or three." I added that "she happens to have been here for over fifteen years prior to that in a number of different statuses. I had to find out, purely by mistake, that she may at this moment still be a lawful permanent resident of the United States." Then I held up Yoko's green card for all to see. "This card turned up in a pile of documents which Mrs. Lennon sent to me. While it is impossible for me, at this point, to determine by her absences and trips to this country whether or not she has retained permanent residence status, and I will have to do so in order to know how to respond to the factual allegations of her Order to Show Cause, finding this card reaffirmed in my mind that we really shouldn't be in these deportation proceedings at all! I submit that there has been such prejudgment and discrimination in this case that the removal of a longtime permanent resident is being sought on the ground that she has merely visited here and overstayed her visit. This is a jurisdictional error and must be corrected."

I knew this bit of drama would cause a shock in the courtroom and worked it for all it was worth.

"Where did you get this green card, the green card you presented, counsel?" demanded the immigration judge. "Didn't Mrs. Lennon tell you that she had been admitted as a permanent resident on one occasion?" He turned to Yoko and asked, "Didn't you know that you had been admitted as a permanent resident, madam, on one occasion?"

No matter how I tried, this remained a case where the judge kept blaming the victim. More to the point, Judge Fieldsteel should have asked the government's trial attorney why we'd never been shown the file that granted Yoko permanent residence.

The judge continued: "Well, I would say, Mr. Wildes, that you have now reached the point that I asked you to reach approximately two sessions ago, and that is, the basis on which you want to proceed with these cases. They are two individuals, they are two separate cases. It would seem to me that the cases should be severed at this point, and when I say severed, I mean legally. I don't have to have them in separate rooms, but they are two separate cases, and apparently stand on two separate legal bases at this point."

It seemed to me that once again, the immigration judge was cooperating with the INS in its efforts to split up my clients. I couldn't allow that to happen.

"I have no objection to the rendering of separate decisions by the same immigration judge," I replied, "but, *under no circumstances* would I consent to separate this inseparable couple insofar as conducting two separate proceedings."

Judge Fieldsteel returned to the green card issue, asking Vinny Schiano, "Is this a surprise to the government?"

Schiano responded, "Yes, it was shown to me this morning. I suggested to Mr. Wildes that we may give separate consideration to this question, without necessarily separating the matters." Even Vinny was changing his tune.

He then went on to address the statements I'd made, saying that the INS had provided all the files I'd asked for, making the third preference petitions available in less than ten minutes after I'd requested them. As to the differences in the approval notices, Schiano claimed they simply reflected the government's attitude "that Yoko Ono might appear to be statutorily eligible for residence, but Mr. Lennon might not be statutorily eligible for reasons already discussed. As far as prejudgment, we are not concerned with any prejudgment. We are concerned with *some* judgment being rendered in reaching that point in these proceedings."

Judge Fieldsteel then turned to me. "Obviously, you are not prepared to concede deportability with regard to Mrs. Lennon, and I can see that there may be some substantial question as to whether she ever abandoned her residence in the United States, but I will not permit you to proceed with descriptions of the visa petitions or the applications for permanent residence until we reach that, and we haven't reached that until we dispose of the question of deportability. Now you can either concede the facts as charged, or we can proceed item by item. What do you want to do, Mr. Wildes? You indicated that Mr. Lennon is prepared to concede the allegations of fact, and I assume, one or both of the conclusions of law in the Order to Show Cause. Is that correct?"

"I did not say that," I stated firmly. "I am prepared to plead, but separately with respect to each allegation of fact and each conclusion of law."

I went on to admit, with respect to John, that he was not a United States citizen, that he was a native and citizen of the United Kingdom, that he entered the United States on a visitor's visa on August 13, 1971, that he was authorized to remain until February 29, 1972, that on March 1, 1972, he was granted the privilege of departing voluntarily on or before March 15, 1972. However, I denied that he abandoned his intention to depart at that time, and, although I admit that he received the letter claiming to withdraw the privilege of voluntary departure, I denied that he remained after February 29, 1972, without authority. As a result, I denied both legal conclusions, namely, that he violated his status and that he overstayed his authorized admission. Although I could have placed the government in the position of having to prove the allegations that I denied in behalf of John, I permitted him to take the stand and respond to Vinny Schiano's first question: "Mr. Lennon, on March 1, did you have the intention of departing from the United States on or before March 13, 1972?"

John's answer put him in the most sympathetic light. "I had no intention either way," he said. "We are looking for the child Kyoko, and neither of us had made up our mind either way at all about it. I just feel it's a matter of if we find the child. Our whole life is built around that."

We then proceeded to deal with Yoko's Order to Show Cause. I admitted, on her behalf, that she was born in Japan and was not a citizen of the United States, but indicated that she might still be a lawful permanent resident. With respect to the other allegations, I indicated that she would respond in the same way that her husband had responded.

Having now pleaded to the allegations of the Orders to Show Cause, we proceeded with our applications for discretionary relief. The immigration judge confirmed that in his view the government had established its case of deportability and that we were now authorized to file those applications. The specific applications that we were filing for John and Yoko were for adjustment of status to that of lawful permanent residents of the United States.

I handed up the applications and the documents filed in support of the applications. At this point, trial attorney Schiano offered John's conviction in evidence. I did not object. The record of conviction stated simply that John was convicted, upon his plea of guilty, of "having in his possession a dangerous drug, cannabis resin, without being duly authorized."

The immigration judge then permitted me to state the gist of my argument, which I'd submit as a legal brief at a future date. I explained that my first argument was that the substance referred to in the conviction, cannabis resin, is not marijuana. I zeroed in on the very circumscribed language in the statute. One of my witnesses, present in the courtroom today, would give testimony on whether the substance "which John pleaded guilty to possessing" was marijuana or not. I also explained that I had other witnesses presently in court who would not be available in the future, and that I would like the court to hear them.

"Perhaps I may be of some assistance," Vinny Schiano offered suavely. "If counsel wishes to recite who would appear and state what, I will stipulate that they would say that without the necessity of presenting the witnesses." This was classic Vinny, offering a clever ploy to avoid the dramatic effect of hearing all the impressive testimony I had prepared.

Even the immigration judge understood that I would never go for that. He responded, "Since Mr. Wildes went to the trouble to get the people here—that he would feel happier if some of their testimony were taken. I certainly will not, Mr. Wildes, accept a parade of some half-dozen witnesses, all of whom are going to testify to what nice people they are."

Rather than enter into a debate with the immigration judge, I simply indicated that I would only call people whose testimony would not be repetitive.

I called my first witness, Lester Grinspoon, M.D., who set aside the large shopping bag of autographed Lennon memorabilia as he rose to take the stand.

Dr. Grinspoon identified himself as associate clinical professor of psychiatry at the Harvard Medical School and director of science and research in the Massachusetts Medical Health Center as well as a member of the Boylston Psychoanalytic Institute. It was obvious from his distinguished appearance and demeanor that he was an important member of his profession.

"Have you done specialized work in the field of narcotic drugs and marijuana?" I asked.

"I have. I have published roughly about sixty papers, most of which have to do with drugs and two books, and my particular interest in this particular drug—marijuana—spans now four and one-half years that I have been in research on it."

To assure that the government was not going to challenge his expertise later, I asked Mr. Schiano, "Does the government have any questions with respect to his qualifications?"

"No," responded Schiano.

"Dr. Grinspoon, will you tell us, as we are all laymen here, with respect to these terms, what is the history and the meaning of the term cannabis resin?"

The doctor explained that cannabis comes from the name of the plant given by botanists in 1753 to a plant that has male and female versions. Cannabis resin is obtained when the female begins to flower. In India, it is called *charas* and in the Turkish world, it is known as *hashish*.

I needed to prove, through this expert witness, that cannabis resin was not marijuana, but was hashish, a different drug, and that it was not a narcotic.

"Do you consider that cannabis resin is hashish?" I asked.

"Yes."

"Is cannabis resin marijuana?" I asked.

"Cannabis resin is *not* marijuana."

"Is cannabis resin a narcotic drug?"

"Cannabis resin is not a narcotic drug."

At this point, the immigration judge seemed intensely interested in the testimony. "I don't want to interrupt you, but you haven't said what marijuana *is*," noted the judge.

"The word marijuana, the etiology of it, is not certain," Dr. Grinspoon replied, "but it is largely thought now to derive from the Portuguese word *Mari bongo*. Regardless of its origin, the word is a North American word for what in India is referred to as *bhang*, and in England, it is also called marijuana but frequently the word *dagga*, which is a term which comes from South Africa. What it actually is—the cut part of the cannabis sativa plant, usually the female, but it may also be female and male, and it's a cutting of these parts usually mixed with stems and seeds and so forth. And as I say, it is a number of things in different parts of the world, certainly in North America it is marijuana. Possibly the term marijuana is used in other parts of the Western World, but there is no question that marijuana refers to just this particular form of the plant, and *not to the resin*," Dr. Grinspoon emphasized.

I closed in for the kill. "Based upon your knowledge and experience and research in this field," I asked, "would I be correct in saying that it is your opinion that Cannabis resin is not marijuana?"

"*Cannabis is not marijuana. Marijuana is not cannabis resin*," he stated emphatically.

"I offer this in evidence," I said to the immigration judge, handing him the witness's book. The judge turned to Schiano, saying, "would you want a short recess so that you could read this, Mr. Schiano?"

"No more than fifteen minutes," replied Schiano with a smile.

"In any event, I assume you have no objection to it being made part of the record?" asked Fieldsteel.

"None," replied Schiano.

Schiano made a valiant attempt to cross-examine the doctor, but was obviously not prepared to deal with the issue of what constituted marijuana from a medical or biological point of view. There was some discussion as to whether he might recall the doctor after preparing a cross-examination, but the immigration judge came to our rescue. He ruled that if Schiano should have some questions in the future, he would arrange for the doctor to answer them without having to come back to New York to testify.

I felt a great deal of gratitude for Dr. Grinspoon. I knew the circumstances of the unfortunate illness of his twelve-year-old son, which made him willing, as a father, to offer his expert testimony. Under other circumstances, I could never have secured him as a witness. I hoped that the autographed records and books that the doctor took home brought some happiness to a young man in his illness.

11

The Testimony Continues

This country's got plenty of room and space.
Let John and Yoko stay!

—Bob Dylan, letter to the INS

I called my second witness, Thomas P. Hoving. At the time of the case, he was in the midst of the ten-year span when, as its director, he completely changed the course of New York's Metropolitan Museum of Art. Hoving testified that he was also a member of the New York State Council on the Arts, had served as the first administrator of arts, recreation, and cultural affairs of the city of New York, and had also been the city's parks commissioner.

"I think the government will concede your knowledge in the field," I said.

"Yes," responded Vinny Schiano.

"Are you personally familiar with John and Yoko and their artistic work?" I asked.

"Yes, I am. I am more familiar with Mr. Lennon's work," Hoving said. "I was at least in part responsible for having Mr. Lennon and the other members of the group, the Beatles, come to New York City and play at Shea Stadium." He explained how, at the height of Beatlemania, he had gone to the group's dressing room with his daughter, "Who I think was worked up to a state of catatonia when she met them. Mr. Lennon at that time talked to me for some significant moments, and was extremely sweet with my dumbstruck daughter, and she began to talk after that. I don't think this is a very pertinent part of the record here, but we discussed various things, and I found him extremely forthright, intelligent, a man of a certain grace and politeness, and was very much impressed with what I saw."

As to John's later career, Hoving commented, "There are few people in the last period of this decade in all of the arts, whether it's painting or sculpture, or architecture or performing arts, who have contributed so much in an extremely deep and essential manner, as Mr. Lennon."

He went on to say, "My basic business in life, sir, is to recognize, exhibit, and teach about artistic qualities. That is the nature of my business, and I believe what Mr. Lennon has achieved and is achieving now is of great artistic importance, and I would consider him a great resource to this city and to the country. Needless to say, as we all know, artists throughout time have sometimes acted in ways that those of us who were more on the bureaucratic side of life might consider a little bit strange. I dare say one of the greatest painters, George LaTour, whose show opened in the Louvre in Paris just the other day, might not have been able to sustain the inquiry of various well-meaning and responsible rules of naturalization. After all, his own town of Springerville got together a petition and condemned him for his acts of public annoyance, which were nothing compared to his great artistic character and, of course, his art remains universal. I don't know that what Mr. Lennon has created is going to become a thing of universal quality. I don't think that it is an issue, but I think that as far as today's times are concerned, the work has been among the very best created."

He continued, "I believe that the basic character of this individual is excellent, and I have no doubt about his artistic ability and qualifications. I would say that if he were a painting, he would be hanging in the Metropolitan Museum, benevolently on the wall, and if he were to ever come to give a series of lectures or what have you on the various sides of art, he would certainly be welcome to do that."

Judge Fieldsteel interjected, with some pride, about his own membership in the museum.

"As far as the work of Mrs. Lennon is concerned," Mr. Hoving said, "I am not familiar with it, but I feel quite solid in my belief that she is very serious in her work."

He then offered a picture of his daughter with the Beatles to the judge, who returned it and thanked him.

"My next witness is Dick Cavett," I said. At this point in his career, Cavett had attained his widest popularity as the thinking person's late-night host. He described himself as "a television performer, a talk show host and comedian, employer of talent in that regard, and I have been in that capacity for about the last four years on an irregular basis. I graduated from high school and Yale University in 1948 and have been pursuing this career since."

I had only one question: "I would ask you to comment, if you will, upon the effect on the entertainment field of refusing to let the Lennons remain here?"

"Well, my opinion is, the Lennons are an important artistic presence in this country." He went on, "They are considered a kind of inspiration by their constant restless activity, constantly testing themselves, fulfilling themselves in challenging artistic ways, and so forth. They seem to be a kind of stimulus on the members of the community that I am involved with and employ on my show. They feel that it's good to have them around, that they are an inspiration not only to other artists, but to—if I'm not rambling on too long—to young people who are in danger of falling into apathy. . . . I believe they set a good example in that sense. The young people who I am concerned with in my audience and who write in, feel that the Lennons *are noted for doing something good with their lives.*"

Neither Schiano nor the immigration judge had any cross examination of this impressive young man.

I admired the way Dick Cavett could organize important thoughts in a few short, pithy phrases. That admiration probably led me to suggest to John and Yoko that they use Cavett's show to announce that, contrary to public rumor, they had no intention of appearing at the Republican convention in San Diego.

I called my next witness.

"My name is Eric Schnapper," he introduced himself. "I'm an attorney, a graduate of Yale Law School, a member of the bar of California. I am now serving as a special assistant to the chairman of the Committee on Drug Abuse of the Young Lawyers' Section of the American Bar Association."

"Are you at this point," I asked, "involved in a program in behalf of the American Bar Association in which the Lennons are participating?"

"Yes. The Committee on Drug Abuse is the largest in that organization," Schnapper explained, "covering forty states in a program which has been ongoing in the last several years, with the law enforcement agency, the Department of Justice. Most of the committee's work is directed toward getting information about hard drugs out to young people. We have asked the Lennons if they would be willing to help us and support us, and to prepare radio and television advertising which we would use in a public announcement service throughout the country . . . we are now involved together in implementing that stage of the work through our Chicago staff. It will take about six months."

Similar efforts had not proven successful, Schnapper said, but he hoped for greater impact with John and Yoko. "They will both take part in the preparation of the ads so that they will reflect their own personal views. When we are settled on the text, they will record it. Our plan is, within the time available, to do a pilot program for the city of New York," he said, "to make sure that we get a formula for these advertisements that is effective, and then to circulate them nationally."

In addition, the association hoped to run a benefit for drug rehabilitation centers throughout the country. As he put it, "Our hope is, but this is still up in the air, to get them to do this throughout the next academic year."

Mr. Schnapper's testimony, as well, went without cross examination.

My next witness was Norman Seaman.

I had grown to know Norman well during my handling of the Lennons' case. He was a kind of fatherly figure to Yoko, heavily involved in show business, or as he put it, "I am an independent concert and theatrical producer, primarily in concerts, because we run concerts in Lincoln Center, Carnegie Hall, and Town Hall. These are primarily classical concerts."

He went on to say that his company's services also involved producing benefit performances for worthy causes.

"Most recently, in January of this year, an organization called AWARE contacted us and informed us that they were raising funds for the organization, which included on its board many distinguished industrialists, a deputy mayor of New York, the vice president of a television network, and asked if we could help on it." As Seaman explained, "One of our main contributions was to invite Yoko and John to participate."

He went on to explain that he had met Yoko Ono around 1961. "At that time, we were very active in introducing the works of new composers, a field we are still active in. . . . we were interested not only in the approved classical end of music, but also in the innovative and experimental end. When I was introduced to Ms. Ono, at that time, I found myself rather fascinated at a lunch that we had in which she showed me the manuscript of a work which she called *Grapefruit*, which is a little difficult to describe as a piece of music. It was probably one of the first that we had, which we call 'multimedia' pieces, the first that I had even seen. I might add that many of the developments in the past ten or eleven years in the field of art, and particularly in the various inter-relating media, were included in that work."

He went on to say, "We put on one or two of her concerts at Carnegie, and we received a rather strange reaction at that time. We found that nobody could watch or react to these programs without communicating. There were those who were violently moved to imply that Ms. Ono belongs in an insane asylum, at best, and to be given some kind of treatment, and there were others who believed that she had a remarkable depth of imagination and the ability to see beyond the normal boundaries of art as we found it described."

He then discussed reviews of her concert by Alan Rich, the music editor of *New York* magazine, and John Crosby, a syndicated columnist. "Both of them wrote it up in terms which implied this was an unusual, imaginative work."

Seaman then added a personal note. "Ms. Ono not only would be an unusual artist, but an unusual person, a person who I felt had an unusually deep humanity. I met her child at that time, Kyoko, and in the course of the many years she lived here, I found that, well, she became a valued friend."

When Yoko went to London, Seaman said, "We kept in touch, and she became engaged and then married to Mr. Lennon. I became privileged to meet Mr. Lennon perhaps four years ago, saw them together at various places here and in Montreal and in England, and mostly in New York."

Yoko's search for Kyoko obviously moved him. "A mother looking for her child, unable to find her, sitting in a courtroom and being cross-examined as to her right to stay here with her husband, and I might add that together, it is coldhearted to think of Yoko alone, now as I think it is for anybody. They have a most unusual marriage, one that is integrated artistically, humanly, socially, and just about every possible way."

He concluded, "All I can say is that personally I feel very moved and very involved with these two brave and intelligent, active, novel human beings whom I see being harassed and whose life is being hassled for no reason. These are people who have an enormous contribution to make, who are a great deal of fun to be with."

Judge Fieldsteel suddenly asked, "Would you state that a narcotics conviction was no reason?"

"I regret to interrupt the immigration judge," I quickly pointed out, "but narcotics convictions are hardly the area of expertise of an arranger and conductor." I turned to the witness and continued: "You obviously had full contact with Yoko over a continuous period of over ten years and with John, over three or four. Is it your conclusion they are persons of good moral character?"

"Definitely," Seaman replied, going on to say, "They work harder for many more hours than most people do. They do not engage, as far as I know, in any wild or unrestrained activities. They are square people basically, as far as their social and moral behavior is concerned."

"I have no further questions," I concluded. There was no cross-examination.

I then announced that there was a statement that would not require testimony, delivered by Reverend Williams of the American Episcopal Church for Bishop Paul Moore. In addition to heading the Diocese of New York, Bishop Moore was the representative for the Church of England in the United States.

A tall, impressive-looking man in clerical garb presented a letter to the immigration judge, who read it. "All right, does the government have any objection to making this part of the record?" asked Fieldsteel.

Schiano replied with a bland, "No."

The judge declared a lunch recess, which probably was just as well. We'd need some fortification before the next witnesses. I expected his testimony to be considerably more contentious.

12

Sharp Exchanges

Be it resolved that John Lennon and Yoko Ono, facing possible deportation by the Immigration and Naturalization Service of the Department of Justice be made honorary citizens of Berkeley, California, enjoying all rights and privileges (as every citizen is entitled to, under law) and that if deported by the government of the United States, be it further resolved that John Lennon and Yoko Ono be allowed asylum in the city of Berkeley to live and work, if they so choose.

—Resolution submitted before Berkeley
City Council by Greg Pyes, May 2, 1972

When we returned from the recess, I called my next witness, who was sworn in by the immigration judge.

"My name is Kenneth Dewey," the young witness introduced himself. "I am an individual artist. For three years, I was director of research and program development for the New York State Arts Council. The last two, I have been one of the five gubernatorial appointments to an eleven-member state commission entitled the New York State Cultural Resources Commission, and I am also presently chairman of the Committee for John and Yoko," which he described as "a spontaneous network of concerned individuals in the arts, education, religion, and from labor, who have felt that the action being taken against John and Yoko at this time is not in their interest."

Dewey handed up a packet of documents to the immigration judge, explaining that there were "in fact a number of groups that have formed spontaneously, and petitions have been sent in by numbers of people, and in other cases, individuals have simply written in their support to an ad hoc committee, the sole purpose of which, everybody agrees, is that the persons who attempt to deport John and Yoko are not acting in the interests of these people."

Vinny Schiano lost his patience. "I have refrained from interfering with this part of the presentation," he spoke up sharply. "However, this is a process of law, and not a procedure of vote-taking or poll-taking. It would be as easy for the government to produce an equal number of letters from people with the opposite opinion."

Dewey, however, was not a man to be shut up. "May I comment on that, sir?" he asked.

With the approval of the immigration judge, he stated, "In my more official capacity I have been in charge for five years with looking after the cultural needs of New York State. The expression of concern that has been registered by those individuals covers a period during which New York State and New York City are considered by many to rank with Elizabethan England, the Renaissance in Italy, and Classical Greece as the creative capital of the world. It is in the interest of those of us who have a firm responsibility in this area to see that those conditions continue, and it is in our strongest interest, as the creative people of our country, to see that artists of the caliber of John and Yoko are a part of that. Sir, the Immigration Service, in my understanding, is obligated to act *in the public interest*. In plain, simple terms, I am here to state that they are not acting in what we construe to be the public interest."

Now Schiano raised a formal objection. "On that basis the documentation is immaterial, irrelevant, and incompetent in the cause of this case."

The immigration judge, however, ruled in our favor. After carefully looking at the documents, he allowed the packet of petitions and letters in, explaining, "Well, certain documentation achieves a weight simply by virtue of who is involved. The people who have written here are clearly representative of—are outstanding representatives of a large-number of various artistic fields. It is an indication that there are a large number of artistic people who are interested in the Lennons."

Dewey continued, "the government is presumably speaking for us. We're here to say that we are being misrepresented by the government in this case."

Schiano noted: "That's a further argument for me. *Objection!*"

"All right," responded the immigration judge, "I'll accept this for whatever it is worth. As I say, it can't be ignored, though I am not entirely sure, Mr. Schiano, whether it is strictly relevant to the issue. When you speak of the Immigration Service, and the immigration law, acting as a public benefit, it is charged with the *enforcement* of the immigration laws. The immigration laws may not coincide with your concept of the public benefit, and there may be a disparity between what you conceive of. I don't think the immigration law can be administered simply for the broad concept of the public benefit. It has to be administered in terms of the law itself. What the law says and where the law gives discretion, then the public benefit may enter into it. But I will take your material and make it part of the record."

So, despite the best efforts by the government's counsel, we managed to get evidence about the public's protests of these proceedings into the record, although Schiano still murmured, "We want to keep this as a trial and not as an election."

Ken Dewey was excused from the witness stand. I was very grateful for his testimony, because not too long after the trial, he unfortunately died in an airplane accident. His loss to the artistic community was felt nationally.

My next witness had insisted on testifying. I was certain that he would be a strong witness but worried that his blunt, abrasive manner might rub Schiano and even Judge Fieldsteel the wrong way. Nonetheless, Allen Klein was sworn in.

"I am president of ABKCO Industries, a management firm which represents the Lennons, and to that extent I am biased." No more than one sentence into his testimony, and Klein already seemed to be baiting the government. I tried to change the direction of his monologue and direct him to a more sensitive approach.

"In addition to your business relationship, have you had an opportunity to have a personal relationship with them? A personal acquaintance?" I asked.

"I have known both the Lennons for three and one-half years. I consider myself a constant friend. When I say constant, I mean I would say that in a normal relationship as though we had known each other all our lives. I consider myself a friend of both of them. I have sat and listened to a host of credible witnesses speak of their artistic work, and I am embarrassed because I think that is self-evident, so if that particular matter is a question of fact now, their merit and ability is noted, I would like to go on to something which may be of less importance in an artistic sense, but to a lot of hungry people, it has a lot of importance."

Klein leaned forward and gesticulated to underline the importance of his next words.

"The Lennons' extensive holdings and interests in the United States, and their businesses do an annual gross volume of $50 million and as such, because this money does not just come in passively, 100 to 150 families are dependent upon them for their livelihood. This does not mean that if they did not live here, these people would not be employed, but were they not happy, they might cease to work. So it stands on its face, the economic benefit to this country is great and would continue to be great or greater if they were allowed to live here and watch over their interests."

With his usual belligerent attitude, John's manager plowed on. "There are two other matters which I would like to touch on. The first is the question which was raised by Mr. Seaman and then someone objected to, that is the relevancy of this particular proceeding with regard to anything, and you rightly said, well, what about the conviction?

"The event of Mr. Lennon pleading guilty in court occurred prior to my meeting him. But when I did meet him and because he wanted to travel to the United States, I became personally involved, and I went through the files and met with the lawyers who represented him in England. And the fact of the matter, which is documented in the lawyers' files, was that when the police came to his personal house, whatever substance was found there was *not his* and his concern was that his soon-to-be wife, Mrs. Lennon, might be charged as a non-resident alien and be deported. In his words to the detective which I had documented, he said, 'If I say that it is mine, will you leave her alone?' And they said: 'Yes.' And because his legal representative said this was something that would be handled with a small fine, he pleaded guilty, I think, not realizing the consequences of his inability to travel, for instance, to the United States. That's why the question of the conviction or his pleading guilty to something he did not do, merely to avoid what he thought might be a more difficult problem, is hard for me to reconcile with all of the energy and time and money which is spent. The detective who made the arrest was one who also arrested –"

At this point, Schiano interrupted Klein's diatribe. "In the interest of saving time, the guilt or innocence is not the subject of this proceeding."

"I beg your pardon?" Klein demanded.

Schiano continued. "I don't think we have to go into the conviction."

"Well just a minute," said Judge Fieldsteel, "what did you mean before when you said this is documented?"

"Mr. Lennon's lawyer has a file," Klein replied. "The statements which were made by him to the police are in the file, and this information was made available to me. I don't say that it is legally relevant, but I say morally it might be."

"All right," responded Fieldsteel, "I have no objection to hear about it. . . . I don't think it has the effect of disturbing the conviction. In other words, Mr. Wildes has indicated that he is attempting to get the competent legal counsel in England to set aside the conviction. That would seem to be the appropriate area to exercise these efforts, because certainly I can't do anything about it. I will not refuse to recognize the conviction where the English court thought itself in a position to sustain a conviction, but I will listen to such matters."

"I was leading to this," Klein continued, "the question of the detective I brought up is one of the reasons that the appeal cannot be lodged. The new information which we are waiting to get is the subject of this investigation by the review board in England as to his conduct, and we can't file the appeal until we get the information which is the subject of this investigation. Until it is concluded and the findings are published, we won't have this information. In any event, and I won't belabor it, but the same gentleman did the same thing to Mr. Jagger and Mr. Richards, who I also represented at the time, and the court of appeals threw out that conviction. I was not involved with Mr. Lennon, or I would never have let him plead guilty at that particular time. In any event, that's the idea of this and I call it a technicality because if a man pleads guilty to something of which he is not morally guilty, he may be guilty *only* legally. And I am approaching this on a *moral* basis, since I am not a lawyer."

Although I appreciated Klein's personal knowledge that the guilty plea in England was not an acknowledgment of true legal guilt and his effort to get that into the record, I wanted to get him back on track. "To get back to the point of your personal relationships," I began.

"I will," Klein continued, "it was just an aside that Mr. Seaman did not have personal knowledge of. In any event, there are just two more matters that I would like to dwell on." And Klein was off again.

"The first is the question of Yoko and her child, and John." He surprised me with this, since to my knowledge, he'd always seemed to dismiss the problem and Yoko and Kyoko. But Klein said, "You can sit and talk about it, verbalize as to the remorse, and everyone can feel sorry in a vicarious way, but you have to have been there and had to travel with them as I have around the world, searching in the outposts of Denmark or Jutland or in Majorca, sitting and trying to reasonably work out an arrangement where she could see her child. And constantly being thwarted and frustrated, each time using these same legal means that are now being used against her and finding her to be physically and emotionally ill by it. It's easy to talk, but it is very difficult to sit and look and listen. It is very hard to reason with that man. Their being deported would be, in effect, a separation. The mother would never get the child, and I don't ever believe that that is the intent of the law of the country of which I am a citizen."

Finally, the judge seemed to show an interest. "How does Mr. Cox make his living since he continually appears to be fleeing?"

"He is a wonderful promoter," Klein replied. "I really don't know. I think—one of the interesting things is that Mr. Lennon and Mrs. Lennon both appeared before a judge in the Virgin Islands, gave testimony, and the judge determined, based upon this testimony that Mr. and Mrs. Lennon were fit and proper people to bring up this child. Mr. Cox then went and took up residence in Texas, where he never lived before, said that he was going to be a resident there, and that is where the child would be brought up. Mr. and Mrs. Lennon picked up and went to Texas even though they had already a decree in their favor. When the Texas judge set down and allowed temporary custody to the Lennons, the man absconded again and there is now a warrant out for his arrest."

Given the way he'd dismissed Yoko in some of our earlier meetings, Klein surprised me with his effective testimony on the humanitarian aspects of the case as he went on. "Now, Cox has already been held in contempt of court and had been jailed. It is not a question of two reasonable people looking for a happy way to live with one child. It is a question of one human being who not only has no concern for the feelings of the mother but has no concern for the court."

Allen was really on a roll. I let him continue.

"John Lennon never really wanted to come to New York. He really didn't like it here. It was really only because of Yoko and her quest for the child that he came here. Now he likes it, and he loves his wife and loves her child and so, to separate them, I think is not really human." He moved on with a rhetorical flourish, pointing to the Statue of Liberty, visible in the harbor beyond Fieldsteel's chair.

"That woman who stands in the harbor with her torch, certainly, I don't think would want to exclude these people."

At last, Klein touched on some of the matters I wanted from his testimony.

"One other thing, and it's a question of humanity. Everyone was talking about what they would do in the future, and how the Lennons would help with this or that. Three years ago, the Lennons began a campaign for peace when it really wasn't very fashionable. An enormous amount of ridicule was heaped upon them, much as that man who pointed his finger at the moneylenders in the temple. And the question is: What is it really all about? Unfortunately, the subtleties are lost sometimes in the media, but it wasn't lost on me, or on George Harrison, or on John and Yoko. Last year, a concert was put together to benefit the people—the children of Bangladesh—and it was a concert sponsored by me. It raised more money than any country had ever given just to help children. Now that's a positive thing. Based on that act alone, they should be granted citizenship in this country. That's a very positive thing. It inspires. If you would speak to the people from UNICEF, they had more calls from concerned human beings, *young people*, who became involved in helping other young people. . . . I don't believe that's the way you treat someone who has done such work."

He went on, "In the second week of June, the highest award that UNICEF gives, called The Father of the Man, is to be given to the people involved in that concert, a grand gesture. The first time something positive really was done and money raised for young, needy children. That had to have a good effect on the people who he is supposed to be influencing. It had a good effect on me, and I am only one. I have lived with them.

"I have been to Mr. Lennon's house in England with Mrs. Lennon and with their children. It just doesn't make sense that people who would give so much to humanity and who have given so much of themselves should be denied what they might have received if they were not who they were."

After a brief exchange challenging the last statement, Schiano had no further questions. The immigration judge then asked Klein,

"Now, when the Lennons came here, you were instrumental in their coming?"

"Yes, I was."

"At that time, you had to seek a waiver of their inadmissibility on account of the conviction?"

"Yes."

"At that time, did you tell the American consul that Mr. Lennon was in fact innocent?"

"Yes, I did."

"Did you state this in writing?"

"No, I told my Congressman, who helped me. That's one of the reasons he helped."

"Not in any of the papers which you submitted, did you say he was innocent?"

"Nor was I obligated."

I suppose it was too much to hope that Klein could answer five questions without challenging the judge.

"I see. You did not advance the argument. You accepted the fact that there was this inadmissibility and you asked to please grant a waiver, so he may come for business reasons to see you?"

"That's right."

After some additional skirmishing, Judge Fieldsteel asked for John's original waiver of inadmissibility to be added to the record. Frankly, I was glad to see Klein's testimony conclude before a full-scale war broke out. As the man left the witness stand, I felt that Klein, though a tough, independent character, had strongly committed himself to the fight for John and Yoko. He came to help, and he did it his way.

I then handed two powerful documents to the judge.

The first was a letter from John Lindsay, mayor of New York, and the second an affidavit from William David Ormsby-Gore, Lord Harlech, former British ambassador to the United States.

Mayor Lindsay's letter was addressed to Raymond Farrell, the commissioner of the Immigration and Naturalization Service in Washington. It pointed out that the Lennons "have personally told me of their love for New York City and that they wish to make it their home." Lindsay continued that, "the only question which is raised against these people is that they do speak out with strong and critical voices on major issues of the day. If this is the motive underlying the unusual and harsh action taken by the Immigration and Naturalization Service, then it is an attempt to silence constitutionally protected First Amendment rights."

Lord Harlech's elegant statement argued that "It may be that there is a theory that no danger arises for the United States of America if someone resides there for six months but that the danger does arise if he stays for seven months or longer." He went on, "This argument is so obviously ludicrous that I make no further comment on it. . . . As a life-long friend of the United States of America, I reject the suggestion that the most powerful democratic country in the world, whose whole constitution is based on individual freedom and human rights, could believe for one moment that it might be subverted by the presence of a single young artist."

After the hearing, the Lennons had their fingerprints taken in Vinny Schiano's office as part of the adjustment of status applications. A crowd of reporters assembled, questioning John and Yoko while Vinny and I looked on. Schiano had already stated that he was a Beatles fan and, as such, derived little gratification from the job of having to deport one of them.

A reporter asked whether Vinny thought it was a "good idea" to kick them out of the country.

He responded, "What I think is not the point. I feel that the law bars him from becoming a permanent resident. The law allows no discretion on that point, and that is it. Even if I loved the Lennons, we could not do anything about that."

When asked whether the law should be changed, Schiano referred to the bill that then-congressman Ed Koch had brought before Congress, which would "allow us to choose between the good guys and the bad guys" and permit a waiver of a minor simple marijuana possession charge.

However, he pointed out, this "was not the law at this time."

Shortly afterward, I overheard Vinny saying, as if to himself, "You know the old saying—sometimes the best guarantee of civil liberties is the inefficiency of the government." Looking at the assembled reporters, he then said, "I think I'd better stop talking. I'm still healing from some old wounds. I had to sue for every promotion I've gotten."

After the hearing, we decided to review the day's developments over lunch in Allen Klein's luxurious office.

As sandwiches and coffee came in, Geraldo Rivera, whom Yoko had invited along, made some comments. He underscored the importance of John and Yoko getting some positive publicity, emphasizing their true pacifist nature. Geraldo felt that John and Yoko were naive compared to professional rabble-rousers like Jerry Rubin and Bobby Seale. With his legal training, Geraldo offered a good analysis.

While we all sat listening around Klein's huge desk, with its seventeenth-floor panorama of New York City through a floor-to-ceiling glass wall, a scaffold with two window washers rose steadily into our vision. The workmen stared at us with a total lack of interest.

Suddenly, John rose from his chair, raised both hands above his head, and shouted at the window washers, "I'm sorry, Mr. Mitchell, I didn't mean a word of it. You're a wonderful attorney general!"

Those few words not only lifted our spirits, but however humorous, also represented one of the sharpest comments on our situation.

13

Left Hanging

*Hell, I think we ought to let him hang there, let him twist
slowly, slowly in the wind.*

—John Ehrlichman, domestic counsel to
President Nixon, on the contentious nomination
of L. Patrick Gray as FBI director, March 1973

Judge Fieldsteel had complicated issues to deal with, but, given the
government's ruthless push to expedite the case as quickly as possible,
I expected a resolution in fairly short order. Instead, we waited for
nearly a year from the end of the hearings in May 1972 until March
of 1973 before the judge rendered his decision.

Not that we did nothing during that period. Right after Judge
Fieldsteel closed the hearing, I filed a letter with the judge request-
ing an additional remedy. To draft my brief on the Lennons' behalf,
I needed to secure a good deal of information from the government.

I explained that I had written to District Director Sol Marks
requesting statistics as to the number of aliens apprehended whom
his service considered were completely deportable from the United

States but hadn't actually deported; the number of cases where removal proceedings were not instituted *at all* and the reasons why they were not instituted. Specifically, I asked for a description of "non-priority" cases and the standards for determining that a case was "non-priority."

My letter to the judge further explained that Mr. Schiano, as the attorney representing the district director of immigration, refused to comply with my request, telling me that such material or statistics must be obtained from the central office of the Immigration and Naturalization Service in Washington, DC.

I concluded by pointing out that the regulations did not permit me to issue a subpoena—that authority resides with INS attorneys, not with lawyers representing aliens. So I asked Judge Fieldsteel to issue such a subpoena, summoning government witnesses knowledgeable about the "non-priority" program so that I could examine them under oath.

The immigration judge responded to me by telephone and letter the next day. "Your request . . . for the issuance of subpoenas for the attendance of government witnesses is denied. The reasons for such denial will be set forth in my decision on the merits of the case." He then warned me that my deadline to file my legal brief was in only a few days.

I filed my brief on the final authorized date. At the same time, the New York Civil Liberties Union, which had requested permission to participate as a "friend of the court" filed its brief as well. I also requested that the immigration judge permit me to file a rebuttal brief after the government filed its brief in opposition to the Lennons' case. It took me seventy-two pages to state the arguments supporting my clients' case.

During this time we also worked with John's British attorneys to have his drug conviction expunged. But there was definite waiting involved, and it didn't go easily. In fact, it was something of a strain.

One of the words most often associated with Richard Nixon's presidency was "paranoia." Unfortunately, that didn't extend just to the president and all his men. The actions of his administration also engendered the same feeling in Nixon's political opponents. I've described John's joking apology to Attorney General John Mitchell when a pair of window washers appeared outside an office where we were meeting—far-fetched eavesdroppers, indeed.

The reality wasn't all that funny, though. My clients and I had no idea why the government wanted to kick them out of the country at a pace never before seen in my practice. We had yet to learn of any "dirty tricks" that had occurred in the case, and at the time remained ignorant of the pressure coming from very high in the Nixon administration to remove John Lennon and his wife from the United States.

We were, however, aware that the government, presumably the FBI, wanted the Lennons to know that they were being followed and purposely harassed. Alleged phone repairmen came to "check" the Lennons' telephone but left promptly when ID was requested. Two men, stationed just across Bank Street from the Lennons' apartment, seemed to be fixing a bike interminably. When John and Yoko got into an automobile, the same two men appeared in a car behind them, following them and making certain that the Lennons *knew* they were being followed. In the jargon of surveillance, this is known as "tailgating" or "an open tail," used to intimidate a subject. In fact, an FBI document specifically recommended the use of this tactic against the New Left because "it will enhance the paranoia endemic in these circles and will further serve to get the point across that there is an FBI agent behind every mailbox." They might not fear the wrath of God, but they certainly would feel the wrath of J. Edgar Hoover. And Hoover specially targeted John Lennon.

Years later, I learned of an FBI program known as COINTEL-PRO. As far back as 1956, the FBI believed that certain "left-wing" and "radical" youth organizations might be manipulated by hostile foreign intelligence agencies. So the bureau set up procedures to "neutralize" such groups in the United States. As time went on, the FBI shifted to surveillance of emerging civil rights, antiwar, and other groups that had no conceivable ties to foreign intelligence agencies. Congress and several court cases later decided that even its operations against Communist and Socialist groups, where foreign intelligence agencies might likely be involved, exceeded statutory limits on FBI activity and violated the US Constitution's guarantees of freedom of speech and association.

The methods of COINTELPRO included infiltration by FBI agents and informers into legitimate organizations, performing various "dirty tricks," such as planting false media stories, distributing bogus leaflets, using forged correspondence, even sending anonymous letters to spouses, employers, landlords, and others to cause trouble for activists. Other tactics included legal harassment and assaults to frighten dissidents and disrupt their legitimate organizations. Without any doubt, these methods were used to discourage young people from protesting the continued US involvement in Vietnam. According to leaked documents, other targets included civil rights leaders such as Martin Luther King and peace activists such as David Dellinger and Phillip Berrigan.

I have to admit that when I took John and Yoko's case, I hadn't realized that the Nixon administration considered rock musicians *persona non grata*. Even before he'd been elected, musicians raised serious questions about the Vietnam War. One singer after another put the horrors of the war in Southeast Asia into music, urging an end to these military interventions. Indeed, the pop music industry emerged as a binding force of a cultural revolution against the war. As I found out later, when FBI files were opened under the Freedom of Information Act, no celebrity garnered more FBI reportage than John Lennon. Hoover feared Lennon's striking popularity and recognized his special ability to influence public opinion, particularly among young people. Lennon kept up a vocal criticism of the US policy promoting the war in Vietnam and never hesitated to express his anti-war stance. Lennon thus became one of the most highly watched celebrities ever to engage the interest of J. Edgar Hoover. Surveillance reports on him ran to literally hundreds of pages.

Also in the FBI file we found references to communications with the CIA. The National Security Act of 1947, which created the Central Intelligence Agency, restricted it from operating in the United States. However, the CIA conducted clandestine operations within the United States for sixteen years, expanding its illegal activities because of the growing problem of student protest against the Vietnam War. President Lyndon Johnson supposedly instructed the CIA to make an independent analysis of the situation. He apparently felt that he couldn't rely on information received from the FBI, which might have been protecting its own turf. As campus protests spread across the country, the CIA implemented two new domestic operations, assigning younger agents to infiltrate peaceful domestic groups of all types. It also used contacts with local police departments, assisting with operations and equipment it considered necessary to stave off the growing "menace" of antiwar campus activity among young people. In 1968, CIA Director Richard Helms consolidated all domestic intelligence operations into the CHAOS Program—which came to an abrupt end in mid-1972 with the arrest of notorious former CIA agents for the Watergate break-in.

Being followed openly was one thing. Having one's phone tapped was another. John came to suspect that some government agency was conducting telephone surveillance on him, and warned me that my own phones might not be safe. He provided a number to me with a Washington, DC area code to test the privacy of my line. If you dialed the number from a suspect phone and got a certain noise over the line, there was probably a tap in progress. Daytime calls from my office and weekend use of my home phone both generated these warning tones.

John complained about being subjected to surveillance and wire-tapping in a TV interview with Dick Cavett. He was also quoted as saying, "We knew we were being wiretapped. There was a helluva lot of guys coming in to fix the phone. I was so paranoid from them tapping the phone and following me; how could I prove they were tappin' me phone? There was no way. . . ."

John Ehrlichman, who was J. Edgar Hoover's contact at the Nixon White House, comments in his book *Witness to Power* that the FBI "dealt excessively in rumor, gossip and conjecture. . . . sometimes a report was based upon 'a confidential source'—the bureau euphemism for wiretapping or bugging." The FBI file on John Lennon is replete with attributions from "confidential sources" for much of the material furnished.

When in 1983 Professor Jon Weiner sued under the Freedom of Information Act to get the FBI's Lennon files into the historical record, the bureau vigorously opposed the case on the grounds of national security. When the court struck down the national security claim, the FBI resorted to the defense of "protecting an unnamed source." Considering Mr. Ehrlichman's comments, those "unnamed sources" were probably illegal wiretaps.

After all these years, I still have no idea who eavesdropped on our phone calls. We launched a lawsuit in 1973 against the attorney general and a host of other officials, claiming illegal wiretapping and surveillance of both the Lennons and myself. In return, the US attorney representing the government responded that the FBI, among seven listed government agencies, had not tapped our phones. That's a hollow assurance, though, considering the hundreds of clandestine government organizations that might have cooperated with the FBI to do their dirty work.

Ironically, J. Edgar Hoover died on May 2, 1972, the day I argued in federal court for an injunction staying Lennon's deportation case until the third preference applications had been adjudicated. However, the machinery Hoover had created continued to grind on. A week after Judge Fieldsteel concluded the hearing, the acting director for the FBI, L. Patrick Gray, summarized the case as follows:

> Sources that Lennon donated $75,000 to organization formed to disrupt the Republican National Convention. Lennon using delaying tactics to avoid deportation claiming that they must locate Ono's child by former marriage who was reported abducted by natural father Anthony Cox. New York developed information that Lennons actually have child hidden at certain residence in Houston Division for purpose of delaying deportation. INS considering filing perjury charges against Lennons if information can be established they furnished false information during hearing. New York has set urgent need for Houston Division to attempt to locate Ono's child and attempt to establish if person keeping child is in contact with Lennons. Actual location of Ono's

child and subsequent prosecution for perjury in this instance is responsibility of INS and Houston being instructed to disregard lead except for contact with established sources only. In view of possible court proceedings, active investigation by FBI in this area could result in FBI agents testifying which would not be in bureau's best interest and could result in considerable adverse publicity.

Thus, the FBI, the primary criminal investigation agency of the US federal government, had reached a conclusion: In the absence of the commission of any actual federal crimes by John and Yoko, the staff would presumably do its best to create such crimes by attempting to prosecute the distraught parents of a missing child for lying under oath. I had heard rumors of this collusion theory being discussed in the INS offices, but it never came up before Judge Fieldsteel—or the reporters of various media outlets from *Rolling Stone* to the *Wall Street Journal* covering the hearings. Maybe the INS feared adverse publicity, too.

On May 9, 1972, President Nixon announced that he was mining North Vietnamese ports and ordering massive new bombing raids. Instead of ending the war, as he had promised in his re-election campaign, he decided to escalate it, trying to bomb the North Vietnamese into submission. Lennon remained part of the antiwar movement, which responded with large demonstrations on college campuses and at military installations.

Despite the daily threat of imminent deportation at the time, and despite the fact that all we could do was file briefs in support of Lennon's position, with Yoko at his side, John joined a public antiwar rally in Duffy Square, urging the US to "get out of Vietnam." Lennon stated, "We ain't used to speakin', but we all know why we are here. I read somewhere that the antiwar movement was over . . . ha, ha! We're here to bring the boys home." He then led the crowd in his song "Give Peace a Chance."

Five weeks later, on June 17, 1972, the DC police apprehended burglars in the Democratic National Party offices located in the Watergate complex. Among those arrested were two CIA-connected individuals, G. Gordon Liddy and E. Howard Hunt. The illegal break-in to plant bugs and photograph documents had been approved by US Attorney General John Mitchell, wearing his "other hat" as head of the Committee to Reelect the President.

Throughout the summer and into the fall, the Nixon administration fought successfully to keep the growing Watergate scandal from getting large enough to affect the election. As part of that effort, John Ehrlichman lobbied for the delay of the confirmation of L. Patrick Gray as director of the FBI. He felt that news of the continued embattled confirmation hearings would deflect media attention from Watergate. That was the reason for his famous comment that Gray should be left "twisting, slowly, slowly in the wind."

When the Watergate burglars were arrested, Nixon planned to claim that they were on a secret presidential mission involving national security, and that when the president determined that a course of action was necessary for national security, it was legal, notwithstanding the methods used to accomplish it. Unfortunately for Nixon, his twisted philosophy of presidential power was tested in the Supreme Court, and the court rendered a decision two days after the arrests at Watergate, ruling that no such presidential power existed. So warped was the government administration of justice at that time that even L. Patrick Gray, the new acting FBI director, apparently took some files home and burned them.

Later in the summer came the nominating conventions for both parties. Since January, and the John Sinclair concert, rumors had flown around mainly thanks to people like Jerry Rubin, about plans to put on a series of concerts raising funds to disrupt the Republican convention, and then for a major concert at the same time as the convention, featuring John Lennon as a headliner. The idea was to attract and fire up young voters to demonstrate against the political proceedings.

My advice to the Lennons was not to attend the Republican National Convention, which had been rescheduled for August 1972 in Miami (rather than San Diego, its original location) for security reasons. I feared that in such a confused, crowded situation, the government could find it easy to plant some sort of drugs on Lennon and then arrest him for an alleged criminal violation—essentially repeating the ugly history with Sergeant Pilcher and the Scotland Yard Drug Squad. In such politically tense times, I thought the United States government perfectly likely to attempt something like that.

Although I subsequently had second thoughts about the advice that I gave, reading the FBI reports and the news about the "plumbers" confirmed my original view. I couldn't take the chance of having my clients set up for arrest or other dirty tricks. Recalling the two New York City Police Drug Squad officers present at every adjourned hearing of the deportation case, my impression remained that the Lennons would be better off staying away from Miami. They accepted my advice.

John took the occasion of a national TV appearance on "The Dick Cavett Show" to make his statement. As I sat below camera view, Lennon said, "They said we were going to San Diego, or Miami, or wherever it is. We've never said we're going, there'll be no big jam with Dylan, because there is too much going on. . . ."

In the end, an item we discovered in the INS files years later convinced me I'd given the right advice. They discussed a plan to arrest the Lennons for crossing a state line to incite a riot if John and Yoko traveled to Miami. I don't believe this was an idle threat. The Miami police received instructions to photograph every person they arrested and to submit the photos so the FBI could determine whether or not Lennon actually appeared at the convention. Some 1,200 unruly persons connected with protest demonstrations on August 22 and 23 were taken into custody. According to an FBI report, examination of those photos and records "failed to reflect that the subject (Lennon) was one of those arrested."

As a side note regarding the quality of the FBI investigation, agents in Miami received a picture to help identify Lennon—actually a drawing of a long-haired young man wearing round wire-framed glasses with the caption, "The Pope Smokes Dope." It wasn't Lennon at all; the picture was of a street singer and Lennon hanger-on named David Peel, whose claim to fame was the song . . . "The Pope Smokes Dope."

George McGovern became the Democratic candidate, and to cheers of "Nixon's the One!" Richard Nixon was nominated for reelection. The Republican campaign, well-oiled with large campaign donations, rolled over McGovern in one of the biggest landslides in American electoral history. By November, the party faithful were cheering that Nixon had won "four more years."

We didn't know it at the time, but FBI records show that after the election, they all but abandoned their investigation into John Lennon.

For John, however, Nixon's reelection came as a crushing blow. Coming on top of the stress of the threatened deportation and governmental harassment, it put strains on his art and on his marriage. In the year afterward, he uprooted himself, went to California, partied considerably too heartily, and made a lot of unfortunate public comments.

A song from this period, "Nobody Loves You When You're Down and Out," pretty much expresses his mood. I tried to console Yoko during this separation, especially as the season came round to Christmas and New Year's. This led to a tradition of exchanging presents for the holidays. Yoko always arranged for a basket of delicacies from Henri Bendel, a very fancy store on Fifth Avenue—and not your usual gift items, but things like lox and wonderful kosher-style foods for myself and my family.

Interestingly enough, on November 8, 1972, Detective Sergeant Norman Pilcher was arrested, charged with "conspiracy to pervert the course of justice," and subsequently convicted and imprisoned. The man who'd planted drugs on John was himself in jail for illegally entrapping and arresting his victims, and we hoped we were a step farther along in the quest to undo John's 1968 drug conviction.

However, as I marked the first full year of my association with John and Yoko, I could not yet point to much in the way of successful accomplishments.

I also couldn't have imagined how long of a haul I was in for.

14

The Hammer Falls

Frankly, we find it more than a little hard to believe that authorities could find no legal way to resolve what is after all a highly unusual set of circumstances. Further, we submit, if the law does not reflect the human equities, it is a law that needs to be changed.

—*Wall Street Journal* editorial, March 28, 1973

By the third week of March 1973, more than a year had passed since I'd met John and Yoko, not to mention ten months since the hearings adjourned, before Immigration Judge Fieldsteel finally reached a decision. I found out about it through a phone call from Sol Marks, who said, "Leon, I'm having a press conference at which the decision will be read. We're inviting you and Mr. Schiano, the prosecuting attorney, to be there and comment on the decision."

I had to wonder about my old friend Sol. He had spent almost forty years in the INS, and he'd never held a press conference before. He was strictly an enforcement officer, a position which suited him well. Sol did not appear to me to have the personality of a public relations person for the INS—I couldn't see him in such a role. The odds seemed pretty good that he had an inside track on how the case was going to break—and wanted to make the most of it.

John and Yoko were not in New York. In an attempt to heal the strain on their relationship caused by the difficult year just past, they'd left their place in Greenwich Village, getting an apartment in the Dakota, a luxury building in Manhattan's Upper West Side. In the meantime, they'd gone off to the West Coast.

I called them, however, reporting the situation and telling them where and when the press conference would take place. As for my own tactics, I explained that I would simply show up and decline to be interviewed about the expected decision of the immigration judge. But I had an idea.

In all the controversy that swirled around us, I noticed that the Lennon case attracted coverage not just by the TV and the usual print media, but in in the underground and music press, publications like *The Village Voice* and *Rolling Stone*, among many. I asked John and Yoko if reporters from these organs had credentials allowing them into the press conference, and could they contact their friends in the newspaper and magazine world to attend? Then I set about drafting questions, which John and Yoko distributed among friendly reporters, who in turn would present them to Mr. Marks. Also, I hired a stenographer to accompany me to the press conference and record every question asked—and every one of Sol's answers.

We went to the fourteenth floor of the INS offices, the site of the press conference—the MASH room. This was an acronym for Multiple Accelerated Summary Hearings, a procedure Vinny Schiano successfully campaigned to copy from criminal court. It allowed for much more expeditious treatment of immigration cases. I have to admit, though, that I felt a little uneasy. INS insiders jokingly suggested that MASH meant "Move Aliens Swiftly Home."

My instincts turned out to be correct. We sat at a table, Mr. Schiano and I on opposite sides of District Director Marks. From the looks of things, both he and Schiano were completely aware of the immigration judge's decision. I received my first copy of that bulky document as I sat down.

However, things did not move as smoothly as Sol Marks might have wished. Before we got started, John and Yoko added their own touch from the other side of the country. A floral deliveryman arrived, presenting a big bouquet of flowers to the district director, while I received a single yellow rose. Sol was never so flustered—and embarrassed. He tried to be as inconspicuous as possible in telling the deliveryman to bring the flowers to his office. But it was impossible to keep the assembled reporters from learning that the bouquet was a gift to the district director from the Lennons.

Sol launched into a prepared presentation on the decision Judge Fieldsteel took almost a year to deliver—a forty-seven-page, single-spaced document. The judge found that John and Yoko had over-stayed their authorized time in the United States, and were therefore deportable as "overstays." He found Yoko to be eligible for lawful permanent residence and exercised his discretion in her favor, granting her that status. With respect to her husband, however, he ruled that John was not eligible for residence because of his conviction for possession of cannabis resin. Fieldsteel granted Lennon "voluntary departure," ruling that John was authorized to leave the United States within sixty days without being deported, but that, should he remain thereafter, he faced deportation to England forthwith.

That went pretty much as Marks had planned. Then came the questions.

"Mr. Marks, did you have to bring this deportation proceeding?"

Sol responded, "Oh yes. I'm required by law to do it."

"Is there a procedure by which you might have avoided doing so, called the 'non-priority' program?"

"No," Sol replied, there was no such procedure.

"Were you told or encouraged by Washington to do this for any political reason?"

Marks stated that he had treated this case "no differently from any other deportation matter," that he had "not consulted with his superiors" in Washington on the case at all, and that he made "all decisions" on his own.

These statements became quite crucial later in the case. I'm afraid poor Sol found himself haunted by the things he told all the assembled reporters at the only press conference he ever held.

Marks then turned to me and asked whether I wished to make a statement to the press. I replied that I would decline until after I had an opportunity to study the extensive decision and discuss it with my clients. However, I indicated that we might choose to have our own press conference, at which time we might disclose our future plans.

Upon hearing of the decision, John and Yoko commented, "Having just celebrated our fourth anniversary, we are not prepared to sleep in separate beds. Peace and love."

When the Lennons returned to New York, I furnished them with copies of the decision, and we met to map out our plans for the future.

Essentially, we faced a "good news/bad news" situation. In Yoko's case, we managed to put the government in a position where it had to approve her application for permanent residency. Judge Fieldsteel had to all but admit that the government had been improper in commencing a deportation proceeding against her.

The finding against John, while painful, was not entirely unexpected—one might almost say "predictable." The judge rendered a well-organized and well-written decision—with one unfortunate exception. He admitted that difficult circumstances that had brought John and Yoko to this country and observed that: "The 'law' which is enforcing the departure of Mr. Lennon from the United States has been unable to enforce its own edict with regard to the custody of Mrs. Lennon's child."

However, he went on to suggest, "There would appear to be some question as to whether the child, in fact, wants to return to Mrs. Lennon. She appears to have called her mother in 1971 and complained that she was being harassed by detectives. As a result the detectives were replaced by people who were personal friends of the Lennons apparently to continue surveillance. It would appear that if the child is able to telephone the respondents, and the detectives and their replacements are able to be close enough to the child so that she feels harassed, her whereabouts are not entirely unknown. In any event the human equities of the situation are apparent, they do not in any way alter the excludability of Mr. Lennon from the United States and his subsequent ineligibility for permanent residence."

I found that a rather harsh evaluation of parents who had not seen their child in two years—or for that matter, had absolutely no reliable information about her whereabouts.

I have to admit, the whole case diminished my high opinion of Ira Fieldsteel. From the very outset, when he attempted to short-circuit our appeal, he disappointed me. But I still held on to the hope that he might consider Dr. Grinspoon's testimony, or even make some new law. The judge frustrated those expectations, however, doing exactly what the INS wanted—or should I say, expected.

Still, I had to face the consequences of what I considered a poor decision. Possible courses of action involved attempting to have the judge's decision reversed and following developments in Britain that might remove John's conviction in the first place. These involved seeking a royal pardon that could expunge the crime, encouraging support for a bill in Parliament expunging certain drug convictions after five years, or possibly reopening John's case based on evidence that might emerge from the prosecution of Detective Sergeant Pilcher.

In addition, we had some legislative remedies. Congress might make a change to the existing law (Congressman Ed Koch already submitted legislation attempting to do this), or a private bill might be introduced to help John in particular. Introducing such a bill in the Senate would have the effect of staying action against the subject of that bill, pending consideration by Congress.

Specifically, we had ten days from the date of the decision within which to file an appeal with the Board of Immigration Appeals in Washington, DC. As I told John and Yoko, our appeal would essentially challenge the determination that John was ineligible under the statute to apply for residence. I also explained that I thought we ought to stage our own press conference, where we could make clear to the public that the government had placed Yoko in the cruel position (as I had foretold) of having to choose between her child and her husband. The Lennons immediately authorized me to arrange such an event.

I decided to hold it at the offices of the distinguished Association of the Bar of the City of New York in midtown Manhattan.

Over the years, the bar association has played host to numerous distinguished guests, both foreign and domestic. Chief justices of the Supreme Court have visited, as well as presidents of the United States. But I'm sure they never gathered such a varied crowd of newspeople as we did on April 1, 1973—April Fool's Day.

The Stimson room was filled with representatives of the newspaper and magazine press, including many friends from the New Left press who were present at District Director Marks' press conference.

I opened with an overview of the status of the legal proceedings against John and Yoko. I went over Immigration Judge Fieldsteel's decision, that Yoko had been granted status as a lawful permanent resident of the United States and that John had been denied that same status because of his possession conviction. That left John sixty days to get out of the country. The judge further ordered that John be deported if he did not leave within that time.

Then I explained that I felt the decision of the immigration judge was legally incorrect because John's conviction was not a conviction for "possession of a narcotic drug or marijuana"—the substance he was convicted of possessing was neither. I acknowledged that I had just filed an appeal with the Board of Immigration Appeals (BIA), which would stay any action by the INS towards removing John until the BIA reached a decision. We would now do our best to convince the BIA that the immigration judge had erred, and, if we were unsuccessful, we would consider taking the matter to the US Court of Appeals, which I thought more likely to correct the error.

I read to the audience a part of the recent editorial of *The Wall Street Journal* in which the editors expressed their disappointment that Lennon was denied the right to remain in this country.

John and Yoko answered some questions, and then, full of surprises as usual, asked to halt the proceedings for an important announcement. Grinning, they waved white handkerchiefs as John read out, "We announce the birth of a conceptual country, NUTOPIA. Citizenship of the country can be obtained by declaration of your awareness of Nutopia. Nutopia has no land, no boundaries, no passports, only people."

The Lennons then got a laugh from the assembled press people by declaring themselves as the ambassadors of Nutopia, which of course granted them diplomatic immunity from any further deportation proceedings. The hankies, they explained, were the flag of Nutopia and had several uses—as a white flag of surrender and, of course, you could blow your nose on them.

The reporters, however, insisted on asking serious questions. Given the government's determined efforts to get him out of the country, did John regret his support for causes like the antiwar movement and the Native American protestors who had occupied the site of the historical massacre at Wounded Knee?

John gave a simple answer. "That would mean being someone else," he said. "I couldn't do that."

Yoko later said that she hoped that I wasn't miffed by the unscripted declaration of allegiance. Besides being a "country with no laws other than the cosmic," Nutopia had no exclusionary proceedings, no deportation proceedings—and therefore no immigration lawyers! Besides lightening the mood, she explained, "as artists, we have to do our thing."

I told Yoko that I could not have been happier with their statement. After all, I had other clients who might want to apply for Nutopian citizenship!

I am reminded of their announcement at the press conference whenever I visit Yoko at the Dakota Apartments. There is a brass plaque on the rear door to her apartment, emblazoned with the caption "Embassy of Nutopia." The embassy could not have chosen a more apt location.

15

The Mystery of Priorities

*A case in which the Service in the exercise
of discretion determines that adverse
action would be unconscionable because
of appealing humanitarian factors.*

—Definition of non-priority case,
INS operations instructions, 1973

The INS insisted on describing its attempt to deport John and Yoko as just another immigration case—and it was, to the extent that we had to make our way through the legal morass of the US Department of Justice. That meant following the next step in the procedure, going before the Board of Immigration Appeals (BIA) in John's case.

However, the handling of the BIA appeal was by no means routine. I filed my legal brief requesting a reversal of the decision against John, and the appeal was set down for oral argument. In a highly unusual step, the entire nine-member board chose to sit and hear my argument. Vinny Schiano was designated to argue the government's case.

I hated to disappoint them, but I informed the board members that I had no present intention to take advantage of my privilege to present an oral argument in the case. By the time the BIA had scheduled those arguments, I'd prepared and filed two separate, important federal lawsuits against the government. The reason I pursued separate cases was because the defendants named in each case were different. My suit under the Freedom of of Information Act demanded access to the immigration cases. The other suit was for violation of my clients' legal and constitutional rights. I wanted to prove that the Nixon administration moved against John and Yoko for political reasons, not for any violation of the immigrations laws, and to show the "dirty tricks" the government had used against them. In the meantime, I asked that the BIA not conduct oral argument nor reach a decision in the case until the information that I demanded in those lawsuits could be made a part of the record of the BIA case.

Once it became clear that the entire board wished to hear my appeal because of the importance of the legal issues I'd raised in the case, I felt I could risk asking the BIA for this rare and unusual remedy. I also had in mind asking the federal court where I'd filed the two lawsuits for the same remedy. This would permit us to discover all the underhanded activities the Nixon administration had secretly performed and offer them for consideration, together with our legal arguments in the deportation case.

By this point, constant media coverage had given the general public a lively suspicion that the Nixon administration had deployed a whole range of unsavory tactics, both in connection with the reelection campaign and for other matters related to his presidency. People may forget today, but the official name of the Watergate hearings was the Select Committee on Presidential Campaign Activities.

Unfortunately, this public awareness apparently hadn't penetrated the BIA. Nor did my reputation with the board for doing a good job on immigration appeal work and even the full board's desire *en banc* to hear my argument help me. The chairman refused to delay the proceedings. So, to get some of my claims before the BIA, I served copies of the complaints in both federal lawsuits on the board as well, making the claims I made in both lawsuits a part of the deportation

The author is pictured with his father, Harry Wildes, in front of
his dry goods store in Olyphant, PA. Circa 1945.
Courtesy of the Wildes family

The author's father behind the counter in
his dry goods store.
Courtesy of the Wildes family

John and Yoko's press conference April 1, 1973, held at the Association of the Bar, City of New York. Yoko had been granted lawful permanent residence and John was ordered deported.

Used with permission. Photo credits: Bob Gruen

To: Leon,
happy New
year!
—we were also
followed by cars
as well as on foot.

John

John was aware
of the Nixon
Administration's
use of the FBI to
surveil him.
*Courtesy of the
Wildes family*

Impromptu press
conference on the steps
of the Southern District
Federal U.S. Courthouse
in Manhattan. Circa 1972.
Courtesy of the Wildes family

Leon (left) and his then associate Steve Weinberg (right) flank
John and Yoko as they leave the old INS offices located at
20 West Broadway. Yoko offers the peace sign to a crowded audience
after an important INS hearing.

Courtesy of the Wildes family

Leon Wildes draws the eyes of the world to John and Yoko's legal plight as the government orders their separation. Press conference 1973, NYC.

Used with permission. Photo credit: Bob Gruen

Once again John and Leon make their arguments public, concerned that
John's case had been prejudged in Washington for political reasons.
Circa 1972.

Courtesy of the Wildes family

John and Yoko declare themselves as ambassadors of the (imaginary) "State of Nutopia" and plead for safe haven and diplomatic immunity. April Fool's Day 1973, NYC.

Used with permission. Photo credit: Bob Gruen

LENNON MUSIC
1370 AVENUE OF THE AMERICAS
NEW YORK, NEW YORK 10019
212-586-6444
TELEX: 148315

june all over.75.

Dear Leon,

I've decided to turn the house into a home!Would you please send all letters etc,etc,to the above address,care of Connie O'Brien.She will bring me what I have to see.(She also has a direct mk phone to the house...) Apart from being otherwise engaged,I dont think It's too good an idea to tie me in too tight with M.r.Anderson...

corderoy,

✝ love John ♡♀

Note from John Lennon when he decided to devote his time to raising his son Sean. Circa June 1975.
Courtesy of the Wildes family

"You can have your father back" John states to Leon's children as he and Yoko leave the INS final hearing granting him lawful permanent residence. July 27, 1976, NYC. *Used with permission. Photo credit: Bob Gruen*

John never forgot Leon's efforts and they developed a strong friendship lasting years after the case was concluded. This 1976 card was typical of John's wit and gratitude. *Courtesy of the Wildes family*

John proudly grasps the new green card he fought so hard to secure.
Beaming, he departs with Leon and Yoko to share an ice cream uptown at
Serendipity's with a famous actor who didn't have a chance to testify.

Used with permission. Photo credit: Bob Gruen

Leon (left) and Ruth (middle) Wildes and their son
Michael Wildes (right) proudly attend the official
dedication of "Strawberry Fields," a living memorial
in Central Park in honor of the world-famous singer,
songwriter, and peace activist.
October 9, 1985.
Courtesy of the Wildes family

The Wildes family are present through the years as Yoko Ono and Sean Lennon continue to honor John's memory and legacy. Top, left to right: Mark, Michael, and Ruth Wildes; Yoko Ono; and Leon Wildes. Bottom, left to right: Michael Wildes, Sean Lennon, and Leon Wildes. *Courtesy of the Wildes family*

The authors' family forged a strong personal friendship with Yoko Ono and her family. Top: Yoko Ono and the author's late wife, Ruth, at an art exhibition of Yoko's work at the Whitney Museum in NYC, February 8, 1989. Below: Leon Wildes (left) and Michael Wildes (right) flank Yoko Ono at an exhibition at the Rock & Roll Hall of Fame Annex in NYC, May 11, 2009. *Courtesy of the Wildes family*

Sean Lennon (left) and Michael Wildes (right) at the Whitney
Museum reflect on their fathers' work as they honor Yoko Ono and
attend Yoko's art exhibition, February 8, 1989.

Courtesy of the Wildes family

Leon Wildes (left), actor Dan Lauria (middle), and Michael Wildes (right) on the set of "Ears on a Beatle," a theatrical off-Broadway adaption of the FBI surveillance involved in John and Yoko's case, co-produced by Daryl Roth and Leon Wildes. 2004. *Courtesy of the Wildes family*

Leon Wildes (left) accompanies his son Michael Wildes (right) as they annually co-teach the doctrines of law derived out of the deportation matter of the Lennon case to law students and honor John's memory at the Benjamin N. Cardozo School of Law, NYC, 2012. *Courtesy of the Wildes family*

YOKO: legal alien

POOR **Yoko Ono** and thousands of other "resident aliens" have had to visit the Immigration & Naturalization Service office at 26 Federal Plaza to pick up new green cards — all because of counterfeiters. There were so many phony green cards being black-marketed, the INS designed a new and improved card. The old ones won't work (at airports) after March 20. Meanwhile, Yoko made the trip as painless as possible, arriving in a stretch limo with her lawyer **Michael Wildes.**

Yoko Ono and Michael Wildes at the Federal Building in
New York City, 1995. The bonds of friendship and trust still prevail.

Courtesy of the Wildes family

Iconic moment: John Lennon signals his message for peace as
he and Leon Wildes step forward, taking action that will change
the face of U.S. immigration law for decades to come.
Federal Courthouse steps, NYC, 1972.

Courtesy of the Wildes family

case appeal record. At the same time, I requested Judge Owen, the federal judge to whom both lawsuits were assigned, to order the BIA to withhold its decision on the administrative appeal until the federal court authorized it.

I made these requests to both the BIA and the court because ultimately the decision in a deportation case is made at yet a higher level, by a federal court of appeals under a legal standard that requires that the decision be made based upon *all* the evidence in the record of the administrative tribunal. So I still strove to get more evidence into the record before the BIA regarding the government's "non-priority" program.

Working in the field of immigration law, I'd heard stories over lunch, at social events, or at bar association meetings, about cases involving aliens indisputably guilty of crimes that made them completely deportable from the United States. Yet, somehow, these people still seemed to be here. Some had never even undergone the painful experience of deportation proceedings. Others ended up in proceedings that were never completed. Some had actually been ordered deported, but were never removed. Why not?

I'd heard of no federal litigation cases to keep them in this country, so I surmised that they either had the benefit of some government program of which I wasn't aware, or they'd paid off government officials to avoid deportation. Among ourselves, immigration lawyers referred to these cases as "non-priority" cases, suggesting that perhaps the government had assigned them no priority whatsoever for their removal, simply placing them at the bottom of the pile.

I remembered attending an immigration bar association liaison meeting with Mr. Peter Esperdy (the former district director of INS in New York and Sol Marks's predecessor in that position). In answer to a direct question about "non-priority" cases, Mr. Esperdy said that there was "no such thing"—no provision of law and no such animal as a "non-priority" case. I accepted his response because I had no basis for challenging it at the time. However, I was also naggingly aware of the existence of some outrageously deportable aliens who were still around. It was almost as if the INS was embarrassed to admit that there might be some mechanism to temper justice with mercy.

Now I found myself involved in a case where the government apparently had made the deportation of John Lennon and Yoko Ono a burning priority. If ever there was a time to learn more about these mysterious non-priority cases, this was it. Should there be a rule based upon a humanitarian ground, the Lennon case presented highly sympathetic circumstances, and John and Yoko would probably qualify.

It seemed to me that John and Yoko's situation fully met all the possible requirements: a loving family being torn apart; a child's future at risk. Yoko's nature, her conception of being the kind of parent she longed to be, involved her husband's companionship. Even with all the heartache of searching for Kyoko, Yoko tried not to be possessive. As she told the press, "I just want to be given a chance to help Kyoko's situation. I think she needs to know that she is wanted by both parents."

When asked what she would do when she did locate Kyoko, Yoko said, "I certainly would not send someone to sneak her away. I would ask someone both Tony and I respect—Dick Gregory, perhaps—to go and talk with him and try to work out a better situation. I know that Tony is very close to her, and I am not about to try to cut that relationship off."

It certainly seemed inhumane to me that the government would force so open-hearted a mother to choose between exile from her child or the removal of her husband. If a remedy based on humanitarian hardship existed, I wanted access to it.

The problem was, the stories I'd heard would all be dismissed as mere "anecdotal evidence." I needed facts and figures to establish the existence of the program, and then I needed to find out how the program ran.

My campaign to uncover this mysterious program had begun in May of 1972, when I wrote a detailed letter to Sol Marks, requesting, under the appropriate statutory authority, a whole series of documents and statistics to show which cases had been declared "non-priority" . . . and for what reasons. When I received no response, I telephoned Vinny Schiano, only to hear that there would be no response to my request.

On June 5, I wrote to Mr. Marks advising him that I considered Schiano's reply to be Marks's official policy, an outright refusal to comply with my request. This prejudiced my efforts to prove that the deportation proceedings should be dismissed by the immigration judge.

Fearing that I could use his failure to respond in my case, Marks wrote me on June 14, referring me to the reading room of the INS and the published decisions and interpretations that might be found there—as though I needed his advice as to how to do my research.

To make my request a part of the record of the deportation proceedings, on June 27, 1972, I'd filed a motion before Immigration Judge Fieldsteel to take the testimony of government witnesses who were aware of the non-priority cases and statistics that I requested. I noted that the INS claimed that it was their "invariable policy" to commence deportation cases against every deportable alien. This was plainly not the truth. However, I couldn't find answers to my questions in the reading room at the INS because the non-priority program was kept under wraps from the general public.

On April 13, 1973, I wrote to Charlie Gordon, the INS general counsel in Washington, DC (another old friend of mine). Gordon was a great scholar and the author of the ten-volume treatise on immigration law, and I had a great deal of respect for his legal ability and erudition. However, my letter didn't get a response from Charlie, but from E. A. Loughran, associate commissioner for management for the INS commissioner's office in Washington. Mr. Loughran informed me that he had authorized Sol Marks to meet with me so that my request might be "presented to the service in less expansive and more manageable categories." He added, "I understand that Mr. Marks has talked to you on the telephone and that it was agreed that you would stop by his office for a meeting."

This letter made me feel that I was making some folks in the INS central office a bit nervous. Still, I was not about to water down my request for information. My letter to Loughran went out on May 21, 1973, explaining that I had been requesting the same documentation for well over a year, and that the INS replies were "to say the least, unresponsive." Since I required this information as a defense against the deportation of my client, I advised Mr. Loughran that I informed

Mr. Marks by telephone that if I did not receive the information within thirty days from the date of my letter to Mr. Loughran, I'd have no alternative other than to institute an appropriate lawsuit in federal court and to examine "knowledgeable parties as to the information requested."

My letter was a subtle suggestion that Mr. Loughran might find himself one of the witnesses whose testimony I might need. Loughran responded on the last day of May, suggesting that I file a certain application form. However, he warned that some of the information I requested "cannot be searched, collected and produced without unduly burdening or interfering with service operations."

I couldn't have cared less.

On June 5, I filed the application form that Loughran had requested. Loughran personally acknowledged the receipt of my letter in an undated response and requested the fee of three dollars for the filing of the application, instructing that it ought to be made payable to the INS. For an associate commissioner, he seemed comfortable doing clerical work far below his level of authority. But I sent the check to his personal attention on June 19.

Loughran's next reply to me, dated July 16, contained more valuable information. Significantly, he never denied that there was a program for "non-priority cases," but told me that there were no statistics *compiled* on the number of such cases. Notably, he defined a "non-priority" case as one "in which the Immigration Service in the exercise of discretion determines that adverse action would be unconscionable because of appealing humanitarian factors." His letter listed the factors as:

1. Significantly adverse effect on subsisting and close family relationships
2. Age of the alien
3. Length of residence in the United States
4. Physical and mental health of the alien

While Loughran referred me to the appropriate sections of the operations instructions dealing with other remedies that the INS doled out, there was no citation to the operations instruction covering non-priority cases, a fact I found significant.

The letter continued: "In addition to 'non-priority' situations, district directors have the authority to grant extensions of voluntary departure time or stays of deportation when 'compelling factors' are present. Extensions or stays under these situations are usually limited to shorter periods of time than 'non-priority' cases. They are usually brief self-executing arrangements whereby a form of relief becomes available, a temporary illness is cured. . . ."

In a letter dated August 1, 1973, I advised Mr. Loughran that his replies to three specific questions did not state specifically whether or not such records are *maintained*. He had indicated that "statistics are not compiled" as to non-priority cases. Indeed, when speaking of other INS remedies, he indicated "that data is not *maintained*." However, his response with respect to non-priority cases was that the statistics were not "compiled," implying that the materials were kept, but that no statistical study had been made. I pointed out that his delay in finally responding to some of my questions had caused significant hardship to my clients; that Mr. Marks's delays had prevented me from offering the information as a defense in the deportation case before the immigration judge, and his "office's continued failure to furnish this information has resulted in my clients' inability to fully document the argument on appeal" before the BIA. As a result, I concluded that "I must, accordingly, respectfully request that this information be furnished promptly."

Finally, I pointed out to Loughran that I had learned that district directors of INS were required by internal operating practice to file a written report on every non-priority case, and that I was disappointed that those written reports had not been furnished to me. They were clearly not exempt from the Freedom of Information Act request I had filed sixteen months earlier.

Thus, I concluded that "I find your failure to furnish this information, which is submittedly a part of your records and not exempt from the scope of the Freedom of Information Act, to be an improper deprivation of my client's due process rights to a full and fair hearing of his alleged deportability from the United States."

I have been an admirer of the Freedom of Information Act since Congress enacted it in 1966. As a piece of legislation, it admirably demonstrates the openness of American law. It requires the disclosure by government agencies about the way these agencies work. Instead of keeping litigants against the government in the dark as to what actually happened in a given case, this legislation enables applicants to apply for copies of official documents and requires that they be furnished within ten days.

Naturally, certain exceptions apply, and typically responses to files contain areas where part of the documentation is blacked out, based on one of the recognized reasons for not making that material available to the public. From the first, historically, this statute stood the government's standard operations, which invariably maintained the secrecy of its internal dealings, on its head. It provided a new set of rules dedicated not to maintaining the secrecy of official files, but rather to their release to members of the public. Accordingly, scholars, journalists, and everyday citizens could use the Freedom of Information Act (FOIA) to review the operation of government agencies, and, on occasion, to discover and expose official misconduct.

Of course, exceptions exist, allowing the government to maintain the secrecy of limited parts of certain documents—for instance, FOIA exempts from public disclosure any material "which reasonably could be expected to cause damage to the national security."

In my law practice, we consider FOIA a helpful friend in assisting my clients to obtain government benefits. An immigration agent might have questioned a client years ago, and now the client may not recall the details. He can learn whether he was arrested, whether he made an oral or written statement, or filed an application. Through FOIA, a lawyer may be able to secure documents no longer available to his client, useful in defending a deportation case.

With reference to the Lennon case, however, this law proved to be of vital importance. Not only was I able to obtain the record of the FBI's interest and investigation of John and Yoko, I was also able to learn why the FBI was so inquisitive. Lennon's FBI file showed me the purpose of investigating the Lennons. It also led to the names of others subjected to FBI surveillance at the same time. A reading of the entire FBI Lennon file clearly disclosed that the government had a political, rather than an immigration/legal, purpose in investigating the Lennons.

But more importantly, FOIA allowed me to strip away the cloak of mystery surrounding the INS "non-priority" program.

It never occurred to me that the INS might actually have a written regulation on the subject. I considered myself highly adept at studying our statutes, regulations, and operations instructions. But I never came upon such a rule. I assumed that there was some unwritten authority by which some deportable persons were permitted to remain here.

If I had any hope of securing a remedy based on the failure of the INS to consider the special equities of the Lennons' situation, I needed to prove that this authority existed and show that it was not used in John's case because of political considerations rather than considerations of humanitarianism, hardship, and family.

By October 1973, thanks to FOIA I had accumulated enough correspondence with various officers of the INS to establish that such a category of case actually existed. But I had no basis for knowing whether my clients qualified for it, and I could see that the government was taking its time in responding to my letters. I had to put more legal pressure on them to hurry up the process.

This urgency set the stage for my legal action against the immigration authorities under FOIA. The Board of Immigration Appeals had yet to reach its decision. I would try my best to get these materials into the BIA record for their consideration and thus possibly for the court of appeals' record as well.

On October 17, 1973, I served a complaint against the former attorney general, the commissioner of immigration, the regional commissioner of immigration, the associate commissioner of immigration, and the district director of immigration in New York, Sol Marks, under the Freedom of Information Act. To my knowledge, this special piece of legislation had never been used before as a litigation tool in an immigration case.

I hoped to find why there were so many aliens still in the United States, completely deportable by law, yet remaining here openly, apparently with the government's full knowledge. District directors of immigration, including Sol Marks, never publicly acknowledged the existence of a "non-priority" program. Indeed, Marks claimed on numerous occasions when questioned about deporting John Lennon that there was no special provision by which Lennon, as a deportable alien, could remain in the United States. Marks claimed only to be doing what the law required of him: the removal of *every* deportable alien.

After a year's worth of inquiries, instituting the FOIA case gained some responses to my questions—at least enough to indicate that such a program officially existed, with records on such cases available in the central office of the US Immigration and Naturalization Service.

I argued that if such cases were "non-priority" and action was deferred, documentation must exist as to their processing. Also, from general information I had heard, internal operating practice required district directors of immigration to prepare a written report on every potential non-priority case, stating the grounds and facts upon which the decision was made in order to delay or defer deportation proceedings in each case. Records of these files must be available and should be furnished to us under the Freedom of Information Act.

From filing the case in October of 1973, I had to wait until March 1974 before the US attorney responded to our action in court. By that time, my oral argument had taken place before the Board of Immigration Appeals, so it was too late to secure the admission of non-priority materials in the record before the BIA. I had, however, taken the precaution of submitting the complaints in both federal lawsuits to the BIA upon oral argument.

By December 1973 I had managed to obtain a blank G-312 "non-priority case summary" form. By April 1974 the assistant US attorney representing the government at the point, Joseph P. Marro, informed me that he had approximately 2,000 final decisions in non-priority cases that he was prepared to forward to my attention. The names and identifying information for the aliens in question were crossed out, and all the forms had been copied. For the cost of duplication, approximately $800, we were offered an opportunity of finally succeeding in our lawsuit.

At last, on June 13, 1974, I received copies of 1,863 approved non-priority decisions. Mr. Marro also attached a request that I stipulate to the dismissal of the FOIA suit, which I wasn't yet prepared to do. In fact, it was not until February 1979 that I received enough information to satisfy me as to the "non-priority" records and procedures.

Even with this quibble, I doubt that any government communication was ever accepted with such joy! My associate and I undertook to study these cases for a prospective law review article in which I planned to bring this important, previously secret information to the attention of the immigration bar, so that others might have the opportunity to take advantage of it.

John made me promise to share our discoveries, and in fact I published several full law review articles on the subject, analyzing all the cases I had for the benefit of potential applicants. In subsequent years, I also fielded hundreds of telephone calls from lawyers and clients about the program as the government continued to tighten its grip on deportable aliens.

The operations instruction containing the non-priority program, originally appearing in the unpublished pages of the government handbook, were moved into the published version by US attorney Paul Curran himself.

As 1973 ended and 1974 began, I focused my attention on winning John's case. That meant pursuing our other federal court case against the US government, not to mention dealing with another adverse decision, this time by the BIA, in the US Court of Appeals.

16

John Winston Ono Lennon vs. the United States of America: The Case of the Cryptic Memo

Can you imagine what must have gone through the judge's mind? Can you imagine the torture and agony he must have felt? Allow John Lennon—ex-Beatle John Lennon, hardly the epitome of middle-class America— allow him to . . . to . . . the word comes hard . . . to investigate the United States Department of Justice?

—*Rolling Stone*, February 13, 1975

While the suit under the Freedom of Information Act to uncover the facts about non-priority cases may have had more far-reaching results, I had filed two separate lawsuits on October 23, 1973, and I had to pursue the other case as well.

Our deportation appeal of John's case now stood before the Board of Immigration Appeals, but I didn't have much confidence that the BIA would reverse the immigration judge's decision to deport John. Yes, the apparent urgency of the proceedings had diminished after the presidential election. Yet even a year and a half after the government first moved against John Lennon, it had not softened its position or offered to accommodate the profound humanitarian needs of a couple that was still doing its best to find Kyoko . . . to no avail.

I recalled how dramatically the situation had changed when I filed my lawsuit, *Lennon v. Marks*. Instead of allowing the government to run out the clock and avoid our efforts to change the Lennons' immigration status, it resulted in a temporary injunction against the proceedings to deport John and Yoko and an order requiring Sol Marks as district director to adjudicate their third preference petitions. Essentially, I'd turned the legal tables completely against the government—all this because I was willing to file a federal lawsuit when I felt it was required!

Now I began to get the same feeling once again. Based on previous experience, I expected that the BIA would simply affirm the immigration judge's decision requiring Lennon to either leave voluntarily within sixty days or be permanently deported, with all the attendant pain for his family. Although I knew I could file a petition to review that decision before the US Circuit Court, I'd have lost the initiative, merely reacting once again to the government's moves. That would never do.

That's why I had drawn up another lawsuit, naming different parties as defendants. The first named defendant was the United States of America itself; then John Mitchell, the (now former) attorney general of the United States; as well as Robert H. Bork, the current acting attorney general; Richard Kleindienst (the former deputy attorney general); Raymond Farrell, the former commissioner of the INS; General Leonard Chapman, the current commissioner; Sol Marks, the district director of the INS New York district; the INS itself; and "persons unknown" in the US government. I wasn't about to let anyone off the hook.

My purpose in filing this lawsuit was to try to prove that the INS abused the immigration law to accomplish a political, rather than a legal, purpose and that Lennon was selectively prosecuted essentially as a political dirty trick. John Winston Ono Lennon, to use his full formal name, was the party suing, claimed that he and Yoko had been the subject of illegal surveillance activity by the US government and that, as a result, his case and various applications he had filed to secure his status here had been prejudged.

Beyond that, the government's actions violated the various rights and privileges that were guaranteed to John and Yoko as aliens in the United States under the US Constitution. For speaking out against the Nixon administration and the Vietnam War, the government punished them by denying their humanitarian need for an extension of time and trying to banish them through an unauthorized deportation proceeding. Even though John and Yoko were not American citizens, they still held First Amendment rights.

They were also denied their Fifth Amendment right to "due process" by the way the government conducted their case, and they suffered other constitutional wrongs under the Fourth and Ninth Amendments. I claimed that the case merited a mandatory injunction against the deportation proceedings and other relief.

In a sworn statement that John submitted in support of both cases, he explained that he and Yoko had a friendship with Jerry Rubin, that they met together at their apartment, went to restaurants and movies together, and spoke frequently on the telephone. They also appeared publicly together during February 1972 to support the cause of Irish freedom.

John also pointed out that during the same period, he met with and talked by telephone with other New Left activists, including Abbie Hoffman, Rennie Davis, Bobby Seale, Huey Newton, A.J. Webberman, Paul Krassner, and John Sinclair. Lennon explained that he met with these individuals in connection with his and Yoko's artistic endeavors, which included promoting the idea that our society had to evolve into a better state. That was a tenet they both held very strongly—"evolution, not revolution."

As a result of these associations, however, the government engaged in unlawful surveillance and instituted baseless and illegal deportation proceedings for reasons other than any violation of the immigration law. The complaint also noted that Lennon had requested the immigration judge to affirm or deny that the government had committed certain unlawful acts, including the use of recording devices and conducting surveillance of his premises—and that his claims had neither been denied nor even acknowledged. Lennon claimed in the selective prosecution complaint that the relief he needed could not be granted by the BIA, where his appeal was currently pending, and that only in US District Court could such claims be adjudicated. We thus felt it was urgent that the district court permit us to delve into the government's illegal activities to prove what was done so it could become a part of the eventual record before the US Court of Appeals, should the BIA deny Lennon's current appeal.

John's suit also recounted that the only way the Lennons had secured the approval of his and Yoko's third preference outstanding artist applications was through an earlier lawsuit in the same court. We also claimed that the INS violated its own procedures in failing to declare Lennon a "non-priority" case, which would have permitted Lennon to remain here indefinitely despite his alleged deportability.

For the first time, Lennon set before the court an undated memo which he had secured concerning "The supervision of the activities of both John and Yoko Lennon." The memo, written in typical bureaucratic language confirming active prejudgment of their case, was sent by the "Supervisor, Intelligence Division Unit 2" to the "Regional Director Group 8." It stated that "John Ono Lennon, formerly of the Beatles and Yoko Ono Lennon, wife of John Lennon, have intentions of remaining in this country and seeking permanent residence therein," and that "this has been judged to be inadvisable and it was recommended that all applications are to be denied." The memo referred to their relationships with Jerry Rubin and John Sinclair, relating that their "many commitments are judged to be highly

political and unfavorable to the present administration" and conclud-
ing that "They are to be judged as both undesirable and dangerous
aliens."

The memo warned, "Because of the delicate and explosive nature
of this matter" the "whole affair" was handed over to INS to handle.
It ended, "Your office is to maintain a constant surveillance of their
residence and a periodic report is to be sent this office."

Unfortunately, the actual origin of the memo and the agency to
which it referred remained obscure. John told me that the document
had been obtained by his driver, a former New York City police officer who currently found himself under investigation. I made some
preliminary inquiries into which intelligence agency might have
a "Unit 2" and report to a "Regional Director, Group 8," but got
nowhere. It seemed that there were so many agencies that had intelligence units it was impossible to ascertain which particular agency
was the source of the memo.

I claimed in our complaint that "upon information and belief"
various officials of the US government "wanted (Lennon) to be
deported or removed and that all discretionary relief applied for by
(him) was to be denied." I argued that this action was not taken by
immigration officials acting under the statutory power conferred on
them to grant or deny discretionary relief according to their own
understanding and conscience, but was based solely on political factors that were not a part of the record and for reasons not inherent
in the immigration law. Our claim was that all our applications had
been prejudged in this manner. "Upon information and belief," I also
claimed in the complaint, "there exists in the federal government a
conspiracy or determined plan to deprive the plaintiff (Lennon) of
his rights, and that this 'conspiracy' was demonstrated by a course
of behavior which was unlawful, unreasonable and contrary to law."

We alleged that the Lennons' and my phones had been tapped
without judicial authorization, that John was subjected to physical
surveillance without court order, that his need for an extension of
stay was ignored, and that he was improperly placed in deportation
proceedings. We also claimed that the only applications approved in
the case had to be secured by a court order in federal district court,

and we'd come back again to federal court for the remedy that we needed. We asked for a hearing to determine to what extent unlawful activity on the part of the government had influenced the decisions made with respect to John's immigration case. Finally we asked the court to enjoin the defendants from rendering decisions based upon such illegal activity.

The Department of Justice, of course, could imagine nothing worse than having John Lennon rummage through its files, examine its witnesses under oath, and ask embarrassing questions. On the other hand, if Lennon was correct and the government had organized a conspiracy to deny his applications for relief and to remove him expeditiously without dealing honestly with his case, an immense violation of law had occurred. I was asking federal judge Richard Owen to permit me to examine under oath the parties whom I had sued, including the attorney general, his deputy, the commissioner of immigration, and the associate commissioner, as well as the New York district director and, hopefully, its chief trial attorney. Balancing the government's equities against my client offered a herculean task, requiring sound judgment and judicial fairness.

Judge Owen had not been on the bench for very long. He'd been appointed by President Richard Nixon, having served in the Justice Department during the Eisenhower administration. The judge was concerned that, while he was willing to allow Lennon to examine the government's witnesses and documents, he thought it inappropriate to open the government's files completely to John. Some of the people I wished to examine under oath were no longer in government service when we reached that point in the case. Both Attorney General Mitchell and Deputy Attorney General Kleindienst had been indicted as co-conspirators in the Watergate case. Commissioner Farrell and District Director Marks had retired, and Chief Trial Attorney Schiano had left government service and was engaged in private practice.

I thought it best to request permission to depose Sol Marks first. My plan was then to move up the ladder, verifying his statements and determining where the decisions in the case actually came from. I planned to hold off on my request to examine Schiano because I felt that his testimony would contain the necessary bombshell to disrupt the government's stonewalling because of his own conflicts while working for the INS.

After the parties agreed to allow the government until March 22, 1974, to respond to the complaint and the usual interrogatories and requests for documents were exchanged by counsel to the various parties, John responded to all of the government's questions.

He acknowledged that they heard a series of clicks and other sounds on the Lennons' telephone prior to March 1972 and that people familiar with wiretaps informed them that their phone had been tapped. He told of a time that "a person who identified himself as representing the telephone company appeared at our apartment on Bank Street and seemed to be working on the phones. When it became clear that he was going to be questioned about his ID, he disappeared."

John also told of observing two individuals who lingered in different guises outside his apartment on Bank Street in Greenwich Village and, who, realizing they'd been observed by John and Yoko, attempted to hide. "We were followed for a period of time by the same two men in a car continuously," Lennon said, "until we commented upon such surveillance on a TV show, when the surveillance was . . . discontinued."

In answer to the question as to the origin of the memo attached to the complaint, he said it was from a former employee, Tom Bassalari, who "was a former narcotics agent or police official of the City of New York and familiar with government investigatory agencies and personnel." Lennon also confirmed that he showed the memo, which was confirmed to be an authentic and believable document, to the Senate Subcommittee on Constitutional Rights, the American Civil Liberties Union, the New York Civil Liberties Union, and other reputable persons.

In answer to a specific question about a staff member of Senator James L. Buckley having stated that the Lennons were considered to be security risks, he indicated that the name of the person contacted was Tom Cole, an executive assistant to the senator, and that the conversation took place around March 26, 1972.

John confirmed, giving a full explanation, all of the court proceedings that transferred Kyoko's custody jointly to Yoko and himself by orders in both the St. Thomas and Texas courts. He noted that the child's father, Anthony D. Cox, was found guilty of contempt of court for his refusal to produce the child when ordered and sentenced to confinement in jail for five days. John carefully pointed out that the court order stated that the child was to reside "within the territorial limits of the United States" and confirmed his and Yoko's joint willingness and desire to raise Kyoko in the United States and give her an American education.

In response to the presumptuous and totally irrelevant questions as to exactly what tax returns he and Yoko had filed in the United States, he simply replied that he was "advised by his tax counsel and verily believes that he complies fully with all income tax requirements of the United States and has filed all tax returns required to be filed."

The government now felt ready to file a motion to dismiss the complaint for failure to state a legal basis for court action. Judge Owen's ruling came down partially in favor of the government, but on two of the three main issues involved, he decided strongly in Lennon's favor.

Judge Owen ruled that if it could be shown that decisions in the case were made based upon non-immigration-related considerations and that Lennon's legal or constitutional rights were denied thereby, the court had full jurisdiction to correct the situation and would proceed to do so. Especially in light of the fact that the immigration judge and the BIA acknowledged that they did not have authority to act in such circumstances, Judge Owen confirmed that he *did* have such authority.

Under the circumstances, he held that it was appropriate to allow Lennon to examine witnesses under oath and inspect government documents to prove his allegations. However, he felt that it was not appropriate to allow Lennon full access to the entire range of pretrial proceedings, as that could prove to be too broad a mandate to give an alien subject to deportation proceedings. Accordingly, he ruled that he would proceed to control the pretrial procedures for the examination of witnesses and documents by periodic meetings with counsel and by making interim decisions. His decision was dated January 2, 1975.

With Judge Owen's decision, it seemed as though I had gained a formidable ally in pressing our case. In fact, I later discovered that the judge had something unusual in common with my client—Owen was also a musical composer. After law school he studied at Juilliard and composed four operas that were well received.

We also had another unlikely ally—Watergate. As I proceeded with the filing of the two federal lawsuits, I sensed an outpouring of support from the media. Where did this sudden sympathy come from? I believe after the steady drumbeat of revelations about the inner workings of the Nixon White House, people began to appreciate what Lennon had been put through in his efforts to legalize his status during the past three years. Many now realized that it was not beyond Richard Nixon's Department of Justice to perpetrate a governmental conspiracy to deny John Lennon any benefit under the immigration law and to remove him as quickly as possible.

One of my more iconic souvenirs from this whole case is a photo of John and Yoko in the US Senate gallery, attending the Watergate hearings that finally forced Nixon to resign as president. I'm sure that's one legal proceeding that they got some enjoyment out of.

Perhaps that was just as well. We still faced some difficult legal proceedings of our own.

17

You Lose Some, You Win Some

Mr. Lennon is simply one of the thousands of tourists who come to this country as visitors for business or pleasure and, lured by the attraction of our nation's economic opportunities and freedom, decided to remain here. Often they do so illegally, as did John Lennon. . . . If upholding the law, as the public pays me to do, is wrong in the eyes of Rolling Stone, *then I plead guilty.*

—INS Deputy Commissioner James F. Greene, writing to protest *Rolling Stone*'s coverage of the Lennon case, 1975

On July 10, 1974, eight months after I handled oral argument in our case, the Board of Immigration Appeals in Washington finally rendered its decision. Although the BIA decided not to grant the extension I had requested, it effectively gave me a good deal of time anyway, permitting me to move ahead with both federal lawsuits. To make a long story short, the decision upheld Judge Fieldsteel completely and rejected all of my arguments.

I certainly felt let down, but I can't call the result unexpected. While the BIA enjoys high regard in the immigration field as the highest-ranking administrative decision-maker in the system, it has no existence in any statute whatsoever. The board was established by a regulation of the attorney general and never reaches beyond its limitations, nor does it generally challenge the decisions of the administration or the immigration courts.

Many arguments I raised in the case could only be addressed to a court, and the BIA has no authority to challenge a court decision, nor does it even have the authority to challenge a regulation promulgated by the attorney general.

The decision, written by the chairman of the BIA himself, Maurice Roberts, was nevertheless a tightly reasoned, self-consistent document. "Maury" Roberts, a dear personal friend, was a highly recognized scholar, referred to by his colleagues as "Mr. Immigration Law." His lectures on recent developments before the BIA received heavy attendance at annual conferences on the immigration field. He had served as editor of the most important periodical in the field, *Interpreter Releases*, for several years before joining the BIA. The position as editor was a prestigious one, one which I myself had to decline because of the tremendous demand on my time it would have created. However, everyone in the field was thankful that Maury Roberts had accepted it for a number of years, and the publication reflected his immense scholarship. He held the position with great distinction before becoming the chairman of the BIA.

Aside from his encyclopedic knowledge of immigration law, he had a sweet disposition and was particularly warm and helpful to me on a personal basis. As the voice of the BIA however, he strictly adhered to the party line.

Approximately a month before the BIA decision, we received copies of 1,863 approved non-priority decisions under our FOIA case. Based on his furnishing of all these decisions, the government's attorney, Mr. Marro, requested that I terminate the lawsuit. In replying to the assistant US attorney, I listed a series of questions regarding the non-priority program that the INS still hadn't answered. I also enclosed a copy of one of the newly arrived files. It detailed the case of an alien convicted of attempted criminal possession of heroin who received non-priority status permitting him to remain in the United States because "expulsion would separate Subject with his wife and 2 minor children."

Certainly John's case involved a much less serious conviction and considerably more serious hardship to Yoko and Kyoko. From the dates of some of the approved non-priority applications, I learned that Sol Marks personally recommended non-priority consideration for cases at the same time as his press conference, where he falsely stated that he was obliged to commence deportation proceedings in *every* case . . . and that John Lennon was being treated "just like any other alien."

Obviously, the district director—and the government—had some explaining to do. And by early 1975, I had the means to force some answers.

Ruling on our selective prosecution case in federal court, Judge Richard Owen allowed us to examine government records and to question other witnesses. By this time, many of the people named in the suit were no longer in government service. John Mitchell and Richard Kleindienst had gone from serving as the chief law enforcement officials of the land to indicted defendants in the Watergate scandal. Vinny Schiano resigned from the INS in December of 1973, and Sol Marks retired in May of 1974.

Based upon the judge's decision, I made my first request for an examination before trial of a witness, a request I knew would bring strong objections from the government. I wanted a deposition under oath from Vincent A. Schiano, my friend and former courtroom antagonist. Vinny had been involved with the case up to and including the oral arguments before the BIA, but now had gone into private practice.

Given his contentious relationship with his superiors over the way the INS handled deportation cases involving Nazi war criminals, the government had to consider Schiano a loose cannon. He could certainly not be relied upon to keep his mouth shut about the existence of documents he might have seen in the secret Lennon files—documents that could prove our contentions of selective prosecution in federal court. No wonder the government began its motion to dismiss our complaint while at the same time requesting an order to prevent our taking a deposition of Mr. Schiano.

The court set the matter down for a conference between counsel and judge to determine the preliminary steps that might be taken for pretrial depositions in the two cases we had filed. To avoid the government-continued motions and filings to terminate our lawsuit, I thought it more appropriate to start by taking the deposition of Sol Marks instead.

I knew that I had a transcript of all of the questions and answers from the press conference Sol held when Judge Fieldsteel rendered his decision. Friendly members of the New Left media agreed to pose individual questions to Marks that I'd drafted, so I had plenty of material to question Marks about. If I successfully proved that he lied to the public at that time, and that indeed he'd received instructions from Washington to bring the proceedings and not to adjudicate any of Lennon's applications, I'd have time later on to follow with an examination of Schiano. Perhaps if Sol knew that Schiano would be examined after his testimony, we might have greater reliance upon the truthfulness of what Marks had to say.

On June 3, 1975, Sol Marks gave his deposition at the Federal Building in New York City.

Since I considered him an old friend, I called in my colleague Nat Lewin to conduct Marks's examination. Nat was an attorney whom I respected highly and had been retained to help draft the court of appeals brief in the case, so he was familiar with the issues. The government was represented by Mary P. Maguire, a special assistant US attorney, who was later to become a member of the BIA after moving to Washington.

Marks left the government in May 1974, after being New York district director for about four years. Lewin asked him whether he had brought all the documentation and records we'd requested. When the government released the non-priority records nearly a year before, we'd already been working for Sol's deposition before he left the INS. Failing that, we stipulated "that he will continue to have full access to all government files and records concerning my client, so that we would not be prejudiced by this witnesses's retirement from government service."

I was shocked to hear, after Marks began to testify, that since being served with the notice to appear in this deposition, a notice both negotiated and approved with the collaboration of Judge Owen, the federal judge in charge of both Lennon lawsuits, Marks had discarded all of his notebooks and private papers on the case.

He explained that he always used stenographic notebooks to keep records of telephone conversations but he destroyed them when he retired from government service. In addition, he testified that he did not have access to the file as a result of his retirement, and Ms. Maguire seemed to be holding the only remnants of the Lennons' files that currently existed.

Rather than engage in a dispute with Marks as to his destruction of his notes and papers, Nat and I decided to pursue his examination from Marks's memory alone, and only toward the conclusion of the examination did Nat raise the issue as to the propriety of a federal witness not appearing with his books and records, as specified by the notice to take his deposition.

We saw no purpose in getting into an argument too early in the examination as the issue could be raised once we had questioned Marks about whatever information we could secure from the documents we already had. Particularly since Judge Owen, in our discussions in chambers, had taken full charge of all depositions and other requests for information, in order to protect the privacy of the government's files, and had indicated that he wouldn't allow an illegal alien to "rummage" through immigration files.

Nat's judgment proved correct. We found it clearly preferable to have Marks identify the documents we already had and use his testimony to establish that our documents were authentic and that he was aware of their contents.

Marks confirmed that he recognized our copy of Senator Strom Thurmond's letter to Attorney General John Mitchell dated

February 4, 1972, and that it had also been in the government's file on Lennon. Thurmond had attached a memo from the staff of the Internal Security Subcommittee of the Senate Judiciary Committee and had advised Attorney General Mitchell that "this appears to be an important matter, and I think it would be well for it to be considered at the highest level." To me, the only level higher than the attorney general was President Richard Nixon himself. Marks confirmed that the letter continued, "As I can see, many headaches might be avoided if appropriate action be taken in time." Below was a handwritten postscript in which Thurmond wrote, "I also sent Bill Timmons a copy of the memorandum." Bill Timmons was the top White House liaison to Congress. It seemed perfectly clear that Thurmond wanted President Nixon notified about Lennon's presence in the United States, his opposition to the administration's policies, and expected the president to take some action to remove him promptly.

Marks testified that he had met the Lennons on one prior occasion, before I represented them, when they needed an extension of stay and that he had checked with the commissioner's office in Washington before granting it. Their purpose was to continue their ongoing search for Kyoko.

He then recalled that after I visited him and advised him that they would need a further extension, he contacted the commissioner's office in Washington once again and received very clear instructions that, except for a one-month extension until February 29, 1972, no further extensions of stay should be granted.

Marks indicated that he reported regularly to the commissioner's office in Washington on anything to do with the Lennon case because of its notoriety—and because of the interest on the part of the INS central office. He stated that even before he became aware of Senator Thurmond's interest in the case, all of his actions were taken from instructions given by the central office. Marks said his initial, personal, impression was that the request for an extension was "deserving," but he did not recall advising the central office of his personal impression. The ultimate decision would be made in Washington by Commissioner Farrell or Associate Commissioner Greene. In answer to questions, Marks stated that if the decision were his, he would have granted the extension, but the commissioner controlled the decision, and he wanted Lennon out of the United States. Marks confirmed that he told the Lennons on March 2, that they should leave the United States by March 15, as he was instructed to do by Washington. He also set the date of the deportation hearing for March 16 as a result of his conversations with Deputy Commissioner Greene. He acknowledged that he signed the Orders to Show Cause commencing deportation proceedings personally, which is rarely done, certainly in no more than five percent of the cases. When asked why he proceeded so quickly with the deportation case, he responded, "I would have gone much more slowly on this case than they directed me to." He acknowledged that if it were simply up to him, he'd have granted a further extension. But, he said, "I didn't know what information was available to the people in Washington." He did not recall having access to Lennon's file. Finally, he admitted flatly that, "I didn't really make the decisions in the case. I was really acting as a conduit."

Marks stated, referring to his own memo, that Associate Commissioner Greene told him, "Under no circumstances should this office approve the I-140 (preliminary petition for third priority consideration as an outstanding artist) filed by Lennon." He understood that the office should simply "sit on it" and not adjudicate the petition until after Lennon was deported. He acknowledged that he instructed his applications chief, Mr. Spivak, not to take any action on the Lennons' I-140 petitions until further instructions came from Washington.

We also asked Marks about his decision to approve both John's and Yoko's third preference petitions when he was sued and the court ordered him to adjudicate the petitions.

Marks indicated that he disagreed with the decision that he actually adjudicate and approve the third preference petitions. "Publicity-wise, it would indicate that here we are willing to concede that the man was of distinguished merit and ability, yet we are forcing him out. It seemed contradictory for the service to have approved it at that point."

Obviously, the order to approve the petitions came from Washington. He also acknowledged that it would be very rare to receive such instructions as he had in this case, especially to issue an Order to Show Cause setting up a deportation hearing on a specified date, March 16, 1972. He could not recall any other case where that had happened. Indeed, he could not recall another case in which Associate Commissioner Greene had instructed him to start deportation proceedings. He acknowledged that this was the only case during his tenure as district director when this unusual action took place.

Nat Lewin finally got to ask Marks questions about his press conference. Marks acknowledged that he held such an event and when asked publicly whether it was true that he had commenced the proceedings entirely on his own, without instruction from Washington, he acknowledged now that he had lied, that it was totally untrue. Although he was not instructed to lie to the public, he stated, "I had the feeling that they would have been unhappy if I had attributed it to them. . . . They would have preferred me to take the flak rather than them, putting it bluntly." He chose to take sole credit for starting the proceedings because he thought if the orders had come from Washington then deportation might be ascribed to political reasons. He did, however, acknowledge that "our commissioner was very political-minded. He owed his job to a political appointment. . . . Conceivably he would have been affected by having to concede that *he* started the proceedings."

"You thought that you ought not tell the truth to the press?" asked Lewin.

"That's correct," answered Marks.

"Merely for publicity's sake, no other reason," Lewin followed, "You were asked in the same press conference on what grounds you had instituted the deportation proceedings. You said that he had been convicted of a marijuana offense . . . that answer was not the reason, that was not true?"

Marks responded, "It was a half-truth."

"It was half-false as well, is that right?" Lewin asked. "You were instructed to deny all discretionary relief, is that right?"

"Maybe not in so many words," Marks replied. "But the clear inference was that we were not to grant him any relief. I understood very clearly from their instructions that we were not to give this man a break."

Mary Maguire, representing the US attorney's office, objected to our seeing the INS files on Lennon, because they were designated "confidential." Marks, on the other hand, had destroyed his personal notes and was no longer the custodian of the government's files, so we were unable to press him for further details. However, we established that he lied to the media at his press conference. He also admitted that all his instructions came from the commissioner of immigration in Washington and that none of the decisions in the case were made by him, even though the law required him to make all the decisions involved. Although Marks tried to defend the actions of his superiors, he did acknowledge that he was instructed to take the action, which he did and took the position that he had no choice to do otherwise. He indicated that he was simply "following instructions" from the INS central office.

The implications were clear: The case was indeed being directed by Washington for political reasons. We had discovered quite a bit by questioning my old friend Sol.

Logically, we should now move up the line of command to verify Sol's statements and determine where the decisions in the case actually came from. I planned to hold off on my request to examine Vinny Schiano, explosive as his testimony might be. Therefore, my second witness was likely to be the associate commissioner of immigration, James F. Greene, as I climbed the ladder.

As the heading on this chapter shows, as late as February 1975, Mr. Greene still continued to spout the party line. His letter to *Rolling Stone* reveals the same misleading and untruthful statements Sol Marks admitted in his testimony. However, Marks had the decency to confess that he had done wrong.

18

Life Goes On

They always say, "Their marriage was a failure," at every divorce. Ours was the other way around; our separation was a failure.

—John Lennon, *SPIN* Magazine, October, 1988
(Interview originally conducted in 1975)

A lot had happened in the three years since I took John and Yoko's case. It had gone from a seemingly hopeless battle against an all-powerful administration bent on deporting my clients, underscored by Nixon's overwhelming electoral victory, to a much more even contest against an administration under fire for multiple abuses of power. In a more personal sense, the struggle had changed our lives as well.

Most notable, perhaps, was the strain that years of struggle against the government had put on John and Yoko's marriage. Shortly after Nixon's electoral victory, they separated for a while, with John going to California and Yoko staying in New York. It was a very difficult time, and I hardly ever discussed the situation with either of them, feeling that this was a personal hardship that they were enduring separately. I knew that I could count on both of them to cooperate with whatever I needed from them in their joint representation. Yoko seemed to sincerely appreciate my personal calls on her birthday, Christmas Eve, New Year's, and so forth, and I tried never to infringe upon their privacy during that strained period.

During the time that John was away, I assume he was quite unhappy, missing Yoko and missing his favorite city, New York. Certainly, the songs he wrote throughout this period reflected considerable confusion and pain. Somehow, I always had the impression that they both believed they would eventually get back together. When that happened, I was personally delighted. I believe that John put his own happiness over the reconciliation into his song "(Just like) Starting Over."

Besides being back with Yoko, I think John was glad to be back in New York. Throughout his fight to stay in the United States, he felt most welcomed by New Yorkers. To him, being in the city was like living in the center of the world. He'd say, "I imagine New York is like London must have been in the Victorian days when Britain was at the height of its power." He'd also compare it to living in Rome at the height of the Roman Empire. New York taxi drivers, who apparently always recognized and respected him, succeeded in making him feel as if he belonged here. He pointed out that no purely "American" type existed—we had Italian-Americans, African-Americans, Irish-Americans, and so forth, all of whom made him feel at home. Despite the pressures placed upon him by his uncertain immigration status in this country, he loved just walking the streets of New York, happily visiting every nook and corner of the city, like the Lower East Side's Little Italy and Chinatown. He was happy to step into a West Side coffee shop for a bite at any time of the day or night, befriending everyday people like the street singer David Peel, whose album "The Pope Smokes Dope" John and Yoko helped produce.

The little apartment at 105 Bank Street had been wonderful. Its front room was not very useful, crowded with files and equipment. The bedroom beyond, two stories high, had a skylight and a wonderful upright bed in its center, where many visitors were welcomed and entertained. John and Yoko often sat in that bed, watching the huge, silent, color TV screen at their feet while surrounded by many friends. One could meet half the world around that bed—radical types like Jerry Rubin or Bobby Seale, oddball musicians like David Peel, poets like Allen Ginsberg, actors like Peter Boyle, television personalities like Geraldo Rivera, or even political operatives like the deputy mayor of New York.

The Lennons had lived in the United States since August 13, 1971, the longest period of time they'd spent together in any single country since their marriage in 1969. John came to America on a number of occasions previously, to perform or to sign contracts for recordings and performances. Yoko, six years older than John, had come to the United States from Japan with her parents when she was only three years old and spent half her life here. She attended Sarah Lawrence College and traveled in and out of the United States on numerous occasions, holding various jobs and staging artistic events, including concerts with John Cage.

In a country so based on freedom of speech, it's not surprising that the Lennons became involved in political activities, especially given their backgrounds. Yoko was a child when atomic bombs fell on her native Japan. John had a partial Irish background and reacted bitterly when the British refused to leave Northern Ireland. He developed a super-sensitivity to class distinctions, having grown up in a working-class community and speaking with an inelegant Liverpudlian accent. His songs about prison, the problems experienced by the Irish, and women's lib all emanated from this kind of personal identification.

In the past, Yoko had stood in Trafalgar Square in London, completely covered by a black bag, holding a sign proclaiming "peace." John, always "the political Beatle," caused a controversy on an American tour years earlier by telling a press conference that he did not agree with the war in Vietnam. His songs "Give Peace a Chance" and "Power to the People" merely continued to express his views.

From the moment of their marriage in March 1969, John and Yoko conducted a series of publicity appearances for peace. These took place first at the Amsterdam Hilton Hotel and thereafter with their "bed-in" appearance in Toronto. Early in their marriage they sent acorns to leaders of many nations, asking that they be planted as a sign of confidence in future peace. Golda Meir of Israel, Pierre Trudeau of Canada, and others responded positively.

Despite his antagonistic relationship with the government, John had an admiration for the United States, which he expressed in the final part of his affidavit to the court of appeals. Describing New York as "a Mecca of the music industry and the arts," he went on to state that, "All of my professional interests are now here in the United States, and naturally my business holdings and financial interests have been transferred to the United States as well."

"Removal from the United States," he concluded, "would be like removing a fish from water, as it would uproot me from the environment which I believe most contributes to my life and work as an artist."

John was pleased at the way his name attracted such huge, devoted audiences around the United States. It took no effort at all, once his name was attached to a project, for the project to grow geometrically. Of course, that fame and John's activism had its downside, motivating the government to feel it had to tail the Lennons and tap their phones.

That was not a fun part of living in the United States, as John told one interviewer: "I felt followed everywhere by government agents. Every time I picked up my phone, there was a lot of noise. Somebody gave me a number that if you call it, you get this feedback sound that confirms your phone is being tapped. And I did it and it did. Suddenly I realized this was serious, they were coming after me one way or another. They were harassing me. I'd open the door, and there would be guys standing on the other side of the street. I'd get in the car and the same guys would be following me and not hiding." He continued, "That's what got me paranoid. They wanted me to see I was being followed. Anyway, after I said it on the air, on TV, the next day there was nobody there. Was I dreaming? No, I wasn't." He even mentioned me. "Look, my lawyer, who's as square as the next one, started to agree. He found his phones were being tapped, and he didn't know how to prove it either."

Continued exposure to John and Yoko took off some of my square edges. Early on in the case, a writer for *The New Yorker* gave this description of one of the deportation hearings: "The Lennons were rather less flamboyantly turned out than the two lawyers who sat flanking them. The one on Yoko's left has a battered face. He wore a Norfolk-cut suit of shiny shantung and his hair, black and wavy, was long enough to cover his collar. The one on John's right has a smoother face, and he wore a more subdued beige spring suit. His fair hair, streaked with grey, was a trifle shorter and his tie was wide and bold, and his glasses were modishly wire-rimmed. John and Yoko whispered amicably with both of them, apparently without discrimination."

The attorney in silk shantung with the longer hair was Vinny Schiano. I was the more conservatively attired figure. But as time went on, I grew my hair longer—and bought my first pair of jeans.

Representing John and Yoko Lennon was a full-time proposition. Although I was hired because of my talent for immigration law, I dealt with a number of professionals in the Lennons' employ—managers, accountants, attorneys, and consultants in the public relations and performance fields. For some reason or other, I found myself taking on the jobs of one after another of these specialists as John and Yoko replaced workers and advisers. There was no question that Yoko had full confidence in my abilities and trusted me to fill in as needed.

On one occasion, Yoko invited me to join her at a lunch meeting with five or six attorneys in a law firm that represented her (a firm, incidentally, that is no longer in operation). I noticed that she asked a lot of questions, and that the attorneys, who seemed to be busy having lunch, made notes and told her they would research and respond to her concerns. I didn't know much about the subject at hand, but it appeared to me that the attorneys should have been able to respond immediately to most of the things Yoko wanted to know.

She invited me to step outside for a moment and then asked, "Do you think these attorneys are taking me for a ride?" I explained that I was not an expert in the areas of their practice, but I was no more satisfied than she was with their responses. She popped her head in the door, told the lawyers that she had an urgent matter to attend to, and thanked me for coming along. I understand she fired the law firm later that day. When Allen Klein's contract with them expired, the

Lennons hired a new manager. However, until they filled that position, they obviously needed someone to arrange their affairs. Once again, I was designated.

From the very beginning, I drafted press releases at every stage in the case, which John and Yoko arranged to pick up and distribute. I also arranged for press conferences at significant points in the case.

My statements of fee were forwarded to an accounting firm, but soon that firm was replaced by another. The business attorneys with whom I dealt likewise got replaced, and I fielded occasional business law questions.

Of course, while all this was going on, I also maintained my usual 9-to-5 immigration law practice, although my famous clients complicated that schedule somewhat. Luckily, the Lennons did not keep normal business hours. John and Yoko often started their workday late in the evening and operated through the night. My telephone, whether in my office or home, could ring at any time of the day or night. I never complained.

I guess I should have figured on the kind of service they'd expect from me when, at our first meeting, Yoko asked for my personal telephone number. I promptly gave it to her, but with this proviso. As an observant Jew, I did not take phone calls from sundown on Friday evening until after sunset Saturday night.

"Oh yes, I know about that," Yoko responded. "That's quite all right."

I never heard a complaint from either John or Yoko with respect to the fact that they could not reach me for about twenty-four hours each week. However, Norman Seaman told me years later that he fielded calls during those hours, and that there were many of them.

On one occasion, I spent the Jewish high holy days, Rosh Hashana, at Grossinger's Hotel. My sons and I were just leaving the room to attend services when the phone rang. The operator, quite annoyed, stated "some wise guy on the phone says he's John Lennon, asking to speak to Leon Wildes."

I took the call. "I am really sorry to call you so close to your holiday, but I have an important question. Can you still talk?" I assured him that I could, and he wished us a happy holiday before he got down to business. I found both John and Yoko highly respectful of my religious observances over the years.

Often, however, we had business that couldn't be conducted by phone. That meant I spent the day at my usual legal work, conducted at the usual business hours. Then I'd have a bite to eat, and around 10 P.M. or so, I'd go to my meeting with John and Yoko. A good deal of the time, they worked in a studio on West 44th Street known as the Record Plant, producing music. When we met there I felt as though I were aboard a spaceship, surrounded by control panels with hundreds of blinking lights. John and Yoko seemed to spend entire days and nights without stepping outside, assiduously preparing recordings of one instrument after another until they blended into a fully completed musical piece. Rock music groups such as Elephant's Memory and individuals such as David Peel joined them and became part of their entourage in this capsule-like musical environment. I'd find myself there until two or three o'clock in the morning and then finally get home. I had always prided myself on my ability to get by with very little sleep. My association with John and Yoko certainly tested that quality.

More important than lost sleep was the fact that these odd hours took me away from my family over a period of several years. That made for some disappointments and difficulties, but my dear late wife Ruth believed in what I was doing, and she, along with my sons Michael and Mark, fully supported me through this time. The boys' contribution to the Lennon case often meant being without their daddy for five long years.

On one of the evenings when I was home, I dozed off during the late TV news, but Ruth continued to watch *The Late Show with David Letterman*. She woke me, urgently pointing to the TV screen. "They're talking about John and Yoko. She is a courtroom artist."

I watched Letterman continue his interview with Ida Libby Dengrove, a familiar-looking courtroom artist.

"Their lawyer was interested in getting the original drawing," she said, while a beautiful illustration that I remembered appeared on the screen. It showed John Lennon and I appearing before Judge Owen in federal court, with the assistant US attorney in the foreground.

"He offered to exchange it for a signed photograph of John and Yoko, but at the time I didn't consider it a fair exchange," she said with some disappointment, "and I did not want to part with it."

After the conclusion of her interview, I called the Letterman show and arranged to get Ida's telephone number. I called the next day and arranged to purchase the picture from her. It still holds a place of honor above my office desk.

Perhaps the most important and life-affirming part of John and Yoko's reconciliation was that they found themselves expecting another child.

This was both exhilarating for the Lennons—and anxiety-provoking. Yoko had suffered several prior miscarriages. In fact, she'd been pregnant in 1968 at the time the drug squad had made their notorious raid and arrest. One of the reasons that John had chosen to plead guilty to the charge had been to spare Yoko the strain of acting as a witness at trial. Unfortunately, Yoko lost the baby only five weeks later. John recorded the unborn child's heartbeat, and he and Yoko included it in their album, *Unfinished Music, No. 2: Life with the Lions*, which came out in 1969. The track, "Baby's Heartbeat," was followed by "Two Minutes' Silence."

Since then, Yoko had undergone major surgery so that she could have a child. Her doctor indicated that this pregnancy was probably her last chance at motherhood. He ordered that Yoko should stay in bed in the couple's apartment and avoid all emotional or physical excitement. The Lennons found that last order pretty difficult to follow, considering the government was still working to deport her husband.

However, I have to commend Assistant US Attorney Mary P. Maguire for showing heart and decency in one of the most interesting moments in my life. Several times in this account, I've mentioned the letter from Strom Thurmond to John Mitchell, essentially the match that ignited the whole deportation debacle. When this infamous letter was revealed, I also learned that it came with a memo attached. Ms. Maguire approached me in federal district court, puzzled by a problem that could only have occurred to an honest lawyer. She admitted to me that there were two memos in the file that might have accompanied Thurmond's letter, but since they were separated from the cover letter in the file, she felt obliged to furnish both of them to me.

That honesty is something I shall remember for the rest of my life. However, while life might go on, so too did our case.

19

Getting to the Truth

*In Fiscal Year 1974, this Service deported 18,824
aliens to all parts of the world, while another 718,740
were required to depart without the issuance of
deportation orders. Admittedly, few, if any, of
these aliens were as well known as Mr. Lennon.
However, I think you will agree, from the number of
illegal aliens expelled, as indicated above, that this
Service has little time or inclination to single out
any alien, be he John Lennon or plain John Smith,
for arbitrary treatment as alleged in your letter.*

—James Greene, associate commissioner,
US Immigration and Naturalization Service, replying
to a letter on John Lennon's deportation

*Your dept. continues to harass him, without his chance
of going thru procedures to become a "lawful" citizen
in your cryptic discriminating terms.*

—Handwritten response from recipient of above letter

Even as our legal struggle to uncover the Nixon administration's unpleasant secrets ran on, a battle for public opinion raged at the same time. One of our greatest allies in getting John's story out was Jack Anderson. While today we may have overdosed on the word, forty years ago, investigative journalism was a new idea. And one of the first practitioners in the field was Jack Anderson. His newspaper column, "The Washington Merry-Go-Round," ran in hundreds of papers across the country and had a significant impact.

Anderson and his associate, Les Whitten, turned up scoop after scoop, uncovering political and corporate corruption. They reported on the shortcomings of the previously sacrosanct FBI and its director, J. Edgar Hoover, earning considerable enmity on Hoover's part. Anderson and Richard Nixon so disliked each other that I've heard it claimed that Nixon had sixteen CIA operatives assigned to keep Anderson under surveillance. To frustrate this, Anderson had his kids dress up like their father and drive off in different directions.

The Anderson-Nixon antagonism apparently grew very serious. In his autobiography, G. Gordon Liddy, a former Nixon campaign operative, recalls discussions with another Nixon staffer, E. Howard Hunt, about "getting rid" of the newsman. According to Liddy, an Anderson column revealed the identity of a CIA source, putting the person's life at risk. Liddy and Hunt talked with a doctor who'd done work with the CIA about what could be done to Anderson. Hunt suggested dosing the columnist with LSD, trusting that the resulting erratic behavior would discredit him. However, Liddy felt the need for stronger measures. They considered breaking into Anderson's Bethesda home and slipping poison into one of his medicine bottles, or a physical attack, mugging or even killing him. As Liddy put it, Anderson "should just become a fatal victim of the notorious Washington street-crime rate." He even volunteered for the job, but in the end failed to get the go-ahead from officials higher up the chain of command. Liddy did, however, participate in the ill-fated Watergate break-in, for which he and Hunt actually went to prison.

It's not surprising, therefore, that Anderson took a serious interest in the Nixon administration's urgency in trying to deport John and Yoko. Jack Anderson gets credit in many quarters with breaking the story of the conspiracy against the Lennons—at least in the mainstream media. Certainly, print and TV news covered what happened in the case. Anderson, however, dug into *why* it happened.

In a critically important column, Anderson wrote in August 1974: "In a case with Watergate overtones, ex-Beatle John Lennon is being hustled out of the United States on a six-year-old hashish charge while more than a hundred aliens with similar or worse drug records remain.

"The singer-composer's major problem does not appear to be his 1968 guilty plea in England to unwitting possession of a small amount of 'hash.' Rather, his offense seems to be outspoken opposition to the Vietnam War, and false rumors that he was going to lead a demonstration against Richard Nixon at the 1972 GOP convention."

Regarding the non-priority files, he reported, "Our investigation turned up aliens not only with heroin and marijuana convictions, but rape, murder, robbery, burglary, auto theft, perjury and even bigamy. All have been allowed to stay in the United States for 'humanitarian reasons.'

"In one case, an alien had different convictions including drug violations and rape, and seven other arrests. Another was described in immigration files as one of 'the largest suppliers of marijuana and narcotics' in his area. At one time, an alien himself admitted to a 'heroin habit costing $80 a day.'

"Compared to these, Lennon looks like a choir boy."

Anderson also devoted considerable space to connecting the dots, describing how "a smear sheet against Lennon" was slipped by Strom Thurmond to Attorney General John Mitchell, how it proceeded to his deputy, Richard Kleindienst, and was then transferred by Immigration Commissioner Farrell to Associate Commissioner James Greene, until in the end this fateful document arrived on the desk of District Director Marks.

On June 14, 1975, Anderson published an article following up on what he called the "Watergate tactics" the government was using to "oust" John from the United States. "Our revelations, combined with the superb legal work of Attorney Leon Wildes, have persuaded the government to consider letting Lennon stay here indefinitely."

This hopeful article discussed the history of the government's deportation attempts and referred to the non-priority materials which I had secured under the Freedom of Information Act. Anderson stated, "Wildes came up with proof, however, that the United States harbors hundreds of ex-felons, many with far more serious drug records, under the 'non-priority' status that permits them to stay in the country."

A famous criminal attorney told me that he believed Jack Anderson never referred to another lawyer's work as "superb." So, beyond taking a professional pride over getting our story into the media, I also took some pardonable personal pleasure from this article.

Anderson returned to the Lennon case in October, discussing Yoko's difficult pregnancy and the ill effects of what he called "harassment" on the part of the INS.

"The Immigration Service has suspended its efforts to deport her husband before the baby is born in November. This decision was taken with great fanfare 'on humanitarian grounds.' But Immigration officials quietly reserved the right to oust Lennon after the medical crisis is over," he wrote, closing the article this way:

"Meanwhile, Yoko is anxiously awaiting her long-wanted baby, with her husband constantly at her side. The Immigration Service won't say whether it will compel John Lennon to leave the country thereafter. Their attorney, able Leon Wildes, has sworn he will fight the deportation with every legal weapon available to him."

Continuing that fight, after I completed taking the deposition of Sol Marks, Judge Owen allowed me to move on to the next witness I had requested, James F. Greene, the associate commissioner of immigration during the time of the deportation proceeding. I decided to question Greene myself. He was now assistant commissioner, having served as the associate commissioner since 1968.

Vinny Schiano referred to Marks as a "capo," a man as loyal to the INS as a crime boss was loyal to the Mafia. Sol was an enforcement agent first and foremost, and that showed when he had to take on the more subtle aspects of his job. Greene, on the other hand, was a highly professional, polished bureaucrat who had more experience being examined as a witness than Marks. Each of his responses to my questions was carefully couched in protective terms—"I have no personal knowledge," "speaking strictly from memory," and phrases made famous by the Watergate hearings and many subsequent congressional investigations: "To the best of my knowledge" and "to the best of my recollection." At the time the government placed Lennon in deportation proceedings, Greene ran the operations wing of the INS. Now he'd taken charge of all branches of the INS under a newly appointed commissioner of immigration and could act for the commissioner in every sphere of authority.

Greene appeared to be a capable official, and I was anxious to see how he would handle himself and the responses he'd give on seeing the communication from Senator Strom Thurmond, and particularly the statement Sol Marks made, which quoted Greene as instructing him to start deportation proceedings forthwith and, in pure prejudgment, not to adjudicate the Lennons' third preference applications.

After a good deal of preliminary questioning, I inquired about the senator's letter. "I was aware that Mr. Thurmond had written a letter to the department that had been referred to the Immigration Service," Mr. Greene replied. When I showed Mr. Greene the letter from Senator Thurmond and the memorandum attached to it from the Senate Internal Security Committee, he identified both documents and acknowledged that he had seen them at about the time they were received by the attorney general. "The letter passed through my hand," he admitted.

However, when I asked whether his service's subsequent actions were made in light of the information attached to the senator's letter (not to mention Strom Thurmond's strong admonition that "many headaches might be avoided if appropriate action be taken in time"), Greene disagreed. "I can't accept your tying those together. The action was taken because his (Lennon's) time had run out. He indicated he wanted to stay here as a permanent resident, and we started deportation proceedings. We felt he was inadmissible to the United States by virtue of his conviction for possession, which is mandatorily excludable, and there is only one way to resolve it: to get it into deportation proceedings.

"I had heard of this document, seen the document when it went through, and that was one thing. The action taken was to start these proceedings, which we did."

Greene's comments with respect to Sol Marks's memo of March 2, 1972, were even more significant to me. In the highly incriminating memo that Marks placed in John and Yoko's file, he admitted that Associate Commissioner Greene had telephonically advised him that "we should immediately revoke the voluntary departure granted to John Lennon and his wife." Additionally, an Order to Show Cause, the document to start deportation proceedings, "should be issued for both aliens and served upon them with a return date of March 16, 1972." Marks's memo continued, "Mr. Greene further stated that under no circumstances should this office approve the I-140 (third preference petitions) filed by Lennon. This is a direction of Commissioner Farrell personally. Further action on the petition will therefore not be taken unless cleared by the undersigned with Mr. Greene."

I asked whether those statements were true, and Greene acknowledged his instruction to Marks. Particularly with respect to the instruction not to adjudicate the third preference petitions, Greene admitted that he instructed Marks not to do his job—clear prejudgment and an absolute violation of Lennon's rights. When I asked about his reasons for the decision, he replied, "We wished to not be in a position where we had approved these petitions and at the same time started deportation. The decision was probably faulty because it was based . . . I mean, his (Lennon's) petition is based on a matter of law, his qualifications, and we recognized or realized that that was an untenable position and we reversed ourselves."

Of course, Mr. Greene did not explain that he and Commissioner Farrell only decided to "reverse" themselves due to our lawsuit—because a federal judge enjoined continuing the deportation proceedings and ordered Marks to adjudicate the applications at once. It gratified me to know that the subtlety of my filing third preference petitions showing that John and Yoko were "extraordinary aliens in the arts or sciences whose presence in the United States was prospectively beneficial of the national culture" had not been lost on the office of the commissioner of immigration. Greene did not want the media to see him declaring two aliens to be extraordinary and then granting residence to one while deporting the other.

When I quoted Sol Marks's testimony that "Marks understood his instructions to be that he was not to give this man a break," Greene agreed it was true, except for Marks's characterization of his instructions about giving Lennon a break. "He was told to proceed in deportation. He was told to not act upon the applications for—on the third preference petitions . . . that's about all he was told. It wasn't a case of break or discretionary relief or what have you." Although he squirmed a bit, he still fully admitted prejudging the applications.

In response to my question as to whether a "non-priority" application had ever been filed for John Lennon, Greene said he never saw such an application by Marks. He responded, "I was not aware of any action of this nature until a year or so ago, when I read in Jack Anderson's column that you had documents which you acquired. . . . with reference to non-priority." He did not recall whether any application had been filed for non-priority consideration on behalf of John Lennon at that time. He confirmed that at the time, a committee existed in the INS central office that would have considered such an application, but, other than reading about the Lennon case in Anderson's column, he was not aware that his service even considered non-priority status for Lennon. Greene also acknowledged that he was aware of the involvement of the Senate Internal Security Sub-committee in the Lennon case.

Although he continued to deny any cause and effect with regard to Senator Thurmond's letter and its attached memo, Greene admitted that the senate subcommittee's interest in removing Lennon had already been expressed to him when he instructed Marks to cancel Lennon's temporary authorization to remain until March 15 and told him to schedule a deportation hearing against the Lennons as of March 16.

And, although Greene's recollection placed it in late 1971, we subsequently showed that it was on February 25, 1972, about ten days after receipt of Thurmond's letter, that a telegram went out to all immigration offices in the United States instructing that the Lennons should not to be given any extensions of their time to visit the

United States. Lennon's status commanded the attention of the com-missioner of immigration and all four of his deputies. The service departed from its usual policies and procedures. Despite this, how-ever, Greene's official responses to people expressing concern over the Lennon case generally ended: "Mr. Lennon is guaranteed and indeed has received the same constitutional rights of 'due process' and 'equal protection under the law' as would any other alien or citizen of this country, and you may be assured that he received a fair and impartial deportation hearing." His testimony put the lie to what Greene stated in the form letter that heads this chapter, "This Service has little time or inclination to single out any alien, be he John Lennon or plain John Smith, for arbitrary treatment."

As Mr. Greene himself commented about these letters, "I would say literally thousands go out over my name in the Lennon case."

When I asked whether the revocation of the two weeks' time for the Lennons' voluntary departure before leaping to deportation proceedings seemed unusual, he admitted, "It was certainly dif-ferent than what we usually follow." And when I asked if he could name other instances besides the Lennons' where this happened, he dodged adroitly: "I believe there have been, but I would have dif-ficulty pinpointing the names and cases." Despite efforts like these and attempts to downplay his service's attempt to sideline the third preference applications—"As I say, the position wasn't sound and we reversed ourselves"—the associate commissioner's statements, along with those of Sol Marks and the memorandum Marks had put in the records, painted a clear picture of selective prosecution, to say the least, as to the way the INS treated this case.

A further memo placed in the file on March 1, 1972, by Carl G. Burrows, assistant commissioner for investigations at the INS central office, shockingly underscores what we later learned. The Burrows memo made it clear that all decisions with respect to the status of the Lennons lay with Washington, and not Sol Marks, contrary to what Marks had consistently and publicly claimed throughout the proceedings. A duplicate copy of the instruction was delivered per-sonally to Sol Marks.

In Burrows's memo, he confirmed what Marks had stated in his memo to the Lennon files and confirmed in his testimony—"Mr. Greene advised Mr. Marks that it was the commissioner's position that we should not approve any third preference visa petition in behalf of the male subject," referring to the third preference petition which had been sequestered in Mr. Spivak's office safe.

However, the next paragraph of the Burrows memo disclosed something I had not previously known, a real shocker. "Mr. Marks had at one time during these conversations notified me that an FBI agent . . . had conferred with an investigator in our New York office concerning the subjects' whereabouts. This unidentified FBI agent indicated to the unidentified investigator that *if the subjects were to initiate travel to Miami* (where, for security reasons, the Republicans had transferred their national convention from San Diego), *the FBI would seek a warrant for subjects' arrest for violation of the federal statute prohibiting interstate travel in the furtherance of any conspiracy to incite a riot.*" I had advised John to stay away from the proposed site of the Republican convention for fear of trumped-up drug charges. This, however, was much, much worse.

I was dumbstruck to read that the INS central office had involved itself so deeply with the Nixon administration's efforts to ensure the president's reelection that they would even collaborate with the FBI to indict Lennon on a contrived, serious criminal charge if he dared travel in this country—to exercise his constitutional right to free speech!

The memo also shows how much scrutiny focused on the Lennons. "This information was conveyed to Mr. Harlington Wood, Jr., associate deputy attorney general, by Mr. Greene together with information that the male subject's attorney, Leon Wildes, had advised District Director Marks that his client had left for Houston yesterday in connection with the female subject's custody suit involving her daughter by a previous marriage. Mr. Marks was directed by Mr. Greene to furnish this information to the New York office of the FBI." He obviously did, as the FBI interviewed and photographed more than a thousand arrestees at the Miami convention, only to report that Lennon was not among them.

Burrows concluded his memo: "Mr. Marks is to report to me concerning any and all developments in this matter."

Although Marks had publicly stated that it was his responsibility and that he personally made all the decisions in the Lennon case, it was clear that the shots were being called in Washington. Mr. Greene, particularly, was involved in passing instructions from Commissioner Farrell and monitoring developments. And, while Marks admitted truthfully that this was the case when he was deposed under oath in federal court, Greene was still unwilling to confirm what the INS commissioner and Immigration Service had done.

20

Breathing Space

Attached are executed forms G-312, Non-Priority Case Summary, and related material furnished by subject's attorney.

—Joe D. Howerton, acting district director, to the INS regional commissioner, September 16, 1975

We may have succeeded in turning the tide against the government at this point, but our antagonists still had plenty of fight in them. When Sol Marks retired in May, 1974, I contacted his successor, acting district director Maurice F. Kiley, requesting to know whether Marks had actually ever filed the G-312 form to recommend the Lennons for non-priority status. Eventually the government admitted Marks had never done so.

Rather than replying to my request, however, Kiley rejected the entire idea. On August 30, 1974, he stated that "non-priority status . . . has been considered by me, and I found no strong equities nor compelling humanitarian factors present to justify granting a stay of deportation." Mr. Kiley's consideration must either have involved psychic abilities or some sort of super power like telescopic vision, since I later learned that at the time in question, the Lennon files were at the US attorney's office. Rather than referring to the files, the acting district director may have been following instructions left behind by Sol Marks.

Luckily, this prejudiced response from the INS had a bright side. On May 27, 1975, the US attorney for the southern district of New York, Paul Curran, after consulting with the assistant US attorneys representing the government in the Lennon case, came to a decision with far-reaching ramifications. He decided that, as a provision of law that was generally applicable to all deportable aliens, the non-priority operations instruction should have been made public, that is, transferred from the blue (secret) pages of the operations instructions to the published white pages. The publication of these previously secret instructions had an immediate beneficial effect upon the immigration bar which continues even today.

At the same time, since it was obvious that Lennon had never received consideration for this remedy, the US attorney sent a letter to Judge Owen, who was hearing the FOIA case on the non-priority issue. "At my suggestion," Curran wrote, "INS, without conceding that its previous action was incorrect or irregular, has determined to undertake a review of the question of possible non-priority status for the plaintiff"—which is to say, John Lennon. So we had now won a "do-over"! Mr. Curran added that, to ensure the fairness of this review, "no one previously involved with the case" would be involved in eventually determining whether John qualified or not.

The US attorney sent a copy of his instruction to Maurice Kiley in his capacity as the temporary replacement for Sol Marks running the INS district of New York. In fact, Kiley wrote to me requesting a series of documents and information in support of the reconsideration. However, his involvement in an earlier denial of the application, despite the fact that the file was not even available to him at the time, automatically eliminated him as the party to rule on Lennon's eligibility. Kiley blew his chances for participation.

Joe D. Howerton, apparently also an acting district director (but never previously involved in the case), was designated to consider the

Lennon non-priority application anew. He had the entire file available to him at the time.

I recently searched through the USCIS online files on the Lennon case to retrieve the form G-312 that Howerton had submitted. It's sort of odd to admit, but despite going over nearly two thousand G-312 forms in the course of analyzing non-priority cases, I had never actually seen this one before.

I had, however, invested considerable work into preparing submissions to accompany my request. It took nearly a month to obtain statements from the obstetrician treating Yoko during her pregnancy, outlining her previous childbearing difficulties, as well as getting business details of the couple's life in the United States from their management consultant.

My presentation started with a legal proposition, pointing out that the operations instruction, now that I had it, stated that the district director of INS, *"shall* recommend consideration for non-priority . . . in every case where adverse action would be unconscionable because of the existence of appealing humanitarian factors." The use of the word "shall" was significant because it was stated as a mandatory requirement for a district director to so designate a case once the hardship was shown. Also as a legal matter, I analyzed the humanitarian factors in the 1,863 non-priority decisions that we'd gained thanks to our freedom of information lawsuit.

Sifting through all these G-312 forms to find circumstances similar to John and Yoko's, we came up with 138 cases involving aliens with some sort of previous drug conviction. These ranged from a man of twenty-four who was arrested for transporting marijuana (John was twenty-eight when he was arraigned for possession) to an alien with a long criminal record (including, in no particular order, auto theft, contributing to the delinquency of a minor, vagrancy associated with being a pimp, rape, burglary in the second degree, disorderly conduct, robbery, suspected robbery, and various narcotics convictions). In that case, non-priority status was recommended "in order to avoid separation of the family."

I pointed out that former district director Sol Marks, who originally received the request for an extension of stay, testified in pretrial proceedings while questioned under oath, that he actually never considered the question of whether Mr. Lennon ought to have been granted non-priority status. He acknowledged that he would have personally granted any extensions that "the Lennons might have requested to continue the search for Kyoko," except that he had been instructed by his superiors in Washington to deny all extensions.

I'd asked Marks, "If thereafter Mrs. Lennon had been found eligible to remain in the United States, as she was, would that have been a case for non-priority consideration?"

He replied, "It would have altered the circumstances. If we then had a legal resident wife and a citizen child and Mr. Lennon, whether he was a distinguished person or not, I *certainly* would have submitted for non-priority consideration." With more than thirty-five years' experience with the INS, Marks admitted under oath that he would have granted non-priority consideration—but he had been expressly told to deny all applications by the INS commissioner's office in Washington!

In addition, I pointed out that Sol Marks himself on March 8, 1972, several days after he commenced deportation proceedings against the Lennons, recommended for non-priority consideration an alien whose crime was "possession of less than one-quarter ounce of marijuana in a car with another person who owned the car." The only family members in the United States were the parents of the alien. The basis for the grant of non-priority in this case was the "emotional strain on aged parents" (who were sixty-three years of age). Yet this did not dissuade Marks from stating publicly and to the press that he had no authority to consider any of the facts and was obligated by the law to start deportation proceedings *in every case* in which an alien was deportable. Under oath, in his deposition, he also later admitted that he had purposely misled the public and that he did so without any instruction from his superiors.

Aside from my presentation for non-priority consideration, I submitted an affidavit from John. It set forth the true, loving nature of a concerned husband for his wife's health and well-being. John detailed the support he gave to Yoko in helping to locate Kyoko and stated, "Unfortunately, despite the entry of court orders granting us custody of Kyoko in the courts of Texas and the US Virgin Islands, where her custody was contested and litigated, we have never succeeded in finding Kyoko. Her natural father has violated the court orders. Our efforts to locate her, which have been documented in court records, have continued for seven years."

John also described the miscarriage that Yoko suffered in England after their arrest by the drug squad, and his insistence on being with her in the hospital at that time, despite the unavailability of a bed. We attached a record containing his songs, "No Bed for Beatle John" and "Baby's Heartbeat," published by Apple Records in 1968, to this affidavit. Given the difficulty of Yoko's present pregnancy, John explained how he constantly attended to her, accompanying her whenever she visited her doctor—"which is the only time she steps outside of our apartment." Given the vital importance he attached to staying with his wife, John explained that he moved all his business dealings from their apartment to the Lennon music office and canceled all his personal appearances, performances, and other obligations—all to help ease the strain on Yoko. He noted that the legal proceedings surrounding his immigration status were "at this point the primary source of strain and would be alleviated if non-priority status were granted."

John offered a lasting tribute to Yoko when he stated: "Ours is a very close relationship, and for the first time it was necessary for us to think about being apart from one another; of not being together on a 24-hour-a-day basis as we had always been. I rely upon Yoko heavily for my well-being and consult regularly as to songwriting. Likewise, she consults with me as to all her artistic endeavors and there is a constant give and take which results in great interdependence. The government's decision placed Yoko in a position where she could travel, particularly to follow-up any leads as to Kyoko's whereabouts, while preventing me from doing the same. A physiological dependence upon one another and the constant support we derive from one another in our professional and personal lives was undermined by the different decisions in our cases. I respectfully submit that separating Yoko and me would cause us extraordinary hardship because of our special closeness and interdependence."

John's affidavit continued with a description of their continuous search for "our child Kyoko" since 1969 when she was spirited away by her father, Tony Cox. "We followed clues," John explained, "which took us to Spain, Denmark, Canada, and France. After exhaustive efforts through private investigators, mutual friends and well-intentioned but mistaken third parties, Yoko has resorted to consulting over ten psychics in her exasperating search to locate Kyoko, even taking two along with her on her recent trip to Japan because of a clue which she wished to follow-up. Hundreds of episodes in her search for Kyoko have cumulatively been physically and emotional draining for us both.

"A typical episode," he continues, "begins with some party holding out a clue as to her whereabouts, only to result in a bitter disappointment or a possible holdup for a large sum of money with no hope of success, even on one occasion, a threat that unless such monies were paid regardless of success the press would be notified that Yoko was not really interested." As a result, John and Yoko decided that the only and best method for them was to follow-up personally on every likely clue, trying as much as possible to avoid publicity. Despite large expense and great effort during those years, no clue ever proved truly helpful.

As for the baby Yoko was expecting, John stated, "In view of my wife's strong ties of more than twenty-five years' duration in this country, it is her desire to raise her expected child in this country, and she would not consider raising her child elsewhere under any circumstances." John pointed out that Yoko felt completely at home in New York and they wished to bring up their child in that city, considering its wealth of educational and cultural opportunities.

John then commented on how non-priority classification would affect Yoko's career. Quoting their good friend and benefactor, Norman Seaman, who followed and encouraged Yoko professionally throughout most of her artistic life, John explained that she'd established her career in this country. She was educated here, started off here as an avant garde artist, and developed her field of multimedia arts in the United States. She, thus, developed her artistic talents here, and all of her friends, colleagues, collaborators, managers, fellow artists, and artistic and business endeavors were in this country. This being so, John's departure from the United States would necessarily affect her health, her career, and the obvious companionship and love which they shared.

The final part of his affidavit dealt with the effect his American sojourn had on his own career. "Through the associations and contacts I have developed here with musicians and other talented people involved in all aspects of the music industry, I have been able to continue growing and producing as an artist. . . . I have gained and benefited from its rich musical environment and have in return generated whatever music I am capable of creating. I trust that there have also been financial and business benefits to the country." If he were required to move from the home he'd made in America, he felt it would disrupt the very basis of his continuing artistic work.

The affidavit was signed on August 26, 1975.

Upon receiving our submissions, Howerton recommended non-priority status for Lennon, stating that deportation "would separate subject from his LPR (lawful permanent resident) wife, who is expected to give birth about November 1, 1975, after a difficult pregnancy." The recommendation was approved by Regional Commissioner Oswald J. Kramer on September 20, 1975, four days after its receipt.

Almost four decades after working with John to draft this crucial affidavit to support his non-priority request, I feel very gratified at having capsulized my client and friend's feelings, expressing his love for his wife, his child, his music . . . and his adopted country.

Also across those decades, I could proudly trace the tremendous impact of the US attorney's decision to remove the shroud of secrecy from the non-priority program. Finally, requests could actually be filed by aliens and their lawyers to secure this classification, which offered the hope of remaining in the United States despite an alien's deportability. John Lennon had accomplished what he had set out to do: to assist not only himself, but other deportable aliens who perhaps could not afford the legal costs of requiring the government to publicize this available remedy, which began to be referred to as the "cure for impossible cases" by immigration lawyers throughout the country.

Achieving non-priority status in our own case meant that after three-and-a-half years of having the sword of deportation hanging over their heads, John and Yoko could take a deep breath and concentrate on bringing their unborn child safely into the world. Whatever the verdict of the court of appeals, they could stay in this country, win or lose.

John greeted the news of his non-priority status as he greeted most of the circumstances in his life, in poetry:

Yoko's pregnant with baby . . .
John's pregnant with hope . . .

He realized, though, that while he could remain in the United States indefinitely, that status would never ripen by itself into legal permanent residence status.

We still awaited the outcome of our petition before the court of appeals. Thanks to the "instructions" from the upper echelons of its central office, the INS deportation procedures had moved along in lockstep, with the initial examination keeping the narrowest focus on John's narcotics conviction and the BIA merely acting to rubber-stamp the immigration judge's findings. While the court of appeals had certain limitations—we couldn't bring in new evidence—it offered the first opportunity for someone with originality to look at the case. We'd done pretty well in the court system, forcing Sol Marks to adjudicate the third preference petitions and then unlocking the files on non-priority status. While we failed in our effort to remove John's conviction from consideration, we'd certainly pushed back strongly against the INS.

I turned again to Nat Lewin to help draft the appeal brief, and he joined me for the oral argument before the imposing three-judge panel. Chief Judge Irving Kaufman had a somewhat controversial background, having presided early in his judicial career over the espionage trial of Julius and Ethel Rosenberg—and imposing the death penalty. In dealing with him, however, there was no question that the man was brilliant. The second judge, Murray Gurfein, had ruled early in the Pentagon Papers case and was a former president of

HIAS, the same Hebrew Immigrant Aid Society where I started my legal career. The third judge, William Mulligan, was a well-regarded speaker who served as dean at his alma mater, Fordham Law School.

The oral argument was intense as Nat and I responded to the court's many questions. I remember one particular question posed directly to me: "If Lennon's eligibility for residence is approved, will you discontinue the action against the attorney general and the other parties?"

I responded, "I would have to consult with my client. As you know, he is justifiably aggrieved by the unusual harshness of the government's proceedings against him. My own inclination would be to terminate the district court proceedings." From my point of view, if we won residence for John, why be vindictive?

The question came from Chief Judge Kaufman, who appeared to me to be inclined to grant our petition for residence. The other judges listened intently, but I wasn't too sure of their reactions. With poker faces like these, I wouldn't care to play cards with those gentlemen.

On October 8, 1975, I received a telephone call. The person on the other end of the line identified himself as a clerk of the Court of Appeals. "Mr. Wildes, I probably shouldn't be doing this," he said, "but I'm a Lennon fan."

And then he told me something I have a hard time believing, even to this day.

21

"Thank God for Tarot Card Readers"

For your information, a petition to review Mr. Lennon's deportation order was filed on September 6, 1974, in the United States Court of Appeals in New York. The petition for review stays Mr. Lennon's deportation pending determination of the petition by that Court.

—James Greene, associate commissioner,
US Immigration and Naturalization Service,
responding to an inquiry on the Lennon case

"I wanted to report to you that you won the Lennon case," the clerk's voice came over the phone. "It was a decision, two to one, and there is a lengthy dissenting opinion. If you would like to send someone over for a copy, I'll let you have it, under the understanding that it should not be released until it is formally entered."

I called Lennon immediately. He answered with the high-pitched, female-sounding voice that he assumed on those rare occasions when he picked up the phone for unknown callers (remember, these were the days before caller ID).

"It's Leon, John, calling with some good news," I announced. "I want to inform you that the court of appeals ruled in your favor, and that you are eligible to get permanent residence."

He responded, a little surprised, "What do you mean, I won? Didn't you say that we might never win?"

"Yes, I assured you that the chances of success were limited, and I didn't want to build your hopes up too high."

Before I could go into any more detail, John said, "Leon, Yoko is at New York Hospital and expects to give birth tonight or tomorrow. I am just on my way over there. Can you stay at your phone? I'll have Yoko call you when I get there, and you can explain it all to her."

I sent someone down to the court of appeals to pick up the decision. It was everything that the clerk said it was. I was elated.

The judges had chosen not to follow my argument challenging the definition of marijuana—that the resin John had been arrested for possessing was not, in fact, the plant. Instead, Judges Kaufman and Gurfein accepted my argument that John's conviction should not be recognized in the United States because it was entered in a country whose drug law had no requirement for *mens rea*—guilty knowledge that one is committing a crime. From a practical as well as a jurisprudential standpoint, that decision probably overturned fewer cases. Judge Kaufman did not let the Nixon administration get away with deporting John, but didn't make sweeping changes to what Congress intended in drafting the law in the first place.

The decision actually hadn't arrived when Yoko called. On hearing that I would have the decision shortly, she invited me and my wife, Ruth, to join her and John in their hospital room to read the decision together. Since I had kept Yoko abreast of each action taken in the case, she was like a copilot. She understood every nuance of the case and appreciated every paragraph of the landmark decision. The court had ruled that Lennon's 1968 British conviction for possession of cannabis resin did not prevent him from qualifying as a permanent resident of the United States. The decision, written by the chief judge, reversed the order of the Department of Justice that held Lennon excludable and had ordered him deported. The court remanded the case to the Immigration Service with instructions to conduct a new hearing on Lennon's residence application. Judge Kaufman stated:

> Although the board (Board of Immigration Appeals) rejected Lennon's selective enforcement defense as beyond their jurisdiction, we do not take his claim lightly. This issue, however, is not presented to us for determination. At oral argument, Lennon's counsel agreed not to press this point unless we found Lennon to be excludable under Section 212(a)(23). We note, nonetheless, that if Lennon's application for permanent residence should be denied for discretionary reasons after our mandate is received, Judge Owen will proceed expeditiously to hear Lennon's claim and accord him the relief to which he may be entitled. The courts will not condone selective deportation based upon secret political grounds.

In referring to Lennon's battle to remain in the United States, the court stated:

> If, in our two hundred years of independence, we have in some measure realized our ideals, it is in large part because we have always found a place for those committed to the spirit of liberty and willing to help implement it. Lennon's four-year battle to remain in our country is testimony to his faith in this American dream.

Judge Kaufman seemed to appreciate what the Lennons had gone through in four years of litigation. John's faith in the American dream had finally been justified.

I couldn't help pointing out to John that, in spite of his well-publicized support for Irish civil rights in Northern Ireland, it was the two Jewish judges who'd voted for him. Mulligan, the Irish judge, had dissented.

After we spent about two hours reading over the lengthy decision, Ruth sensed that Yoko was becoming uncomfortable and thought we should leave. She asked John, "If the baby is born during the night, please call and tell us." He assured that he would.

Before leaving, John turned to Yoko and said "Can I tell him now?"

"All right," she replied, "go ahead."

"Leon," John stated seriously, "you are the only lawyer I understand, and my wife loves you. But you know why we stayed with you all these years when these fancy Washington lawyers wanted to handle the case? It's because Yoko's tarot card readers all said—'stick with Leon, he is going to win the case for you.'"

Not quite sure how to respond, I said, "Thank God for tarot card readers." We kissed Yoko and left.

We must have arrived at home at about 1 A.M. The next thing I recall is hearing the phone ring. Half asleep, I answered. "This is John calling," the caller said.

I'm afraid I was still groggy, because I asked, "John who?"

"John Lennon, and I have a beautiful boy!"

Sean Lennon entered this world on October 9, his father's thirty-fifth birthday. Despite all the plans for natural childbirth, he was born by Caesarian section and weighed eight pounds, ten ounces. Since Julian, his half-brother, was officially named John Julian, John and Yoko chose Sean, the Irish version of John, and Taro, the traditional Japanese name for a boy. The hospital staff had never seen such an excited new father.

John chose Elton John to be Sean's godfather. The reason, as I heard it, was that John felt that since Elton was gay, he was not likely to have children of his own to leave his money to.

Soon after Sean's birth, the Lennons set out to reorganize their lives. John decided that he wanted to raise Sean, and Yoko decided that she was going to handle the business. John's dealings would be filtered through one part-time secretary who would take all the calls. John reported to me that this arrangement showed him how most of his calls were of more value to others than they were to him, and it cut his work down precipitously.

The arrival of Sean changed John's life completely. Never had changing a diaper been such an interesting experience. Although there was a nanny on duty, John undertook raising Sean as his primary task, and no detail was too small for John's attention. He would make up for any paternal neglect that Julian might have experienced.

On hearing the happy news, my wife and I had invested in a very expensive plush toy for Sean. But we felt we ought to offer something more permanent to celebrate Sean's birth. I had dealt with John Ryan, a transplanted British craftsman, to make the furniture for my office. Now we decided to have a special English style armchair built for Sean and engraved with his name, birth date, and our good wishes. We chose it from two samples that had been delivered to our home. A skilled woodworker did the necessary engraving, and the final product turned out beautifully—so beautifully that Ruth said, "What about our own sons? They're special, too."

So, each of the sample chairs was engraved, "Michael's Chair" and "Mark's Chair" with the date, "1975." Their contribution to the Lennon case involved many, many hours of not being with their father during the period of nearly five years while I was involved with the case, so they deserved a reward.

Both chairs still enjoy pride of place near Michael's and Mark's desks, and now they're even being used by another generation.

Not long after the court of appeals decision, I heard from John. "Leon, you'll love this," he said. "George Harrison called me to tell me the American embassy informed him that he was no longer ineligible for a visa 'under the Lennon doctrine.'"

John's former bandmate had also fallen afoul of the notorious Sergeant Pilcher and his drug squad. But in January 1976, the State Department issued an instruction to American consuls worldwide that the US immigration law "does not apply to convictions under statutes which extend to 'innocent' drug possession." (That is, where a statute imposes absolute liability without regard to whether the accused person knew or was aware of the nature of the substance possessed—our old friend *mens rea*.)

Luckily for George, the memo went on, "the British Dangerous Drug Act was such a statute." However the State Department did point out that in July 1973, the British statute was amended requiring "criminal knowledge" as an essential element for conviction.

Even today, the "Lennon doctrine" still stands. I imagine John would take some pride in that. Certainly, he found a lot of humor in the situation. "Can you imagine?" he asked. "I'm now a doctrine."

22

A Card-Carrying Victory

*From the discussions I have had with congressional
and other leaders, I have concluded that because
of the Watergate matter I might not have the
support of the Congress that I would consider
necessary to back the very difficult decisions
and carry out the duties of this office in the way
the interests of the nation would require.*

—President Richard M. Nixon's resignation
speech, August 8, 1974

The decision of the US Court of Appeals didn't mean that we'd auto-matically won. A majority of judges on the appeals panel reversed the holding by Immigration Judge Fieldsteel that John's conviction could be used to deny him permanent residence, just as I had argued. They "remanded" the case to the Board of Immigration Appeals to reverse its decision. In turn, the BIA returned the case to Judge Fieldsteel so that he could exercise his discretion on the question whether John should become a permanent resident.

However, there was really no question now about John's eligibility for permanent residence. In fact, considering what he'd gone through during the past five years, the only appropriate action was to grant it to him gracefully.

Since Vinny Schiano had left his position as chief trial attorney, his colleagues, Allen Shader and Bill Dunlap, were designated to complete the trial of the case. Frankly, I missed Vinny's presence—and not for a chance to score a win over him. Schiano was a sharp operator and would have been smart enough to complete the processing of the case in a way that let the INS put the best face on what could be a publicity disaster.

When I met with Shader and Dunlap, I offered some thoughts on how the government might show itself in the most positive and cooperative light. I suggested that they offer me the courtesy of permitting a number of important witnesses to testify briefly as to John's eligibility, and stress the benefit to the United States of having John Lennon reside here. If possible, the INS might actually prepare John's green card in advance, so that the agency could confer it upon him with dignity at the hearing. My respected opposing counsels never thought to object that I was recommending a kind of prejudgment!

As I anticipated, Shader and Dunlap were not inclined to be so gracious. They first tried to avoid all testimony entirely, suggesting I join in a stipulation as to what the witnesses would have said. I explained to them that after five years of hard work on my part and five years of enormous pressure upon my clients, I was not about to agree to avoid the testimony of some people who had anxiously awaited this happy moment.

I proposed that we should have no more than six or seven witnesses. They recommended that we have "one or two." We also agreed upon the other documentation to be submitted. Of course, they wanted a letter from the Lennons' accountant or business manager showing that John was not likely to become "a public charge," and that he had paid whatever US taxes were due.

The next day, I met with John and Yoko at their new apartment in the Dakota. I reviewed my meeting with the INS attorneys, and we decided to consult with Norman Seaman as to which witnesses would be appropriate to present.

We mentioned the name of Bishop Paul Moore. He was actually the bishop of the Church of England in the United States, and quite clearly an appropriate choice. Other names mentioned included former mayor John Lindsay, who had taken a strong stand on behalf of John and Yoko early on, and Leonard Bernstein, both for his prominence in the world of music and because he was also a neighbor at the Dakota. The sculptor Claes Oldenburg and Eric Larrabee, head of the New York State Council on the Arts, were mentioned, as was Paul Simon. Other possible witnesses spanned the worlds of politics, entertainment, music, and the arts—Congressman Ed Koch, Mike Douglas, Roger Hall, Peter Boyle, Joan Davidson, Theodore Bikel of Actors Equity, Penny Singleton of AGVA, talk show host Geraldo Rivera, author Norman Mailer, Gloria Swanson, Stevie Wonder, the sculptor Isamu Noguchi, the composer John Cage. We faced no shortage of character witnesses for John Lennon!

During our meeting, John thought it might be interesting to obtain copies of his and Yoko's FBI files under the Freedom of Information Act. However, he suggested that I consider holding off on such requests until some time in the future, once he was granted permanent residence. I told him that I felt I should ask for my FBI file as well. We concluded our business as they signed whatever papers I needed at the time. John and Yoko were planning to spend time at a place in Montauk for the summer, where they could not be easily reached. We arranged that Edith Chang would be the go-between during that time.

We also discussed the possible discontinuance of the federal lawsuits. The Freedom of Information Act suit had served its purpose. In fact, I'd even published my first law review article analyzing the 1,863 decisions we had received, believing that others faced with deportation proceedings would find it useful. As to the selective prosecution suit, I advised my clients not to make any premature decisions. We had to guard against the possibility that the government might turn out to have further tricks up its sleeve.

John said that he would prefer to maintain a "low profile" from then on. He would try to avoid getting a "record" again—his "auntie" had once told him that was very important in life. On hearing that, I assured John that his conviction in the United Kingdom had been totally expunged under the British Uniform Rehabilitation of Offenders Act. I explained that I would have another discussion with the government trial attorneys to assure that the proceeding went as smoothly as possible. I'd also meet with John again to talk over his own testimony for the final hearing. Finally, I also expected to confer with the immigration judge to prepare for the final hearing and with Federal Judge Owen as well.

Norman Seaman thought that once we decided who would appear as John's witnesses, we ought to have a party for them to meet one another before the final hearing date.

I also reviewed the prospective witnesses with Michael Tannen, John's new manager who replaced Allen Klein. I was particularly happy to meet with him—since he'd taken the job, my life became much easier. For a while I'd found myself performing some managerial duties during the interregnum between Klein and Tannen. Michael recommended Sam Trust, the head of ATV Music, as a witness. Trust had years of contractual dealings with Lennon and had published Lennon's music. Yoko, her business advice sound as ever, confirmed most of our decisions.

As things turned out, Congressman Koch judiciously declined to testify. He thought it inappropriate for a congressman to appear as a character witness because it might affect his judgment on pending legislation. Bishop Moore also regretted that he could not appear, as he was out of the country, so I arranged to have his delegate deliver a letter to the immigration judge at the hearing.

Although we started all these arrangements, they'd have to wait on a final okay from Immigration Judge Fieldsteel. Both trial attorneys Shader and Dunlap appeared for the government, and I appeared for Lennon. Fieldsteel indicated that he would have no objection to the presence of witnesses. Although he recognized that their testimony might not be very necessary, he would not deny us the opportunity to show our stuff at this time. I explained to him that the INS had no real objection to granting John residence at this time. I also confirmed I would limit the time that each witness took and that the government's trial attorneys would limit any potential cross-examination.

After arranging the more routine aspects of the anticipated final hearing, I delivered my own message to the immigration judge and the government's trial attorneys. The decision of the Court of Appeals had been very explicit. Should the government deny the case upon any discretionary basis, the decision ordered Judge Owen of the district court to vigorously proceed with the selective prosecution action. In that respect, I'd already taken testimony of Marks and Green. I warned that I would then be taking the testimony of former chief trial attorney Schiano, Commissioner Farrell, former attorney general Mitchell, and possibly others.

Without acknowledging that they would waive cross-examination of my witnesses, the government lawyers indicated that they had no expectation that such questioning was at all necessary. I particularly warned them about challenging Norman Mailer, who might respond forcefully if provoked. I also told the trial attorneys that I would not appreciate any questions being posed to John about his stay in San Francisco during the period of time when he and Yoko had separated temporarily.

After the pretrial conference ended with everyone congratulating me on what they always considered an impossible outcome, I returned to my office, arranging to meet privately with each witness.

I well recall July 27, 1976, the date of the final hearing, because it was the birthday of my younger son Mark. He turned nine years old, and I consented that Ruth bring him and his older brother, Michael, to the hearing. Michael was already fully engrossed in the details of the case despite the fact that he was only twelve.

Ruth was somewhat shy about attending a hearing for one of my clients, particularly John Lennon, but I assured her that this was a special occasion that would probably remain with all of us as a happy memory for years to come. I wanted my boys to be there.

We were once again visiting John's application for adjustment of status to permanent residence. Judge Fieldsteel would conduct what I expected to be the final hearing in the case, more than four years and four months after we'd first appeared in this hearing room. According to the mandate of the US Court of Appeals, the case was "remanded" to the immigration judge in order for him to exercise his discretion and adjudicate the application.

Since the Court of Appeals had ruled that the British conviction could not be considered, the immigration judge was prevented from considering John's drug charge as a disqualification for permanent residency. I was confident that no other problems would arise, but one never knows. We'd certainly encountered enough surprises so far in the case.

The hearing room at 20 West Broadway was packed with media people, even more than the last time around. However, the atmosphere was more hopeful because of the favorable decision from the court of appeals.

John and Yoko and I got into an elevator on the main floor. Ruth and the boys were at the back of the elevator, but John noticed them and greeted Ruth in his usual friendly, outgoing manner. Ruth explained about Mark's big day, and John offered his best birthday wishes as we got out of the elevator.

Judge Fieldsteel called the court to order. "For the purpose of those of you who are present who are not familiar with the posture of the case," he noted, "I might give you some background so that you know what the case is about." Fieldsteel had been properly dressed down by the Court of Appeals, which overruled practically every word of his order of deportation. So perhaps he felt he had some explaining to do. "This is an application originally for permanent residence which came before me sometime in 1972. I entered a decision in March 1973, in which I found that Mr. Lennon was not eligible for permanent residence on the basis of the law as I construed it. There was an appeal taken from that to the Board of Immigration Appeals, and the Board of Immigration Appeals sustained my position. It then went to the Court of Appeals for this district, and the court of appeals reached an opposite conclusion and the case was remanded for completion. So the posture of the case now is an application for permanent residence in which the one impediment considered by the Court of Appeals has been removed.

"Now, I think that approximately three or four years have elapsed since the original application. I think that the original application should be brought up-to-date.

"Mr. Wildes, as I understand it, Mr. Lennon no longer lives at his 105 Bank Street address. Would you correct the application and put in the appropriate address and any other changes that may have taken place since this application?"

I responded, "I'll be pleased to." Then I thought that the judge's recap of the case was incomplete and offered a further contribution. "If I may add to Your Honor's review, I would like to point out for the review that Your Honor granted residence in the original decision to Yoko Ono, Mr. Lennon's wife." The judge agreed and confirmed that her case was no longer before him. "I indicated the new address," I continued, "which I will not call out publicly, and I have added the happy circumstance of the birth of Sean Ono Lennon on October 9, 1975, who resides with his parents, John and Yoko Lennon, at the same address."

The immigration judge then acknowledged that the government had found some of its paperwork and completed some of the necessary procedures in advance of the final hearing. They had already obtained a visa quota number under the third preference portion of the quota for Great Britain, which was currently available for the case. The judge then acknowledged that, "Mr. Lennon has been physically and medically examined and found to be medically admissible to the United States. The government has checked the records of the Federal Bureau of Investigation and finds nothing adverse there." I could have made a long speech concerning adverse information in those records, but I restrained myself from doing so. The judge then confirmed through the trial attorney, Mr. Dunlap, that the records of the American embassy in London had been checked and that nothing adverse to Lennon had been found. Judge Fieldsteel asked Mr. Dunlap whether he was satisfied, on behalf of the government, that the Lennons' tax situation had been appropriately met. Dunlap confirmed that it was satisfactory. I truly missed having Schiano present at the hearing, because he was more animated, a real presence in the courtroom. However, I was perfectly happy to have the accommodating Mr. Dunlap on the job—he seemed to have been programmed to cooperate. Dunlap acknowledged that the government had John's birth certificate and the tax letter, and confirmed once again that he was satisfied on all grounds.

Then Judge Fieldsteel turned to me and asked whether I had "anything further to offer in behalf of Mr. Lennon." I stated that I had and asked John to take the stand and be sworn in.

"Mr. Lennon," I asked, "other than the original conviction, with which all of our litigation over the past five years has concerned itself, have you ever been convicted of any crime or offense anywhere in the world at any time?"

Lennon answered with one word—"No."

"Have you ever been a member of the Communist Party or any other party or organization whose purpose might be to overthrow the United States government by violence or force?" I thought that Schiano might have had fun with a question like that and perhaps would have asked John about his association with Jerry Rubin and Abbie Hoffman, among others, and whether their organizations had the intention of overthrowing the US government.

In this case, however, Lennon dutifully responded, "No," without any comment from the government's attorney.

In response to my question "Do you subscribe to the principles of our government?" He responded, "Yes."

"Do you intend to make the United States your home and to reside together with your wife, Yoko, and your son, Sean?" I asked.

He responded, "I do."

"Will you continue your work here? What are your plans?"

"I hope to continue living here with my family and making music." He had a way of conveying a message in a few well-chosen words. Some of the reporters started writing feverishly.

My final question was, "Is there anything further that you would like to add at this point, in connection with your request that you be granted permanent residence at long last, by the Immigration and Naturalization Service?"

Lennon straightened up and said, "I'd like to publicly thank Yoko, my wife, for looking after me and holding me together in those four years, and giving birth to our son at the same time. So many times I wanted to quit and she stopped me. I'd also like to thank the cast of thousands, famous and unknown, who have been helping me publicly and privately for the last four years, and finally, last but not least, thank you, my attorney, Leon Wildes, for doing a good job well and I know this is the end of it."

I responded simply, "I won't try to add anything to that."

Trial Attorney Dunlap had some routine questions as to whether John had left the United States since he entered on August 13, 1971, and Lennon acknowledged that he had not.

It was now time for our witnesses. Judge Fieldsteel, never patient with bringing many witnesses to his courtroom, asked for "an offer of proof" as to what we are attempting to establish.

"These witnesses," I told him, "will testify as to their knowledge of Mr. Lennon's character and to his qualifications for the exercise of your discretion in granting him residence. These are people who have had business dealings with him, know him socially, and can assist Your Honor in the exercise of your discretion." Although Fieldsteel was not happy to see a procession of witnesses take the stand, he was essentially a true gentleman, and after an admonition to keep their testimony brief, he allowed me to have them testify.

My first witness was Sam Trust, the president of ATV Music Corp. He stated that his company was "one of the largest music companies in the world and administers the rights to John Lennon's works." He was the past president of Capitol Records Music Publishing Company and for ten years before that of Broadcast Music Inc., "one of the leading licensing organizations throughout the world." He also acknowledged that before that he was a member of the Cincinnati Symphony Orchestra and a working musician. He was also a member of the US Navy Band. His credentials in the music industry were easily recognizable. I asked whether he would comment upon his impressions of John Lennon's character as derived from many meetings with him. His reply was clear and forceful.

"First of all, I'd have to say that any time I would wish to locate John, there was no problem. Whenever there was a meeting, he was there. When a business decision was needed with his approval, it was not unreasonably withheld. I believe that he treated all business matters objectively rather than subjectively, which he might have done, being a writer and artist of his stature."

I thought it best not to let such an industry expert leave the witness stand without asking one further question. "Would you care to comment upon the potential effect on the music industry of John Lennon's remaining and doing his work, as he testified that he would, in the United States, rather than in some other country?"

"There would be two positive major effects if John were to reside here," Trust responded. "One, it is generally acknowledged that the United States music scene is in the doldrums right now, as evidenced by the resurgence of Beatles material, since the Beatles were probably the most powerful innovation or force in music in perhaps the last thirty years," he said. "The staying power of the copyrights that John composed and participated in as a singer is back on the top of the charts and selling better than anything else. I believe if we have a creative force such as John in the US scene we can look forward to some new type of innovation in the music business, or what is referred to as a new 'kick' in the music business. In addition to that, John Lennon is a revenue generator. Wherever John is, he will create excitement and revenue."

Trust continued, "The center of the revenue generation will be in the United States, meaning that works of the recorders here will be distributed and sold abroad, and the United States will be the center for the reception of revenues earned outside of it. In other words, it would be a very positive financial effect for the US government."

I had met Sam Trust for dinner the night before the hearing, and he did not disappoint me in his testimony.

For my next witness I called Norman Mailer, who introduced himself by stating, "I am a writer, and I've published about twenty books. The best known would probably be *The Naked and the Dead*,

The American Dream, and *The Armies of the Night*." With my urging, he acknowledged that "I did receive a Pulitzer Prize in 1968." Mailer's very presence in the courtroom made everyone take note.

"I think John Lennon is a great artist," Mailer said with confidence. "I would hesitate to interpret his character because I think artists often have a character that is so complex that one doesn't jump in. Besides, I do not know Mr. Lennon firsthand. We have many friends in common, and I've heard splendid things about him for many years, but I come here really to speak about his, what I consider his enormous contribution, not only the public concept but to art in general. I think that he is one of the great artists of the western world and I've thought that it is a terrible shame that we had to lose Henry James and T.S. Eliot to England. We've only gotten Mr. Auden back, and I think under the circumstances it would be a pleasure if we could have Mr. Lennon as well."

There was no cross examination.

My next witness was Geraldo Rivera, a friend of John and Yoko who became personally involved with them over the years of their immigration proceedings. Through his encouragement, my advice that the Lennons participate in a major charitable function to benefit handicapped children resulted in a very successful Madison Square Garden performance where the best seats were occupied by the special youngsters, enjoying the show as well as its proceeds.

Geraldo described himself this way: "I'm an attorney admitted to the bar in New York State and in the southern district. I'm a correspondent for ABC News, and I am the son of immigrants." I always admired his uncanny way of recapitulating facts and making forceful presentations.

As Geraldo went on to explain, "I met Mr. and Mrs. Lennon in late 1971. It might have been very early in 1972. We were drawn together by our mutual interest in music and the cultural life in this city. Sometime after that I did a story on an institution for the mentally retarded called 'Willowbrook.' It was the world's largest institution for the retarded at that time and certainly one of the Western world's poorest institutions. I did the exposé and highlighted the problem but I was very frustrated and very bitter because I didn't know what to do in terms of a solution . . . I wasn't very well known at that time, and we needed to raise money.

"I called John and Yoko. They were at that time in San Francisco, and John had not, up until that time, done a concert in quite a number of years, if I'm not mistaken. He and Mrs. Lennon agreed to come back to the city of New York from San Francisco and do the concert for us. As a result of two sold-out concerts in Madison Square Garden, we raised over $90,000. Still, the Lennons did not think that that was a sufficient contribution, so out of their own pockets they donated $50,000, so the net total was $140,000.

"Now to talk in abstracts, to talk in terms of money is not sufficient, I believe, to truly define the character of these two people, particularly the person who is before the bar today. That money liberated at least sixty severely and profoundly retarded children from the pits of hell, the worst institution anywhere, and set them up in small, clean community-based residences where they could be cared for on a one-to-one basis. That was very new at that time, we're talking about 1972 now, so it had a domino, snowballing effect. Not only were those children helped subjectively, but the point that was made by that effort continues today. I truly believe that what was started in 1972 by John Lennon and by Yoko and by other artists will continue and it will be marked in history as a turning point in the care of the mentally handicapped. If ever there was a person who deserves to stay in this country, it's him."

The audience seemed to be writing as quickly as it could, taking down every precious word about the children John and Yoko had helped.

My next witness was Isamu Noguchi.

After being sworn in, Noguchi stated that "I am a sculptor. I've done many works all over the world, including the UNESCO garden and a garden in Israel and many works in this country, no doubt some of which you know—the Chase Manhattan Bank here, garden and works which are in Washington and the Metropolitan Museum of Modern Art and so on. I've occupied myself with things having to do with the land and place a good deal, since I am myself half Japanese and brought up as a child in Japan, although I was born here. I've known Mrs. Lennon for many, many years, at least ten years, and I never had the privilege of meeting Mr. Lennon until the day before yesterday. When I met him and spent the whole day with him and, you know, played with the child and so forth, it brought back to me my own childhood and my own difficulties. I am convinced that for a child of mixed parentage such as theirs, the United States is the one and only place where they can have a real even chance of developing normally. I wish Mrs. Lennon well, and I pay respects to Mr. Lennon, and I think that their child also deserves the privileges and bounty that comes from America."

Before Noguchi left the witness stand, Judge Fieldsteel told him that he had a coffee table designed by the artist in his home, which he liked very much.

I thought it important to have a man of the cloth in court. Knowing that the Rev. Paul Moore, Jr., the bishop of New York, was the highest ranking clergyman in the country representing the Church of England, I was happy that a member of his staff, in clerical garb, submitted a letter from the bishop in which he concluded that John's presence in the United States "Will be beneficial to our culture and his presence in our country is a positive force, especially among our young people." He noted that "Idealism, gentleness, and integrity are rare qualities in a public figure," and concluded, "I covet their influence for our country." The presentation of Bishop Moore's personal letter added a colorful note to the proceedings.

Now came my final witness, Gloria Swanson. It might seem strange to call on an actress who enjoyed her greatest fame in the Roaring Twenties, even though Ms. Swanson got an Academy Award nomination as the fading silent-movie star in *Sunset Boulevard*. But John and Yoko specifically asked for her, for a reason far removed from what Swanson called her "many, many, many, many years" in film, television, and the stage.

"I recently was sworn in by Mayor Beame as an honorary commissioner for the youth and physical fitness of New York City," she testified, "and I can't tell you how much this means to me. Because as one grows older, one realizes that the youth of this country have to really save this planet, because it seems to be in a dreadful mess and for many years I've been interested in physical fitness.

"Of course, I have fallen short of that many times because I don't exercise enough. But I have been interested in the food situation and it so happened that a friend of mine met Mr. and Mrs. Lennon at a health food store and saw a book she said she was carrying and my husband had written it. They got to talking about it and he said would you please give Mr. Dufty and Ms. Swanson my card, Mr. Lennon to these two people, because we understand what the problem is about the food.

"Well, soon after that, we invited them to our home and, to find that we were very much interested in the physical well-being. My feeling is that most of the crime of the youngsters today comes from absolute malnutrition. There is too much junk food that they have in schools, and this is one of the things I'm interested in. I hope very much that the Lennons may be privileged to stay in America so that they may also help, because professional people, I do believe, have a sense of indebtedness to the public. I think that as you get on in life you want to be able to repay them in some way and this is what I hope that I can do.

"I hope that I can see that youngsters can at least have some good nutrition. And I am hoping that the Lennons will also help in this. Many times young people won't listen to older people, especially great-grandmothers, but they will listen to someone who is more or less in their age bracket. So this is why I'm here today, Your Honor, because I hope that they will be allowed to stay in this great country, which we must fix. Many things are wrong with it now, but I'm sure the young people will do something about it."

My witnesses had all testified.

In conclusion, I said, "I hope that we will be forgiven for what Your Honor may have referred to as gilding the lily, in bringing witnesses which may or may not be an over-effort in proving our case. Our experience in the past few years has taught us not to leave any stone unturned with respect to this particular case. We wanted to permit you, in the exercise of your discretion, to have the opinions of people from different walks of life, in different arts particularly, as to the prospective benefit to our country of having Mr. Lennon remain and settle here."

Judge Fieldsteel then asked me, as Lennon's lawyer, and Mr. Dunlap in behalf of the government, whether we wished to sum up our respective cases. He especially asked me to be brief.

My summation began, "Mr. Lennon, under the Immigration Act, to my mind, has always qualified, and now in accordance with the ruling of the court of appeals, has been certified as a matter of law to qualify statutorily for adjustment of status under Section 245 of the Immigration and Nationality Act. He was duly admitted to the United States in a non-immigrant status. He has a third preference petition that was approved for him as an outstanding artist, which is valid, a quota number available to him, and does not have any disabling conviction or any element which might present a statutory ineligibility ground.

"We have presented today all of the evidence which we felt was necessary in order to convince Your Honor that in the exercise of your discretion, on a discretionary basis, Lennon ought to be granted residence. This is true not only because of the personal circumstances which might permit him and his wife and baby to live and settle in this country, which he loves so dearly, but also because of the interests of the United States which the Immigration Act is an aspect of. The discretion of the Immigration Service should always be exercised in what we consider to be the public interest. I think it will indeed be a happy page that we turn in the particular book of John Lennon's five-year experience with the Immigration Service, if he were granted permanent residence on a discretionary basis today."

Mr. Dunlap was even briefer. "The government has very little to say. The government feels that in view of the present record, there is no objection to John Lennon becoming a permanent resident of the United States."

The immigration judge then dictated his oral decision in the case, recounting that he had previously held Lennon to be ineligible for permanent residence, that his ruling was upheld by the Board of Immigration Appeals, but later reversed by the US Court of Appeals. He recited that the court of appeals had instructed that the case be remanded to the immigration court with instructions that the conviction not be considered as a part of the decision of the immigration judge. He acknowledged that the witnesses had provided evidence of his good character and potential value, both artistically and economically, to the interests of the United States. He concluded that Lennon was statutorily eligible for residence and, in the exercise of his discretion, he approved John's application for permanent residence.

The hearing concluded. As we left the courtroom, amid the congratulations and good wishes from members of the media and even government officials, John and Yoko approached my sons; John again wished Mark a hearty "Happy birthday." Yoko gave Mark a kiss, wished him a happy birthday, and gave him his best present when she said, "I'm giving you back your daddy." She kissed Ruth as well.

John and Yoko outdid themselves with gratitude, thanking me profusely for living through this with them on a daily basis. As for John, I knew from experience with other artist clients that his joy would translate itself into a spurt of artistic energy and imagination and that we could expect to hear some extraordinary new music from this gifted musician and composer. Each of his witnesses spoke from the heart, and it was clear to me that their truthful testimony would bear fruit now that he could live a more normal life in New York City.

As we left, we were instructed to join Maurice Kiley, Sol Marks's successor, in his office. As we were escorted up to the offices of the district director, I was still suspicious that the INS had some unpleasant surprise in store for us. When I earlier requested the use of a room where we could have a brief press conference after the hearing, Mr. Kiley had refused. Only after members of the press were also invited and I saw a TV crew already there, did I begin to feel somewhat secure.

I had no reason to trust Kiley. He had played along with the government completely at earlier stages in the case. After all, when I first obtained the previously secret information on non-priority consideration, Mr. Kiley told me that Lennon did not have the equities needed for such a remedy, without even reviewing John's file, which was not at the INS office at the time. Photographers who took our pictures as we came in to the room recorded my wary expression, but my doubts turned out to be unjustified. In fact, the government went out of its way to be nice to Lennon, perhaps particularly because the media was present. They'd actually prepared his green card in advance so that they could present it to him before the TV cameras and other media. As the TV interviewer Sara Lee Kessler began her spiel, I started to relax as the significance began to sink in—I'd finally won the case. After what we'd suffered through, it would take my clients and me some time to be comfortable with normal government immigration proceedings . . . and frankly, to be more trusting of the government.

After John posed with his green card for innumerable photos, it was finally time to go. Yoko had asked me to have someone else in the car with her and John and myself, someone who could stand at her other shoulder for security purposes. Naturally, I invited my partner, Steve Weinberg. Steve had assisted me diligently on the Lennon case, and more important, picked up the load on many of my other cases when I was busy with the Lennons.

We left the building through the usual crush of media people and fans outside and proceeded to Serendipity, a delightful restaurant where John, Yoko, Steve, and I looked forward to all kinds of wonderful foods (even if Gloria Swanson might not have approved of the fare). Peter Boyle and his girlfriend would also join us for the celebration.

During the car ride on our way from the hearing to Serendipity, John and Yoko were especially kind to me, thanking me profusely for my continued devotion to their cause. Yoko particularly said that I should take a great sense of personal gratification for having accomplished such an extraordinary result for John—attaining a resolution other lawyers hadn't even considered possible.

We reminisced briefly about the original conditions of the case when I was first retained. I complimented Yoko on her "sixth sense" by which she understood what was likely going on in the minds of our adversaries in Washington. John felt that life was what happens "while you are busy making other plans." He suggested, however, that I ought to write a book about the case. I replied that I thought it wasn't a bad idea, when I could get to it.

23

Ever After?

*God willing, there are another 40 years of
productivity to go.*

—John Lennon, *Playboy* Magazine, January, 1981
(Interview conducted in 1980)

It was the kind of déjà vu that creates chills. Yoko called me to discuss some current business I'd been handling for her, asking me to meet her at a recording studio. I remarked that the invitation conjured up old memories of the Record Plant, where I often joined John and Yoko during their music session for legal discussions that went late into the night. She, too, well recalled those hours, although she said that the current studio was light-years ahead of the technology of the old one.

At 7:00 in the evening, I joined Yoko in the control room of the studio. Silently she motioned me to follow her, so I didn't get a chance to find out who or what was being recorded.

In the private lounge where we spoke, she mentioned that Sean was working on a song for a new documentary movie to be released on his father's upcoming birthday. He would be singing one of John's songs and playing the piano.

After our discussion, she returned to the studio and then, for the first time, I saw Sean's face at the far end of the space. He gave a silent but friendly response to my wave and continued to sing "I Am the Walrus." After a while he came around, hugged his mother, and extended his hand in a warm gesture of friendship.

"Hi, Leon, how are you?" he said as he ran a hand through the long, wavy hair that fell almost to his shoulders. He was tanned and looked very happy and at ease as he went back to recording.

From that moment on, I observed how Sean walked, how he brushed back his hair, strummed his electric guitar, and generally displayed so many long-forgotten mannerisms of his gentle father.

Even the humor was his dad's. The way he managed to take himself less than seriously, urging the recording staff to "hit me with a radiator" when he obviously sang a note off-key, struck me as the humor of John Lennon.

Sean joined me in the lounge after I was called there to take a phone call.

"Sean, I have to tell you that I am literally covered with goosebumps. Your gestures, your appearance, even your humor, they're all so much your dad's." Sean listened intently to my war stories about our legal fight to keep his father in the United States, although undoubtedly I must have seemed merely to be an old man with a long memory. He smiled gently to hear the comparisons with his illustrious father as I spoke about those long-past meetings at the Record Plant to plan the strategy for his parents' defense.

In a way, this conversation from some years ago illustrates the basic principle underlying all immigration law—keeping families together. Whatever else I accomplished in the long, difficult fight against the Lennons' deportation, I gave John five years with his son.

I have to admit that I had a very busy, very productive few years after the Lennon case. Using the 1,800-plus non-priority cases we'd pried out of the INS files through FOIA, I published five law review articles on the case. This included a whole summer's work with David

Grunblatt, a young lawyer who helped me as we delved into the files and creating a statistical study, trying to analyze the mass of cases and organize them into different categories. Then I undertook the work a second time a couple of years later to see if I could pry more facts out of the data—to ascertain if the INS continued to carry out the non-priority program as equitably as previously.

We faced an odd legal problem since our analysis lacked any denied cases. When I asked about them, the INS told me that if a case was denied, the request was destroyed in Washington. So, because we had no denied cases, some courts held the view that they couldn't determine whether a case should be approved for non-priority status just because it fell into one of the categories I'd established—possibly some similar cases had been denied. Judges felt that they couldn't determine where the waterline was, below which you couldn't get non-priority status and above which you would.

On the other hand, the Ninth Circuit Court of Appeals, taking a more thoughtful approach, often held that if a case was similar to any of the categories I had established in my articles, non-priority status would be approved.

It would be nice to think that my efforts represented an important landmark in immigration law. I consider it a real find, managing to prove what I instinctively thought was the truth, that such a remedy for "impossible cases" actually existed. I didn't expect to find it written so clearly in black and white—or rather in black and blue, since the material appeared in the unpublished blue pages of the operations instructions. But I knew the government had to have some procedure available for situations in which it would prove too heartless or embarrassing to remove someone. Imagine how news coverage of a deportable paraplegic being forced aboard a plane would look? And the fact is that they did have provisions for treating special cases and even had a nice operations instruction on it, despite the way they hid it from the public to avoid being besieged by requests.

On the whole, I'd say that my work had a permanent influence. However, the INS kept changing the wording of the operations instructions, watering them down. Non-priority treatment became a voluntary kind of thing that a district director could do if he felt it was appropriate. He couldn't be forced to do it and couldn't be sued if he failed to do it, even if he'd done so in similar cases.

Finally the reference to non-priority status disappeared entirely from the operations instructions, after Homeland Security absorbed the INS, splitting its duties among three separate agencies. Immigration and Customs Enforcement took over the job of deporting people. And, while written regulations covering non-priority status are not as easily found, the procedure has actually expanded, no longer being restricted to district directors. As a type of prosecutorial discretion, it is currently available more broadly than before.

John made an interesting life choice after winning his green card, deciding he wanted to get away from the business end of music. Yoko would go downstairs to the ground floor of the Dakota building where the office was, and she'd run the business while he took care of Sean. John became a house-husband well before the title gained currency.

That didn't mean that John abandoned music, though.

I visited the Lennons' apartment in the Dakota a number of times, usually delivering gifts for Sean. One of these was a children's toy synthesizer, a little piano or music box with buttons on it—you pressed them to hear notes. Although we intended the gift for Sean, Yoko reported that John was usually the one playing with it.

Some time later, I got involved with a more serious musical instrument of John's. I was visiting at the Dakota, waiting for John and Yoko in their magnificent living room, where the furniture and carpeting were all white, including the grand piano—the same instrument he'd played in the video footage of "Imagine." I understand that fairly recently, a furor broke out among Lennon fans when a picture of Lady Gaga playing this piano appeared on the Internet. I hope I won't be in for the same when I admit that I sat at this iconic instrument playing a beginner's piece I'd recently learned from my kids' piano teacher.

John entered and said in surprise, "Leon, I didn't know you could play the piano. You know, I don't really know how to play. All I can do is pick out chords."

Leaning over me, he stretched out his fingers to hit a chord.

I remember trying to be smart, saying something like, "I wouldn't worry about it, John, it won't affect your career."

A little embarrassed, I explained that we had this piano teacher who came in the evening once a week for the boys, giving each one a lesson, and afterward I would keep him an extra half-hour while he tried to do something with me—a hopeless case, I'm afraid.

Then Yoko joined us. John announced that I was learning to play, adding, "When Sean is old enough to learn, I'm going to take lessons with him, like Leon does with his boys."

I told Ruth the story when I got home. "He's going to do something in music because of the way I did," I said, still amazed. I didn't consider myself a person who could teach John Lennon anything about music . . . about law, maybe, but not music.

Unfortunately, John never got to fulfill his plan. In 1980, just as he was launching his first musical project since completing the deportation proceedings, John was fatally shot by a disturbed young man, Mark David Chapman, at the entrance to the Dakota building.

I'm told that the day had been extremely mild, reaching 64 degrees—a record for December 8. At 5:00 in the evening, Chapman actually spoke with John as he and Yoko left the building. John signed an album for the young man, who said of Lennon, "He was very kind to me."

But when the Lennons returned to the Dakota shortly before 11 P.M., Chapman fired five shots at Lennon, four of them hitting him in the back. Although John was rushed to Roosevelt Hospital, he was declared dead on arrival.

While all this happened, I was completely unaware, vacationing with my wife down in Aruba—I haven't been there since.

We stayed in a hotel that really took the notion of "getting away from it all" to extremes. They kept only one copy of the *New York Times*, and it was never available. If you weren't in your room to receive a telephone call, the management didn't leave messages— apparently they thought that was helpful for occupants, so they'd have a good vacation.

What this meant was that we never got the call from Ruth's mother, who worked with our babysitter Louise to take care of the boys. Upon hearing about John getting shot, both Michael and Mark began agitating to go to the planned vigil at the Dakota. They had friends across the street, so there should have been no problem. But Ruth's mother wasn't about to allow it. The call we never got was essentially to say that Louise was having trouble. However, we never got wind of this problem—or the tragedy that caused it.

Ruth and I were on a blanket out on the beach when we heard two girls on the next blanket saying something about John Lennon being shot. For years during the deportation proceedings, John had told me about his fear of something like that happening. To me, it sounded like a joke in very bad taste. I think Ruth said, "Don't talk like that!"

Of course, then we found out that it was no joke—that it actually happened the day before, and a vigil had taken place. You can imagine how devastated we felt, not even to be around. I think I put something in the *New York Times* when we got back as a memorial for John.

Ruth and I did our best for Yoko after John's tragic death, and some years later, she was able to return some of that consolation when Ruth passed away. I'm afraid nobody could talk to me at that time. But my son Michael related an experience he had with Yoko. By this point he was a young lawyer and had taken over immigration legal matters for her, and they suffered a minor traffic accident while going downtown to the INS offices. "I sat in the Dakota with her to have a cup of coffee," he said, "and she explained that one of the reasons she especially appreciated you was because of Mom. Yoko always felt that the compassion Mom showed was so genuine. She was very comforting to us, remembering the kindness both of you had shown."

Yoko didn't have other friends like Ruth, someone with family and a lot of close personal friends. In Yoko's life, she was surrounded by a lot of single people—artsy types. I can recall how John often got upset—"We've got a dozen people around here, and she's making coffee for them all."

I think one of the primary reasons for the good relationship I always enjoyed with John and Yoko was the fact that I never asked for any favors. In fact, the only time I requested autographs was for the music and memorabilia I collected for Dr. Lester Grinspoon's critically ill young son, a great fan of John's, when I was trying to persuade the good doctor to testify at the deportation proceedings. Heaven knows, there was no shortage of occasions when individuals and organizations approached me because of my friendship with the Lennons, for one favor or another. I never pursued either John or Yoko on any such matter.

There was one odd exception, when a Japanese attorney, a partner in a major law firm in New York, contacted me. He explained that he knew a Japanese artist whom he described as being on "John Lennon's level" who could work well with Yoko. Yasushi Akimoto had written a one-act play entitled "Homeless" and wished to present it at an international film festival. However he needed an actress to portray an older woman, a street person, pushing a baby carriage with all her personal effects. He requested that I ask Yoko whether she would play the part.

I'd learned over the years that Yoko was a person of immense human compassion who identified with those down on their luck. So I called her to ask whether I could arrange for a meeting with this Japanese artist/filmmaker. Her immediate response was, "Leon, in all the years I know you, you have never asked anything of me. Why is this so important?"

I responded, "I don't know—he's trying to do a film about a homeless person in New York, and I think you would have an affinity for the character involved."

"I certainly do have a feeling for homeless people. There but for the grace of God go all of us." She asked me to arrange to bring Mr. Akimoto to the Dakota. So I met him, along with a translator, and accompanied him to Yoko's apartment. As we came in, we found slippers at the front door, and I removed my shoes to put on a pair. Akimoto and the translator did the same.

"Old American tradition," I said, attempting a mild joke. "We remove our shoes upon entering as guests." Akimoto didn't understand what I said, and his translator never even smiled. I worried that I was delivering a couple of duds without a sense of humor.

Yoko met with them for about an hour and a half while I cooled my heels in the famous white living room. When they were about to leave, she thanked me graciously for giving her the opportunity to get involved with this project. She'd accepted the role of the homeless person.

I think I still have a copy of the film at home. Both she and Akimoto were very happy that she agreed to play the part, and I felt that the years had given me a profound understanding of Yoko Ono Lennon.

We still exchange holiday greetings and gifts and, as my son Michael puts it, we remain on her "A-list" with invitations to her projects.

Some years ago, I attended a reception at the Japan Society for an exhibit of Yoko's art and film work and had the privilege of tying up one of the more troubling loose ends of the Lennon case. Yoko and John had come to this country primarily in search of Yoko's daughter, Kyoko. Although they spent many years on this quest, their efforts never led to success.

Jon Hendricks, Yoko's faithful and competent colleague, came up to me. A quarter of a century had not changed his youthful appearance, although the years had added some weight to his graceful frame. "Kyoko is here," he said, "and I want to introduce you to her." I needed a moment, feeling emotionally overwhelmed.

He brought me to an attractive young woman who greeted me charmingly. When I told her that I considered the attempts to find and help her to be one of the most significant factors in my handling of the five-year-long deportation proceedings, she was fascinated.

I asked what she'd gone through all those years earlier, but she had very little recollection. She knew practically nothing about John and Yoko's efforts to see her, as her father had kept that sort of information away from her. She was only seven years old when she moved into a religious commune with her father and his new wife, spending seven years there and then an additional seven years in another commune. The atmosphere was always guarded, with any attempt to contact someone in the outside world considered a suspicious circumstance. Kyoko even lost her name, living under several assumed identities.

After attending college, she decided that she would like to be a teacher. For about five years she taught third and fourth grade students and enjoyed her work thoroughly. But when she was expecting her own child, she gave up teaching—and made an important decision, at long last revealing her whereabouts.

"When I anticipated becoming a mother in 1994, I finally decided that I should contact my mother." With her husband's support and encouragement of what they both knew was the right thing to do, she contacted her mother. Once she entered motherhood herself, she knew how important it was for a child to communicate with her mother. And with two children, Kyoko was thrilled she was able to find a babysitter so that she and her husband could attend the opening of her mother's art show.

For myself, I felt happy for Yoko, reunited with her daughter and her grandchildren at last.

The last time I was at the Dakota, Yoko invited me for tea and took me to task on the subject of writing this very book. "Leon," she said, "this is a historic document that you have been working on, and I would like you to finish it."

Certainly, a lot of other people, writers and filmmakers, approached me for information while doing their projects about John's life, his time in New York, and his battle against the government. For the most part, they seemed to find most of whatever I had to say either too technical or not sexy enough to include. Usually, they bridge the period from 1971 to 1975 with a blanket, "Lennon was fighting deportation." If they go any deeper, they confuse deportation proceedings with court actions where I claimed constitutional violations or where I invoked the Freedom of Information Act.

In writing this book, I've come to realize the amount of legal stuff involved here that has to be explained to the general public. From a lawyer's point of view, though, this is an extremely sexy case about the misuse of the law by the government itself.

One of the problems with trying to put a period on the end of this story is that the case continues to influence the law even to the present day. I've spent more than forty years trying to get information out of a very recalcitrant government.

Working in my branch of the law, the FOIA is a very important tool. We use it all the time. Clients will come in and we'll ask, "Were you arrested?"

They'll respond, "Well, I don't know if it was an arrest. They picked me up."

Then, when we ask if they signed anything, they can't recall.

Clients can't remember all the facts, except for knowing that they had some sort of contact with the government—an arrest or investigation or appearance. To get the documents on what the problem may be, we often file a request with the client's authorization and have the information sent to our office, just to know what the government may have on the client. Otherwise we could end up wasting a lot of effort.

These reports should arrive in ten days, according to the statute, but in the real world, within that time you get a reply saying there are many others ahead of you. And then the process can take a year.

Much of the information in this book was mined from records of government agencies involved—much too heavily involved, I think—with John Lennon.

What Lennon was trying to do—getting on college campuses, teaching young people to exercise their right to vote, trying to update them on what was going on, the current events of the time, to pique their interest—those were all completely legal things. Even trying to "dump" Nixon was a perfectly legitimate undertaking. Hubert Humphrey wound up running in 1968 because of a "dump Johnson" campaign.

Dumping a president, campaigning against his reelection, represents an absolutely legal exercise of constitutional rights. What we learned going through John's FBI files—at the time, that was pretty shocking to me. Where I grew up, you idolized Hoover's G-men. And using the US immigration process, where I'd spent fifteen years of my life working, to eliminate potential political opponents, simply wasn't the America I knew. I remember a discussion I had in Yiddish with my father, who'd seen other, more dangerous parts of the world. "If you're born in this country, you don't realize what you have," he told me. "You have a right to vote, you use it."

Today, thanks to FOIA and the efforts of public opinion, you can go to the US Citizenship and Immigration Service web site and see the Lennon files. Thanks to other legal efforts, you can also view some of the FBI's files on the case. The principle we fought so long and hard a battle over is how the government improperly used the legal process in attempting to get John out of the country and to avoid giving him the facts of his own case. If, at the initial deportation proceeding I'd been able to present Marks' memo about receiving orders from Washington not to adjudicate Lennon's applications, the whole process would have been a lot shorter. All I can say is, I lost respect for a good deal of what our government agencies did, spending their time and our money hiding incidents that might be embarrassing to them if discovered by the general public.

Frankly, I wonder if these dangling ends will ever be resolved, if the past forty years of effort haven't succeeded. We accomplished something very significant, though. Besides the music that so many people around the world continue to enjoy today, John Lennon left a legal legacy that still represents a huge contribution to the practice of my profession.

In the field of immigration law today, no one has done more for people under deportation than my old friend John. Whether you call it non-priority status, deferred action, or prosecutorial discretion, as it's become known more recently, this remains the only remedy available in many of the most difficult immigration cases.

Ultimately, we persevered and found out about this well-hidden INS program, thanks to John's character. Reporters would often ask him as he left deportation court why he wouldn't stop giving the government so much trouble. He'd reply, "We're artists. We have to tell it like it is." He wasn't going to change his opinion just because the government threatened to deport him, even though they scared the daylights out of him. He saw that his phones were probably being tapped, that people were following him. I could see that these developments disturbed and frightened him, but never enough to scare him off.

Thanks to his willingness to fight and the human resources he put into that fight suing the government, we managed to discover and helped create a remedy for impossible cases. Even if it seemed completely black with no chance of success, we learned that the government essentially had a heart, that indeed any enforcement agency has the authority to determine when and to what extent to use its authority. They can decide to defer certain action, to put it off temporarily for the well-being of a person involved, to avoid public embarrassment of the government, or for simple humanitarian reasons, to avoid hardship. John helped us all to ascertain that the government had such authority, although it did its best to hide the fact, even declaring that such authority didn't exist.

John asked me at the time to make sure the information we discovered got distributed as widely as possible in the public domain, so that people who couldn't afford to stay in court for all those years to accomplish what he was able to do, would still have this remedy available to them.

And this legacy continues, with deferred action revived in an unusual way. On June 12, 2012, President Obama used his executive powers to establish Deferred Action for Childhood Arrivals (DACA), based on the Dream Act, a piece of legislation that could not get passed through Congress. Under this program, young people below the age of thirty-one, who entered the country illegally while under age fifteen, are presently in school, in possession of a high school or college diploma or a G.E.D., or an honorable discharge from the armed forces, can gain at least a temporary working status and protection from deportation. Over 600,000 young people have benefited from DACA.

I can add a personal footnote here. Rabbi Aharon Bina, dean of an Israeli rabbinical school that my son Mark had attended, interceded with me to aid a top student. The young man was an "illegal American," Rabbi Bina explained, who had entered the country before he was sixteen—obviously a candidate for DACA. When asked if I could help this student, I replied that with the help of John Lennon, I already had.

John's legacy is a broad attempt to reform the immigration process in a humanitarian way for hundreds of thousands of applicants. John always aimed his work and attention to the younger generation. In fact, his immigration troubles began because of his perceived influence on youth. Perhaps it's only fair that over a half a million young people could have their lives influenced for the better because of his commitment and successful efforts.

If John could see this, perhaps he'd be enjoying the last laugh.

APPENDIX

Important Documents from the Case

For more information see:
www.wildeslaw.com

UNITED STATES DEPARTMENT OF JUSTICE
Immigration and Naturalization Service

FILE: A17 597 321

DATE: August 11, 1971

IN RE: John Winston Lennon

APPLICATION: Temporary admission to the United States pursuant to
section 212(d) (3) (A), Immigration and Nationality Act

The applicant(s) has (have) been found by a [X] consular officer [ ] immigration officer to be ineligible to receive a nonimmigrant

visa under Section(s) 212(a) ___23___ of the Act.

Nationality:	Date and Country of Birth:	Country of Residence:
Great Britain	9-10-40 - England	England

Occupation:	Employer:
Musician	Self-employed

Purpose in seeking entry into United States and destination:

To edit film and consult with business associates at ABKCO Industries, 17 Broadway, New York City and Capital Records in New York City in connection with record release in September 1971 and to attend custody hearing in St. Thomas, Virgin Islands on September 16, 1971.

Plans regarding travel to United States and period of temporary stay:

One entry during August or September for six weeks.

Basis for favorable action:

To promote American Business Interests and for Humanitarian reasons.

ORDER: It is ordered that the application be granted for the above indicated purpose, subject to revocation at any time, valid as set forth below.

ENTRY: One during August or September 1971

PERIOD OF TEMPORARY STAY: Six weeks on condition that the activities and itinerary of the applicant shall be limited to those set forth above and that no extension of stay or change in activities or deviation of itinerary shall be authorized without prior approval of the District Director, Washington, D. C.

Section 212(a) (28) cases only.
Basis of excludability

Assistant Commissioner, Adjudications

TQ:NJM:hcm
Form 594
(Rev. 5-15-71) Y

Telephoned to Mrs. Gilchrist, Visa Office 2:30 PM, 8/11/71.

File Copy

Authorization for issuance of visitor's visa to
John Lennon despite statutory ineligibility

FILE

CO 212.24-C
January 14, 1972

Assistant Commissioner
Adjudications

John W. O. Lennon, A17 597 321 and Yoko Ono Lennon, A19 489 154

Mr. R. H. Ffrench, Deputy Regional Commissioner, Southeast Region,
telephonically advised today as follows concerning subjects:

> The written statement requested from subjects has been
> submitted. It does not appear that there have been
> deliberate violations of status by engaging in unauth-
> orized performances. The subjects did make several
> appearances for which they received no compensation.
> A letter will be written to the subjects explaining
> to them that they may not give any performances, live
> or taped, regardless of whether or not they receive
> compensation unless a nonimmigrant visa petition for
> the performances has first been approved. It will be
> further explained to them that a nonimmigrant visa peti-
> tion is not required only when all performers, entertainers
> and musicians involved in a charity show receive no com-
> pensation.

> Mr. Ffrench stated that in addition the subjects requested
> an extension of stay because a court hearing has been
> scheduled in Houston, Texas in connection with the child-
> custody litigation.

> Mr. Ffrench also stated that the petitioner (Mike Douglas
> Show) plans to have subjects cohost five 1½ hour shows.
> All of these will be taped in January and will be televised
> in February. The taping cannot be completed in less than
> the 17 days requested by the petitioner.

> Mr. Ffrench recommended that the subjects' classification
> be changed to H-1 until January 31, 1972. The subjects
> will be instructed to file an application on Form I-506
> for that purpose and to file an additional application on
> that form to be changed back to B-2 classification upon
> completion of the performances which they will be taping
> in the latter part of January. Upon approval of the appli-
> cation to be changed from H-1 to B-2, an extension of stay
> will simultaneously be granted to February 29, 1972.

CC: W/F - John LENNON   CC: A17 597 321

TE:SB:dmm   CC: A19 489 154 (File held in NYC)

One-month extension of stay granted to
John and Yoko, to February 19, 1972

235

January 26, 1972

MEMORANDUM FOR THE FILES

SUBJECT: John Lennon

FROM: Jack Norpel

(cc: Thomas L. Hughes; Carnegie Foundation;
Finances; California; Communes; Anarchy)

John Lennon, a former member of the British music group known
as The Beatles, and his wife Ono, entered the United States in the
latter half of 1971 at the Virgin Islands. Lennon was reportedly born
September 10, 1940, in England.

A commune group from Washington, D. C., is to transfer to
California in preparation for disrupting the Republican Convention
later this year.

A confidential source has learned that the activities of this group
are being financed by Lennon. The group is now said to be in New
York City for training and preparation for disruption of the convention.

Another Government source confidentially advised that Lennon's
visa was of interest to Thomas L. Hughes, former head of the INR
in the State Department and now Director of the Carnegie Foundation;
to one L. Mathias who wrote a letter to the State Department on
January 14, 1972; and to Congressman Bingham of New York.

EXHIBIT B

Document submitted by Senator Strom Thurmond
in lieu of the committee's actual memo

LEON WILDES

Report of Associate Commissioner of Immigration Greene
on report of INS District Director Marks on Lennon case

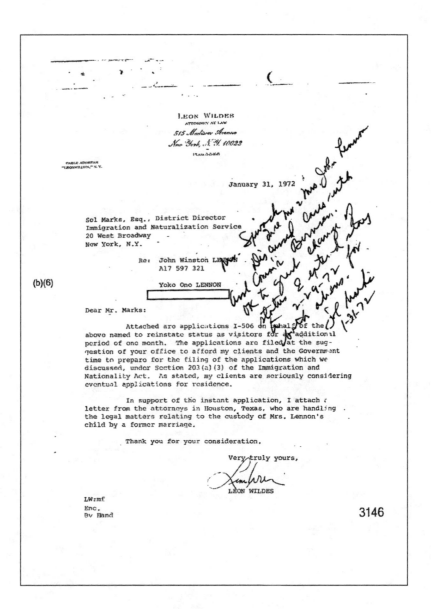

LEON WILDES
ATTORNEY AT LAW
515 Madison Avenue
New York, N.Y. 10022
PLaza 5-2460

CABLE ADDRESS
"LEONWILDES," N.Y.

January 31, 1972

Sol Marks, Esq., District Director
Immigration and Naturalization Service
20 West Broadway
New York, N.Y.

Re: John Winston LENNON
      A17 597 321

(b)(6)   Yoko Ono LENNON

Dear Mr. Marks:

        Attached are applications I-506 on behalf of the
above named to reinstate status as visitors for an additional
period of one month. The applications are filed at the suggestion of your office to afford my clients and the Government
time to prepare for the filing of the applications which we
discussed, under Section 203(a)(3) of the Immigration and
Nationality Act. As stated, my clients are seriously considering
eventual applications for residence.

        In support of the instant application, I attach a
letter from the attorneys in Houston, Texas, who are handling
the legal matters relating to the custody of Mrs. Lennon's
child by a former marriage.

        Thank you for your consideration.

                            Very truly yours,

                            LEON WILDES

LW:mf
Enc.
By Hand   3146

Letter from Leon Wildes to Sol Marks

238

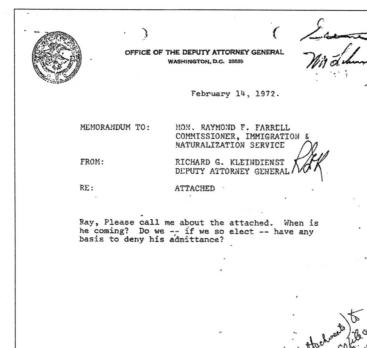

OFFICE OF THE DEPUTY ATTORNEY GENERAL
WASHINGTON, D.C. 20530

February 14, 1972.

MEMORANDUM TO: HON. RAYMOND F. FARRELL
                 COMMISSIONER, IMMIGRATION &
                 NATURALIZATION SERVICE

FROM: RICHARD G. KLEINDIENST
                 DEPUTY ATTORNEY GENERAL

RE: ATTACHED

Ray, Please call me about the attached. When is
he coming? Do we -- if we so elect -- have any
basis to deny his admittance?

RGK:tl

FEB 1 6 1972

ASSOCIATE COMMISSIONER
OPER

3143

Senator Strom Thurmond's letter to Attorney General Mitchell
forwarded by Deputy Attorney General Kleindienst to INS
Commissioner Farrell, who reported back to Kleindienst

JACK LEMMON

Sirs:

I respectfully offer my support for
extended United States visas for Mr. and Mrs.
John Lennon. In my view, they will offer a
welcome and spirited diversity to U.S. Arts
and Letters.

Sincerely,

Jack Lemmon

February 15, 1972

Letter from Jack Lemmon

FRED ASTAIRE

February 16, 1972

TO WHOM IT MAY CONCERN:

I have met Mr. and Mrs. John Lennon and understand that they wish an extension of their legal stay in this country. They are two extremely talented people and I am pleased to recommend that the extension be granted.

FRED ASTAIRE

FA/bj

Letter from Fred Astaire

DAPHNE
PRODUCTIONS
INC.
The Dick Cavett Show
DICK CAVETT

February 28, 1972

United States Immigration Service
c/o Leon Wilde
515 Madison Avenue
New York, New York

Gentlemen:

I submit this letter as whole-hearted recommendation and support of
the granting of a permanent working visa for John Lennon. His many
accomplishments and abilities----literary, musical and artistic----
are matters of public record, well-known to the world at large.

He has been hailed as a giant in the particular world of music by
too many distinguished critics, essayists and journals of opinion
and aesthetics to require any reiteration of his accomplishments in
this field by me. In a field where he (and his former associates)
were at first assumed to be merely a faddish, passing phenomenon of
contemporary taste, he has established himself as a major artist
about whose talent the word 'classic' has been applied in its fullest
sense. (An essay in a prominent music journal comparing his work with
that of Schumann and other classical composers comes to mind as representative of many such estimates.)

It is in my role as a figure on national television (THE DICK CAVETT
SHOW-in its fourth year on ABC television) that I have come to know
John Lennon and recognize him as a man of substantial character
beyond his artistic achievements. The effect of his personality and
mind on the viewers of my television program has led me to the conviction that his continued growth as a writer, musician and film-
maker will have a profound effect on the generation whose consciousness
he has entered so dramatically. I think it is something akin to this
that Peter Marin refers to in THE NEW YORK TIMES, where writing about
the book, "Lennon Remembers" he refers to "Lennon's struggle...the
struggle of a whole generation, or, for that matter,all of us, to
wrest from the confusions of media and our collective infancies the
truth of our own experience." Or, in another part of the same piece,
where he refers to Lennon's "decency and common sense...(and) instinct
for moving himself and his fans past their delusive fantasies."

There is, I feel, a major contribution to be made here that perhaps

1790 Broadway, New York, New York 10019. Suite 1301. Tel.(212) 765-2820

Letter from Dick Cavett

The Dick Cavett Show

DICK CAVETT

page 2

only John Lennon is in a position to make, and if he finds it con-
ducive to his talents to pursue this work in the United States,---
perhaps even essential to do so---I do not think it overstates the
case to say I feel it would be a kind of artistic or cultural crime
not to facilitate his doing so.

His latest works in the medium of film, as seen on my program, have
been highly acclaimed and indicated an extraordinary skill in communicating in this medium as well.

I cannot imagine how standards of acceptance for working visas are
established, but if it is necessary to be as peculiarly blessed with
talent discipline and accomplishment as John Lennon is, their
issuance must be rare indeed. I can urge and support it in his case
without reservation.

Sincerely,

DICK CAVETT

1790 Broadway, New York, New York 10019. Suite 1301. Tel. (212) 765-2820

Petition to Classify Preference Status of Alien
(pages 244–245)

PART III—OATH OR AFFIRMATION OF PETITIONER OR AUTHORIZED REPRESENTATIVE

33. This petition was prepared by: ("X" one) ☐ the petitioner ☐ another person.
If petition was prepared by another person, item 35 below must also be completed.
The petition may be subscribed and sworn to or affirmed only by the following persons:
In third preference cases—by the beneficiary himself, or by the person filing the petition on the beneficiary's behalf. If the petition is being filed by a person on behalf of the alien beneficiary, item 34 below must be completed by that person.
In sixth preference cases—by the employer who desires and intends to employ the beneficiary. If the employer is an organization the petition must be signed, subscribed and sworn to or affirmed by a high level officer or employee of the organization.

I swear (affirm) that I have examined the contents of this petition and the accompanying documents and that the statements in this petition and the accompanying documents are true and correct to the best of my information and belief.

NAME John Lennon (Print petitioner's full, true, and correct name) SIGNATURE JL John Lennon (Petitioner's full, true, and correct name)

TITLE

Subscribed and sworn to (affirmed) before me this 29th day of February A.D. 19 72

at New York, New York

(SEAL) My commission expires (Signature of officer administering oath) (Title)

34. DECLARATION OF PERSON FILING PETITION FOR THIRD PREFERENCE ON BEHALF OF ALIEN BENEFICIARY

I declare that I have been requested and authorized by the alien beneficiary to file this petition on his (her) behalf.

(Signature) (Address—Number, Street, City, State and ZIP Code) (Date)

35. SIGNATURE OF PERSON PREPARING FORM, IF OTHER THAN PETITIONER

I declare that this document was prepared by me at the request of the petitioner and is based on all information of which I have any knowledge.

Leon Wildes (Signature) 515 Madison Av.,N.Y.,N.Y.10022 (Address—Number, Street, City, State and ZIP Code) 2/29/72 (Date)

TO PETITIONER: DO NOT FILL IN THIS BLOCK—FOR USE OF IMMIGRATION OFFICER

a. Corrections numbered ( ) to ( ) were made by me or at my request. (Date) (City)

(Signature of petitioner or authorized member of petitioner's organization) (Title)

b. The person whose signature appears immediately above was interviewed under oath and affirmed all allegations contained herein.

(Date) (City) (Signature and Title)

INSTRUCTIONS

Failure to follow instructions may require return of your petition and delay final action

1. HOW TO PREPARE PETITION.

a. Print legibly in ink or use a typewriter.
b. Submit one copy only for each alien beneficiary.

2. WHO MAY FILE A PETITION.

a. *Third preference petition.* A petition to accord an alien a third preference classification for issuance of an immigrant visa may be filed by the alien himself or any person on his behalf. The alien must be a member of the professions, or a person who because of his exceptional ability in the sciences or arts will substantially benefit prospectively the national economy, cultural interests, or welfare of the United States.

b. *Sixth preference petition.* A petition to accord an alien a sixth preference classification for issuance of an immigrant visa may be filed by any person or organization desiring and intending to employ within the United States an alien who is capable of performing specified skilled or unskilled labor, not of a temporary or seasonal nature, for which a shortage of employable and willing persons exists in the United States.

c. *Western Hemisphere natives.* A petition is not required and should not be submitted on behalf of an alien who was born in any independent foreign country of the Western Hemisphere or in the Panama Canal Zone or the spouse and children of any such alien if accompanying or following to join him.

3. WHERE TO SUBMIT THE PETITION.

a. *Outside United States.* A person executing the petition outside the United States must take the completed petition to the nearest Immigration and Naturalization Service officer or American Consular officer. That officer will administer the oath or affirmation and furnish the address of the office of the Immigration and Naturalization Service in the United States to which the petition should be sent by the petitioner.

b. *In United States.* A person executing the petition in the United States must take or mail the completed petition to the office of the Immigration and Naturalization Service having jurisdiction over the intended place of residence of a third preference alien, or over intended place of employment of a sixth preference alien.

4. SPOUSE AND UNMARRIED CHILDREN UNDER 21 YEARS OF AGE OF BENEFICIARY.

Do not submit petitions for beneficiary's spouse or unmarried children under 21 years of age. When a third or sixth preference petition is approved, the beneficiary's spouse, and his unmarried children under 21 years of age, if accompanying or following to join him, will automatically be eligible for the same preference status as the beneficiary.

5. CERTIFICATION BY THE SECRETARY OF LABOR.

a. *General.* A third or sixth preference alien may not be admitted to the United States unless the Secretary of Labor has certified that (a) there are not sufficient workers in the United States who are able, willing, qualified, and available at the time of application for a visa and admission to the United States and at the place to which the alien is destined to perform such skilled or unskilled labor, and (b) the employment of such alien will not adversely affect the wages and working conditions of the workers in the United States similarly employed.

Application for the certification of the Secretary of Labor (or his designated representative) must be made on Labor Department Form ES-575A, or Form ES-575A and B, in accordance with the Instructions for Completion of Application for Alien Employment Certification. The forms and instructions may be obtained from any Immigration and Naturalization Service office, consular office, or State Employment Service office.

The Department of Labor publishes lists (Schedules) of occupations in Part 60, Title 29, Code of Federal Regulations. "Schedule A" is a list of occupations for which the Secretary of Labor has issued a blanket certification for qualified persons. "Schedule B" is a list of occupations for which the Secretary of Labor will not issue a certification for the reason that sufficient workers are available in the United States or the admission of an alien for employment in such occupations will adversely affect wages and working conditions of workers in the United States similarly employed. "Schedule C—Precer-

A17 597 321
A19 489 154

March 1, 1972

Mr. John W. Lennon
and Mrs. Yoko Ono Lennon
105 Bank Street
New York, N. Y.

Dear Mr. and Mrs. Lennon:

The records of this Service indicate that your temporary stay in the United States as visitors has expired on February 29, 1972.

It is expected you will effect your departure from the United States on or before March 15, 1972. Failure to do so will result in the institution of deportation proceedings.

Please notify this Service of the date, place and manner of your departure at least two days in advance of your leaving by calling Mr. Orville R. Conley at 264-5896.

Very truly yours,

SOL MARKS
District Director
New York District

(4)   P × 11 vd
7/7/75

First notice of temporary stay expiration

March 2, 1972

MEMORANDUM FOR FILES:

Re: John LENNON - A17 597 321 (Conf.)
     Yoko Ono LENNON - A19 489 154 (Conf.)

Associate Commissioner Greene telephonically advised today that
we should immediately revoke the voluntary departure granted to
John Lennon and his wife. An O.S.C. should be issued for both
aliens and served upon them with a return date of March 16, 1972.

Mr. Greene further stated that under no circumstances should this
office approve the I-140 filed by Lennon. This is a direction
of Commissioner Farrell personally. Further action on the
petition will therefore not be taken unless cleared by the
undersigned with Mr. Greene.

Mr. Spivack has been advised.

SOL MARKS
District Director
New York District

cc: Mr. Spivack

Memo for Lennon's files confirming prejudgment
of Lennon's third preference petition

LEON WILDES
ATTORNEY AT LAW
515 Madison Avenue
New York, N.Y. 10022
PLAZA 3-3468

CABLE ADDRESS
"LEONWILDES," N. Y.

March 2, 1972

Immigration & Naturalization Service
20 West Broadway
New York, New York 10007

Re: LENNON, John
A17 597 321

Gentlemen:

I submit herewith the third preference petitions, to be considered as a joint submission of Mr. & Mrs. John and Yoko Ono Lennon. The adjudicator is invited to consider references and critical reviews attached to each of the petitions as being submitted in behalf of the other since many refer to the joint artistic efforts of both artists.

Perhaps no other living artist has contributed in a greater degree, both qualitatively and quantitatively, to the culture of his generation than has John Lennon. Both individually and as an outstanding member of The Beatles, he has achieved a stature in the art and entertainment world unequalled in our generation. It is hardly possible, in most countries throughout the world, to find a young person who is not aware of the immense contributions of John Lennon, particularly in the field of rock music. By sheer volume of gold records sold, he probably has composed and performed more records than any other living composer and performer. As the acknowledged leader of The Beatles, John Lennon gained international prominence for his outstanding writing of the songs performed by the group, and The Beatles fast became the most popular personal appearance act in show business history. The revenues from their sales had impressive economic implications for England, where they were thought to have made a major contribution to Britain's balance of payments.

Recognition of the outstanding individual and group contributions of Mr. Lennon came from many sources. Not the least of these was Queen Elizabeth's having named The Beatles as members of The Most Excellent Order of the British Empire (M.B.E.) as a result of John's outstanding efforts. John Lennon's personal

Letter from Leon Wildes to INS
(pages 248–250)

Page Two.

contribution to The Beatles' success cannot be overstated; not only was he the major composer of most of The Beatles' hits but his mode of presentation of lyrics is considered by most of the critics to have been the main driving force to the outstanding success of The Beatles.

To assess the true impact of Mr. Lennon's song writing talents, individually and as a member of The Beatles, would require a careful analysis of thousands of critical reviews appearing throughout the world, too numerous for inclusion in an Immigration Service file.

The reader is respectfully referred to the attached biography (Current Biography, December, 1965) offering a review of his major accomplishments until 1965. Several excerpts from Who's Who in America, Who's Who, etc. are attached and it may be safely assumed that John Lennon has been included in every important compendium of major contributors to the culture of our generation.

There are submitted herewith numerous articles, most of which are critical reviews appearing in well-known magazines and newspapers, which treat with the talents and contributions of Mr. Lennon as an individual and as part of the group in the fields of musical composition, filmmaking, internationally acclaimed recordings, acting, and the authorship of two immensely well-known books.

Also submitted are a selection of articles covering the enormous financial impact of the record sales and other promotional activities which add an economic dimension to the outstanding cultural impact which John Lennon's talents would have on American culture.

Some of the articles specifically cover the creative period subsequent to the splitting-up of The Beatles where John Lennon emerges as the individual artist of greatest prominence; others cover his joint artistic endeavors with his wife Yoko Ono, whose third preference petition is submitted simultaneously. Only an abundance of personal modesty on the part of the artist has limited the number of personal references to a selected few.

Page Three.

There can be no doubt that John Lennon has exceptional ability in the arts and that his presence in the United States will substantially benefit the national economy, the cultural interests and the welfare of the United States. He distinguishes himself by a sense of language, a sense of humor, and a sense of humanity. His talents carried over into other media and he published books of drawings and philosophy considered to be brilliant by acknowledged critics. The movies he made and in which he appeared as an actor demonstrate new and original talents in other art media, likewise acclaimed by the critics. As stated by Elia Kazan and his wife Barbara Loden, "John Lennon is one of the most influential and stimulating artists of our time." A failure to accord him third preference priority would be, in the words of Dick Cavett, "a kind of artistic or cultural crime." It is respectfully requested that the petition be approved.

I have requested the granting of deferred departure in these cases and my application has thusfar been denied. It is hoped that these applications will demonstrate that it is in the best public interests of the United States to grant such deferred departure privilege to these applicants to enable them to remain here without the institution of deportation proceedings so as to facilitate the completion of all necessary procedures preliminary to the filing of applications for permanent residence. Since our deferred departure policy in third preference cases stems from our national interest in availing ourselves of the services of outstanding artists and professionals needed in this country, it is respectfully submitted that to proceed upon a course of action requiring deportation proceedings in these cases would be contrary to our nation's best cultural interests and hence an abuse of discretion. I trust that this will not occur.

Very truly yours,

LEON WILDES

LW:de
encls.

Table of Contents of Documentation in Support of
Third Preference Petition in Behalf of JOHN LENNON

1. Biographic data
   Current biography, December, 1965, four-page analytic
   review of exceptional accomplishments and biographic data

2. Excerpt - Who's Who, 1971

3. Critical reviews, newspaper and magazine articles, etc.
   Seventeen, August, 1965, 'The Scene with the Beatles'
   Time, May 1, 1965 (review of book 'In His Own Write')
   New York Times, January 15, 1967, 'Beatle on the
       Battlefront' (review of John Lennon as a film actor)
   Look Magazine, December 13, 1966, 'John Lennon: Beatle
       on his Own', by Leonard Gross, Look European Editor
   Los Angeles Times, undated, 'John Lennon Relives his Life
       on a New Album'
   Rolling Stone, October 28, 1971, records (a review of
       'Imagine'
   Village Voice, February 25, 1971, 'Songs of Experience'
   The Evening Star, Washington, D.C., October 16, 1971,
       'Lennon's Album? As Good as Beatles!'
   Boston Herald Traveler, December 26, 1971, 'Imagine'
   Rolling Stone, November 1, 1969, 'Two Virgins'
   Saturday Review, December 30, 1967, 'After "Sargent Pepper"'
   Saturday Evening Post, March 21, 1964, 'Beatlic Grapho-
       spams'
   Cue, June 12, 1971
   The Nation, June 8, 1964, book review of 'In His Own Write'
   Cashbox - film reviews
   New Republic, August 7, 1965, 'In the Echo Chamber' (a
       book review)
   Time, August 12, 1966, 'An Interview with John Lennon'
   Dallas Times Herald, January 6, 1972, citation of litho-
       graphy art show in Dallas, Texas
   New Yorker, June 24, 1967, review of Beatle albums -
       reference to John Lennon
   Newsweek, June 26, 1967
   Newsweek, October 4, 1965, relates to business successes
   Newsweek, May 27, 1968 (same)
   Newsweek, March 1, 1965, relating to success of stock in
       corporation

Table of Contents of documentation in support of
third preference petition
(pages 251–252)

Table of Contents - John Lennon

Page Two.

4. Letters of reference
    Whitney Museum of Modern Art, David Bienstock, Curator of
      Film
    Elia Kazan (four times awarded best director of the year
      by the New York Drama Critics; received Academy Award
      twice for best film director; founded Actor's Studio;
      original director of the Lincoln Center Repertory
      Theatre)
    Barbara Loden Kazan (received Antoinette Perry Award for
      her portrayal of Maggie in Arthur Miller's 'After
      the Fall'; wrote, directed and acted in 'Wanda',
      winning international critics prize for best film
      at the Venice Film Festival)
    Dick Cavett, host, The Dick Cavett Show

5. Evidence of awards received (Emmy, Academy Award, gross sales
    volume and number of gold records achieved, etc. to be
    attached)

      Note: Due to the outstanding and well-known qualifications
of John Lennon, a random sampling of critical review has been
assembled for submission. Further references and clippings abound
and will be made available for submission, should further evidence
be required. However, it is thought that the attached documents
amply demonstrate third preference qualifications. The letters of
reference submitted with the application for Yoko Ono are being
submitted jointly with this application, and should be read by the
adjudicator.

CONFIDENTIAL

xxx

3/2/72 50.0 CO 837-C

Carl G. Burrows, Assistant Commissioner
Investigations, C. O., Washington, D. C. 626-1347

Sol Marks, District Director
New York, New York 212-264-5943

John W. Lennon, A17 597 321
Yoko Lennon, [   ] (b)(6)

I had several discussions with Mr. Marks concerning the cases of the subjects.
He advised me that the subjects' immigration attorney, Leon Wildes, had, today,
in response to Mr. Marks' telephone inquiry, advised that the subjects will not
depart prior to March 15, the date fixed for their voluntary departure. It was
determined that when Mr. Wildes appears at the New York Office tomorrow, March 3,
1972, to file an application for a third preference petition in behalf of the
male subject, Mr. Marks should reiterate his inquiry as to whether subjects
intend to leave by March 15th, and if the response is again in the negative,
he should furnish Mr. Wildes with a letter advising him that in view of the
subjects' refusal to depart within the time specified an Order to Show Cause
and deportation proceedings will issue (and will be served upon Wildes as the
attorney of record) notifying the subjects that a deportation hearing will be
set for March 16, 1972. U

Mr. Greene advised Mr. Marks that it was the Commissioner's position that we
should not approve any third preference visa petition in behalf of the male
subject. U

Mr. Marks had at one time during these conversations notified me that an FBI
agent from the New York Office of the FBI had conferred with an investigator
in our New York Office concerning the subjects' whereabouts. This unidentified
FBI agent indicated to the unidentified investigator that if the subjects were
to initiate travel to Miami, the FBI would seek a warrant for subjects' arrest
for violation of the federal statute prohibiting interstate travel in the
furtherance of any conspiracy to incite to riot. This information was conveyed
to Mr. Harlington Wood, Jr., Associate Deputy Attorney General, by Mr. Greene
together with information that the male subject's attorney, Leon Wildes, had
advised District Director Marks that his clients had left for Houston yesterday

DECLASSIFIED
M. MOSKOWITZ
BY ASSOC. REG. COMMISSIONER
MGMT. 2/18/82 CONFIDENTIAL

Excluded from automatic
Downgrading and
Declassification

3373

INS Commissioner's office concerns that if the Lennons were to
attend the Republican National Convention in Florida they would be
criminally indicted for crossing state lines to incite a riot!
(pages 253–254)

CONFIDENTIAL

- 2 -

in connection with the famale subject's custody suit involving her daughter by a previous marriage. Mr. Marks was directed by Mr. Greene to furnish this information to the New York Office of the FBI.

All of the foregoing information was furnished to Mr. Joel Lisker, Internal Security Division, Department of Justice, subsequent to its communication to Mr. Wood.

Mr. Marks is to report to me concerning any and all developments in this matter.

CC: District Director, New York, New York
     Personal Attention: Sol Marks
     The FBI Current Intelligence Analysis, Volume II, Number 4, dated
     February 25, 1972, on page 3 reflects the following information;
     classified CONFIDENTIAL - GROUP 1 -
     "YOUTH ELECTION STRATEGY (YES)
          British musician John Lennon, New Left activist Rennie Davis,
     and former Yippie leader Jerry Rubin are behind the recent formation
     of Youth Election Strategy (YES), which is to be the audio-visual arm
     of the Election Year Strategy Information Center (EYSIC) (Volume II,
     Number 3). YES plans to make arrangements for videotapes, films,
     and other forms of entertainment to raise funds for financing
     EYSIC's upcoming demonstration activities at the Republican National
     Convention in August." (c)

                                              Carl G Burrows

NOTE: Copy endorsed to New York is classified based on quoted excerpt of
       FBI Current Intelligence Analysis.

CC: WF John W. Lennon
     WF Yoko Lennon

DC:CGB:dmw

MAR 10 1972

RECEIVED
DISTRICT DIRECTOR

CONFIDENTIAL

A17 597 321
A19 439 134

March 6, 1972

Mr. John Lennon and
Mrs. Yoko Ono Lennon
105 Bank Street
New York, New York

Dear Mr. & Mrs. Lennon:

Your temporary stay in the United States as visitors expired on February 29, 1972.

On March 1, 1972, we advised you in writing that you were expected to effect your departure from the United States on or before March 15, 1972. It is now understood that you have no intention of effecting your departure by that date. We are therefore revoking the privilege of voluntary departure as provided by existing regulations (Title 8, Code of Federal Regulations 242.5(c)).

Very truly yours,

SOL MARKS
District Director
New York District

cc: Leon Wildes, Esq.
515 Madison Ave.
New York, N.Y. 10022

S:FEB:mn

Second notice of time expiration, revoking
the privilege of voluntary departure

UNITED STATES DEPARTMENT OF JUSTICE
Immigration and Naturalization Service

ORDER TO SHOW CAUSE and NOTICE OF HEARING

In Deportation Proceedings under Section 242 of the Immigration and Nationality Act

UNITED STATES OF AMERICA:

In the Matter of _____)
)
LENNON, John Winston   )
                    Respondent.   )

To: __John Winston Lennon__   File No. ___A17 597 321___
        (name)

105 Bank Street, New York, New York
Address (number, street, city, state, and ZIP code)

UPON inquiry conducted by the Immigration and Naturalization Service, it is alleged that:

1. You are not a citizen or national of the United States;
2. You are a native of __Great Britain__
   and a citizen of __United Kingdom & Colonies__;
3. You entered the United States at __New York, New York__ on
   or about __August 13, 1971__
              (date)

4. At that time you were admitted as a nonimmigrant visitor for pleasure and were authorized to remain in the United States until February 29, 1972.

5. You remained in the United States after February 29, 1972, without authority.

AND on the basis of the foregoing allegations, it is charged that you are subject to deportation pursuant to the following provision(s) of law:

Section 241(a)(2) of the Immigration and Nationality Act, in that, after admission as a nonimmigrant under Sec. 101(a)(15) of said act you have remained in the United States for a longer time than permitted.

WHEREFORE, YOU ARE ORDERED to appear for hearing before a Special Inquiry Officer of the Immigration and Naturalization Service of the United States Department of Justice at __20 West Broadway, New York, N. Y. - 14th floor__ on __March 16, 1972__ at __8:45__ a.m, and show cause why you should not be deported from the United States on the charge(s) set forth above.

Dated: March 6, 1972   IMMIGRATION AND NATURALIZATION SERVICE

Form I-221
(Rev. 3-30-67)   (Signature and title of issuing officer)
                                        DISTRICT DIRECTOR
Bond Review Yes ☐ No ☑   NEW YORK DISTRICT
T.A. Assigned Yes ☑ No ☐   (City and state)
                          (over)

Original deportation charge

NOTICE TO RESPONDENT

ANY STATEMENT YOU MAKE MAY BE USED AGAINST YOU IN DEPORTATION PROCEEDINGS

THE COPY OF THIS ORDER SERVED UPON YOU IS EVIDENCE OF YOUR ALIEN REGISTRATION WHILE YOU ARE UNDER DEPORTATION PROCEEDINGS. THE LAW REQUIRES THAT IT BE CARRIED WITH YOU AT ALL TIMES

If you so choose, you may be represented in this proceeding, at no expense to the Government, by an attorney or other individual authorized and qualified to represent persons before the Immigration and Naturalization Service. You should bring with you any affidavits or other documents which you desire to have considered in connection with your case. If any document is in a foreign language, you should bring the original and certified translation thereof. If you wish to have the testimony of any witnesses considered, you should arrange to have such witnesses present at the hearing.

When you appear you may, if you wish, admit that the allegations contained in the Order to Show Cause are true and that you are deportable from the United States on the charges set forth therein. Such admission may constitute a waiver of any further hearing as to your deportability. If you do not admit that the allegations and charges are true, you will be given reasonable opportunity to present evidence on your own behalf, to examine the Government's evidence, and to cross-examine any witnesses presented by the Government.

You may apply at the hearing for voluntary departure in lieu of deportation. Moreover, if you appear to be eligible to acquire lawful permanent resident status the special inquiry office will explain this to you at the hearing and give you an opportunity to apply.

You will be asked during the hearing to select a country to which you choose to be deported in the event that your deportation is required by law. The special inquiry officer will also notify you concerning any other country or countries to which your deportation may be directed pursuant to law; and upon receipt of this information, you will have an opportunity to apply during the hearing for temporary withholding of deportation if you believe you would be subject to persecution in any such country on account of race, religion, or political opinion.

Failure to attend the hearing at the time and place designated hereon may result in your arrest and detention by the Immigration and Naturalization Service without further notice, or in a determination being made by the special inquiry officer in your absence.

REQUEST FOR PROMPT HEARING

To expedite determination of my case, I request an immediate hearing, and waive any right I may have to more extended notice.

Before:

(signature of respondent)

(signature and title of witnessing officer)

(date)

CERTIFICATE OF SERVICE

This order and notice were served by me on _7/March 6, 1972_ in the following manner:
(date)

by personal service(English)language

(signature and title of employee or officer)

Interpreter

LONG DISTANCE TELEPHONE CALL REPORT

DATE	ACTIVITY	FACILITY: FTS XXX	AMOUNT (DO NOT-FILL IN THIS BLOCK WHEN CALL IS HANDLED THROUGH A SERVICE SWITCH BOARD OR WHEN FTS IS USED.)	FILE NO.
3/7/72	50.0	COMMERCIAL		CO 837-C

FROM: (NAME)	(OFFICE)	TELEPHONE NUMBER CHARGED
Mr. Sol Marks, District Director New York, New York		212-264-5943

TO: (NAME)		TELEPHONE NUMBER CALLED
Carl G. Burrows, Assistant Commissioner Investigations, C. O., Washington, D. C.		626-1347

CERTIFICATION: I CERTIFY THAT THIS OFFICIAL TELEPHONE CALL WAS NECESSARY IN THE INTEREST OF THE GOVERNMENT.

APPROVAL:

Carl G. Burrows

SIGNATURE OF EMPLOYEE MAKING THE CALL.

SIGNATURE OF APPROVING OFFICER. (REQUIRED ON COPY ONLY.)

JUSTIFICATION: WAS THIS CALL MADE AT THE REQUEST OF THE CENTRAL OFFICE OR REGIONAL OFFICE? ☐ YES ☐ NO
IF "NO" IS CHECKED, ENTER JUSTIFICATION.

SUBJECT MATTER:

John W. Lennon, A17 597 321
Yoko Lennon, ☐ (b)(6)

Mr. Marks called to verify service of a revocation notice and Order to Show Cause on subjects and their attorney. He will send us a copy of the revocation notice and of the Order to Show Cause.

The Lennons have returned to New York and are residing at the Bank street address. I inquired whether either the Order to Show Cause or the revocation notice made any reference to the fact that the ground of inadmissibility in subject's case had been waived and that the waiver order was also revoked. Mr. Marks checked the documents and advised that there was no such reference. After a very brief discussion, he agreed to issuing a superseding Order to Show Cause which will be accompanied by another letter of notice that the waiver had been revoked.

Copies of those documents will be mailed to us also. The hearing date remains set for March 16, 1972, in New York City.

CC: WF John W. Lennon
    WF Yoko Lennon

DC:CGB:dmw   Work Folder

     ...tions Log
     ...stigations Log

ORIGINAL TO CASE FILE, SUBJECT FILE OR WORK FOLDER: COPY TO FINANCE

FORM G-40 (REV. 3-1-60) UNITED STATES DEPARTMENT OF JUSTICE Immigration and Naturalization Service

3136

Long distance telephone call report, March 7, 1972

"CONTINUATION SHEET"

IN THE MATTER OF   March 7, 1972

LENNON, JOHN WINSTON   A# 17 597 321

4. At that time you were admitted as a nonimmigrant visitor for
    pleasure and were authorized to remain in the United States
    until February 29, 1972.

5. On March 1, 1972 you were granted the privilege of departing
    the United States voluntarily on or before March 15, 1972.

6. You abandoned your intention to depart from the United States
    on or before March 15, 1972.

7. On March 6, 1972 the privilege of voluntary departure to March
    15, 1972 was revoked.

8. You remained in the United States after February 29, 1972
    without authority.

    AND on the basis of the foregoing allegations, it is charged
    that you are subject to deportation pursuant to the following
    provision(s) of law:

        Section 241(a)(9) of the Immigration and
        Nationality Act, in that, after admission
        as a nonimmigrant under Section 101(a)(15)
        of said Act, you have failed to comply with
        the conditions of such status.

        Section 241(a)(2) of the Immigration and
        Nationality Act, in that, after admission
        as a nonimmigrant under Sec. 101(a)(15) of
        said act you have remained in the United
        States for a longer time than permitted.

Continuation sheet, March 7, 1972

```
[2202-2261]
                    UNITED STATES DEPARTMENT OF JUSTICE
                        Immigration and Naturalization Service

                  ORDER TO SHOW CAUSE and NOTICE OF HEARING
                In Deportation Proceedings under Section 242 of the Immigration and Nationality Act

UNITED STATES OF AMERICA:

In the Matter of                          )          (SUPERSEDING)
                                          )
LENNON, JOHN WINSTON                      )
                                          )
                    Respondent.           )

To:   John Winston Lennon                      File No. A 17 597 321
           (name)

      105 Bank Street, New York, New York
      Address (number, street, city, state, and ZIP code)

              UPON inquiry conducted by the Immigration and Naturalization Service, it is alleged that:

          1. You are not a citizen or national of the United States;
          2. You are a native of_____ Great Britain
             and a citizen of_____ United Kingdom and Colonies    ;
          3. You entered the United States at New York, New York                          on
             or about August 13, 1971
                        (date)


                       See Continuation Sheet attached X
                       hereto and made a part hereof.



          AND on the basis of the foregoing allegations, it is charged that you are subject to deportation pursuant
      to the following provision(s) of law:


                       See Continuation Sheet attached X
                       hereto and made a part hereof.



          WHEREFORE, YOU ARE ORDERED to appear for hearing before a Special Inquiry Officer of the
      Immigration and Naturalization Service of the United States Department of Justice at
      20 West Broadway, New York, New York 14th. floor
      on  March 16, 1972          at    8:45 a.m., and show cause why you should not be deported
      from the United States on the charge(s) set forth above.


      Dated: March 7, 1972                           IMMIGRATION AND NATURALIZATION SERVICE

      Form I-221   Bond Review  Yes ☐ No ☑
      (Rev. 3-30-67) I.A. Assigned Yes ☑ No ☐   DISTRICT DIRECTOR
                                                 NEW YORK DISTRICT
                                                  (City and State)
                                          (over)
```

Amended deportation charge

NOTICE TO RESPONDENT.

ANY STATEMENT YOU MAKE MAY BE USED AGAINST YOU IN DEPORTATION PROCEEDINGS

THE COPY OF THIS ORDER SERVED UPON YOU IS EVIDENCE OF YOUR ALIEN REGISTRATION WHILE YOU ARE UNDER DEPORTATION PROCEEDINGS. THE LAW REQUIRES THAT IT BE CARRIED WITH YOU AT ALL TIMES

If you so choose, you may be represented in this proceeding, at no expense to the Government, by an attorney or other individual authorized and qualified to represent persons before the Immigration and Naturalization Service. You should bring with you any affidavits or other documents which you desire to have considered in connection with your case. If any document is in a foreign language, you should bring the original and certified translation thereof. If you wish to have the testimony of any witnesses considered, you should arrange to have such witnesses present at the hearing.

When you appear you may, if you wish, admit that the allegations contained in the Order to Show Cause are true and that you are deportable from the United States on the charges set forth therein. Such admission may constitute a waiver of any further hearing as to your deportability. If you do not admit that the allegations and charges are true, you will be given reasonable opportunity to present evidence on your own behalf, to examine the Government's evidence, and to cross-examine any witnesses presented by the Government.

You may apply at the hearing for voluntary departure in lieu of deportation. Moreover, if you appear to be eligible to acquire lawful permanent resident status the special inquiry office will explain this to you at the hearing and give you an opportunity to apply.

You will be asked during the hearing to select a country to which you choose to be deported in the event that your deportation is required by law. The special inquiry officer will also notify you concerning any other country or countries to which your deportation may be directed pursuant to law; and upon receipt of this information, you will have an opportunity to apply during the hearing for temporary withholding of deportation if you believe you would be subject to persecution in any such country on account of race, religion, or political opinion.

Failure to attend the hearing at the time and place designated hereon may result in your arrest and detention by the Immigration and Naturalization Service without further notice, or in a determination being made by the special inquiry officer in your absence.

REQUEST FOR PROMPT HEARING

To expedite determination of my case, I request an immediate hearing, and waive any right I may have to more extended notice.

_____
(signature of respondent)

Before:_____

_____
(signature and title of witnessing officer)   (date)

CERTIFICATE OF SERVICE

This order and notice were served by me on _March 7 1972_ in the following manner:
(date)

by personal service(_ENGLISH_)language. _a copy of OSC was personally served_
upon Subject att'y, Leon Wildes, 515 Madison and IJC and aujt. copy of OSC was
served on Miss Sarah Segal at Subject' att'y _____
105 Bank St NYC.   (signature and title of employee or officer)

Interpreter _____

CO 703.1080

Dear Mr. Terry:

Reference is made to your letter of April 11, 1972 with enclosure from Mrs. J. R. Heard concerning Mr. John Lennon.

Mr. Lennon is ineligible for a visa and admission into the United States because of a conviction of possessing marijuana. An alien convicted of such an offense may not be admitted for permanent residence. However, his entry may be authorized under a special provision of law for a temporary visit.

Mr. Lennon's present visit to the United States was authorized under this special provision of law for business purposes and to attend a custody hearing in court proceeding in connection with Mrs. Lennon's child by a previous marriage. His entry was authorized for these purposes upon the recommendation of the Department of State after all of the factors in his case had been carefully evaluated.

Since Mr. Lennon did not depart from the United States within the time authorized, he is presently the subject of deportation proceedings.

Sincerely,

Raymond F. Farrell
Commissioner

Honorable John H. Terry
House of Representatives
Washington, D. C.   20515

Enclosure

CC: A17 597 321 (NYC)

(c)   CC: W/F - John Lennon [   ])

TC:KJM:anb

333

Raymond F. Farrell memo

UNITED STATES DEPARTMENT OF JUSTICE
IMMIGRATION AND NATURALIZATION SERVICE
20 WEST BROADWAY
NEW YORK, NEW YORK 10007

April 24, 1972   A17 597 321
A19 489 154

Leon Wildes, Esq.
515 Madison Avenue
New York, New York

Re: John Lennon
Yoko Ono Lennon

Dear Mr. Wildes:

Your letter of March 15, 1972 contains the request that
deportation proceedings relating to the above-named aliens be
cancelled pursuant to the authority of 8 CFR 242.7.

The information you submitted as well as other relevant
material has been carefully reviewed. You have been aware
that it is the Government's position that the male respondent
is not eligible to adjust his status to that of a permanent
resident in view of his conviction in England. The arguments
that you have presented both in your communications and at
the deportation proceedings are not sufficiently persuasive
in view of the male respondent's conviction and other circumstances in this case. Accordingly, your request is denied.

Of course, you have already been advised of this decision
orally and this merely constitutes written confirmation of
the decision already furnished to you.

Very truly yours,

SOL MARKS
DISTRICT DIRECTOR
NEW YORK DISTRICT

Denial of previous motions

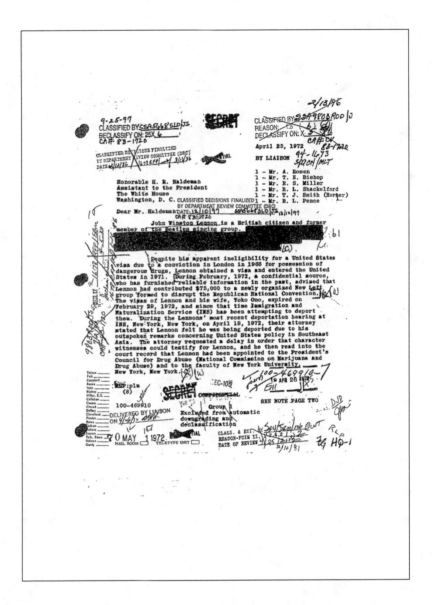

A typical FBI report to the White House

Honorable H. R. Haldeman

    A second confidential source, who has furnished reliable information in the past, advised that Lennon continues to be a heavy user of narcotics. On April 21, 1972, a third confidential source in a position to furnish reliable information advised that there was no information available indicating that Lennon has been appointed to the National Commission on Marijuana and Drug Abuse. A fourth confidential source in a position to furnish reliable information advised that Lennon has been offered a teaching position at New York University for the Summer of 1972.

    This information is also being furnished to the Acting Attorney General. Pertinent information concerning Lennon is being furnished to the Department of State and INS on a regular basis.

                Sincerely yours,

NOTE:

    Classified "Confidential" since information is contained from ███████████████████. First confidential source is ███████████; second confidential source is ███████████; third confidential source is pretext inquiry by WFO with ██████████████████ National Commission on Marijuana and Drug Abuse, Washington, D. C.; and fourth confidential source is ███████████████, New York University, New York, New York.

    See memorandum R. L. Shackelford to Mr. E. S. Miller, 4/21/72, captioned "John Winston Lennon, Security Matter - New Left," and prepared by RLP:plm.

CONFIDENTIAL

- 2 -

CONFIDENTIAL

HQ-13

THE CITY OF NEW YORK
OFFICE OF THE MAYOR
NEW YORK, N.Y. 10007

April 27, 1972

Hon. Raymond F. Farrell
Commissioner
Immigration and Naturalization Service
United States Department of Justice
119 D Street
N.E., Washington, D.C. 20536

Dear Commissioner Farrell:

I am writing this letter to you on behalf of John Lennon and
Yoko Ono who are currently facing deportation proceedings inititated
by your Department.

I consider it to be very much in the public interest, from the
point of view of the citizens of New York as well as the citizens of
the Country, that artists of their distinction be granted residence
status.

They have personally told me of their love for New York City
and that they wish to make it their home. They have made me familiar
with the tragic hardship involved in their desperate effort to find
Yoko's 8 year old child, Kyoko. I believe this is the type of hardship that our Immigration laws must recognize and the removal of the
Lennons from this Country would be contrary both to the principles of
our Country as well as the humanitarian practices which should be implemented by the Department of Immigration.

The only question which is raised against these people is that
they do speak out with strong and critical voices on major issues of
the day. If this is the motive underlying the unusual and harsh action
taken by the Immigration and Naturalization Service, then it is an attempt to silence Constitutionally protected 1st Amendment rights of
free speech and association and a denial of the civil liberties of
these two people.

Mayor Lindsay's letter to INS Commissioner Farrell

Hon. Raymond F. Farrell   - 2 -   April 27, 1972

In light of their unique past and present contribution in the fields of music and the arts, and considering their talent to be so outstanding as to be ranked among the greatest of our time in these fields, a grave injustice is being perpetuated by the continuance of the deportation proceeding.

Very truly yours,

John V. Lindsay
M A Y O R

cc: Attorney General Richard G. Kleindienst
     Commissioner Sol Marks
     Senator Jacob Javits
     Senator James Buckley

FROM: Superviser, Intelligence Division, Unit 2.

TO: Regional Director, Group 8.
SUBJECT: THE SUPERVISION OF THE ACTIVITIES OF BOTH JOHN AND YOKO LENNON.

It has come to the futher attention of this office that John Ono Lennon, formely of the Beattles and Yoko Ono Lennon, wife of John Lennon, have intentions of remaining in this country and seeking permanent residence therein, as set forth in a previous communication this has been judged to be inadvisable and it was recommended that all applications are to be denied.

Their relationships with one (6521) Jerry Rubin , and one John Sinclair (4536), also their many committments which are judged to be highly political and unfavorable to the present administration. This was set forth to your office in a previous report. Because of this and their contriversal behaviour, they are to be judged as both undesirable and dangerous aliens.

Because of the delicate and explosive nature of this matter the whole affair has been handed over to the Immigration and Naturilization Service, to handle. Your office is to maintain a constant servaillence of their residence and a periodic report is to be sent this office. All cooperation is to given to the INS and all reports are to be digested by this office.

EXHIBIT D

Unidentified report about the activities of John and Yoko implying they were under surveillance

IMMIGRATION AND NATURALIZATION SERVICE

```
------------------------------------X
                                    X
In the Matter of :                  X
                                    X
JOHN WINSTON ONO LENNON             X File No. A17 595 321
                                    X
------------------------------------X
```

RIDER TO NOTICE OF APPEAL TO THE BOARD OF
IMMIGRATION APPEALS

The decision should be reversed because:

Deportation proceedings were improperly and discriminatorily
instituted and should have been terminated; their institution
and continuance were an abuse of administrative discretion;
maintenance of deportation proceedings which prevent complian
with U.S. Court orders is improper.

As to the sole ground for deportability sustained by the Immigration Judge, the government failed to prove that the disput(
allegations of fact were true by clear, unequivocal and convincing evidence.

The Immigration Judge committed error and denied Respondent due
process in refusing to terminate the proceedings, in refusing
to permit Respondent to depose a knowledgeable representative
of the Immigration Service, in refusing to grant adequate time
for submission of rebuttal briefs, and in refusing to defer his
decision to await the outcome of proceedings in England relating
to the Respondent.

Respondent's application for adjustment of status should not
have been denied and he should not have been held excludable
under Section 212(a)(23) of the Immigration and Nationality Act
as his conviction is not included in Section 212 (a)(23); the
Immigration and Nationality Act contains no definition of the
term "marijuana" and since deportation visits great hardship
upon an alien, the language used by Congress should be strictly
construed and any doubt as to its meaning resolved in favor of
the alien; the statute under which Respondent was convicted
permitted a conviction to be entered without proof of "mens rea"
and punished a type of possession not contemplated by Section
212 (a)(23) of the Immigration and Nationality Act; only convictions for possessing marijuana under certain circumstances
which would enable the accused to traffic in the forbidden
substance are included in Section 212 (a)(23); the use of the
British conviction as a bar to residency would deny Respondent
due process; the legislative history of Section 212(a)(23)
confirms that Respondent's conviction is not therein included.

Respondent's conviction should have been considered a petty
offense under Section 212(a)(9) and his application for permanent residence should therefore have been granted

Notice of appeal of the deportation order to the BIA
(pages 269–270)

-2-

Section 212(a)(23) of the Immigration and Nationality Act
is unconstitutional insofar as it relates to the "illicit
possession of marijuana"; its application to the Respondent
effectively denies him due process of law and the equal
protection of the law and violates the right to privacy.

In view of the novelty of the factual and legal issues and
the complexity of the proceedings as well as of the decision
rendered herein, Respondent respectfully requests that he
be granted until October 2, 1973 to file his brief in support
of this appeal.

Respectfully submitted,

LEON WILDES, ESQ.
Attorney for Respondent,
JOHN WINSTON ONO LENNON
515 Madison Avenue
New York, New York 10022

UNITED STATES DEPARTMENT OF JUSTICE
IMMIGRATION AND NATURALIZATION SERVICE
WASHINGTON, D.C. 20536

OFFICE OF THE COMMISSIONER

PLEASE ADDRESS REPLY TO

JAN 1 0 1975

AND REFER TO THIS FILE NO.

CO 243.129-C

(b)(6)

I have your letter of November 23, 1974, regarding the deportation matter of John Lennon.

In Fiscal Year 1974, this Service deported 18,824 aliens to all parts of the world, while another 718,740 were required to depart without the issuance of deportation orders. Admittedly, few, if any, of these aliens were as well known as Mr. Lennon. However, I think you will agree, from the number of illegal aliens expelled, as indicated above, that this Service has little time or inclination to single out any alien, be he John Lennon or plain John Smith, for arbitrary treatment as alleged in your letter.

Thank you for your interest in this matter.

Sincerely,

James F. Greene

James F. Greene
Deputy Commissioner

Deputy Commissioner Greene's letter regarding
the deportation of John Lennon

United States Department of Justice

ADDRESS REPLY TO
"UNITED STATES ATTORNEY"
AND REFER TO
INITIALS AND NUMBER

PJC:ets

UNITED STATES ATTORNEY
SOUTHERN DISTRICT OF NEW YORK
UNITED STATES COURTHOUSE
FOLEY SQUARE
NEW YORK, N. Y. 10007

BY HAND   May 27, 1975

Hon. Richard Owen
U.S. District Court Judge
Customs Court Building
One Federal Plaza
New York, New York 10007

                    Re: John Lennon v. United States, et al.
                              73 Civ. 4543

Dear Judge Owen:

     At my suggestion, INS, without conceding that its previous
action was incorrect or irregular, has determined to undertake
a review of the question of possible non-priority status for
the plaintiff in the above-captioned action. Initial review
and recommendation will be made by a District Office official,
an intermediate recommendation will be made by a Regional
Office official, and final review and determination will be
made by the Central Office Non-Priority Committee. None of the
participants in the review will have had a previous connection
with the determination to institute and prosecute the deportation
case. I will notify the Court and plaintiff's attorney of the
outcome of the review, which will be commenced immediately.

     Since plaintiff's Service file may not be current with
respect to facts relevant to the non-priority status review, the
plaintiff may be requested to furnish information. We trust that
Mr. Lennon and his attorney will cooperate in any such request.
His attorney has been furnished a copy of this letter.

                              Sincerely,

                              PAUL J. CURRAN
                              United States Attorney

CC: Leon Wildes, Esq.

     Maurice F. Kiley
     District Director
     Immigration & Naturalization Service

US Attorney Paul Curran memo

June 12, 1975

REQUEST FOR INFORMATION UNDER
THE FREEDOM OF INFORMATION ACT

Senator James O. Eastland
Chairman,
Subcommittee on Internal Security
Committee on the Judiciary
United States Senate
Washington, D.C.

Re: Mr. John Lennon

Dear Sir:

I represent the above named, a noted musician, in legal
proceedings before the United States Department of Justice
arising out of the attempt to effect his deportation from
the United States in the early part of 1992.

It now appears that the deportation proceedings brought
against my client were not based on a purported violation
of the immigration law, but were founded upon political
reasons contained in a secret memorandum prepared by the
staff of your Subcommittee transmitted by him to then Attorney
General John Mitchell, and promptly communicated to the
Commissioner of the Immigration and Naturalization Service
by Mr. Mitchell's deputy, Richard Kliendienst. Senator
Thurmond likewise sent a copy of the memorandum to the
White House. Copies of Senator Thurmond's letter and
memoranda from your file are attached.

Accordingly, and contrary to the assertion of one Jay
Sourwine, Esq., of your staff, it clearly appears that your
Subcommittee maintained a file on my client, as originally
confirmed to the Undersigned by the office of Senator
James Buckley of New York. I respectfully request that I be

..../.

Memo from Leon Wildes to Senator James O. Eastland
(pages 273–274)

Senator Eastland contd...   page two
                                             June 12, 1975

furnished with a copy of my client's file, and would be
pleased to cover the cost of photostating involved. Since
it now appears that the data which formed the basis for
the above-mentioned memoranda was derived from investigatory
sources within the executive department, you are advised
to consider this request under the provisions of the Freedom
of Information Act, 5 U.S.C. 552 et seq., as amended.

I respectfully request that the copy of my client's file
be furnished within ten (10) days of the date of this letter.
In the alternative, I shall consider this request as being
a sufficient basis for having exhausted administrative
remedies under the afore-mentioned statute, and seek
appropriate judicial relief.

Very truly yours,

LEON WILDES

LW:jh
Encls:
Certified mail: Return receipt requested

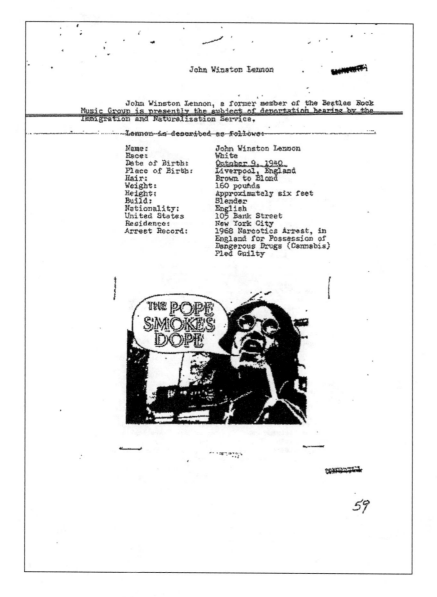

Erroneous photo (not of John Lennon) sent to Miami police
authorities by the FBI to help identify Lennon, should he appear there

LEON WILDES
ATTORNEY AT LAW
515 Madison Avenue
New York, N.Y. 10022

PLAZA 3-3468

CABLE ADDRESS
"LEONWILDES," N. Y.

August 26, 1975

Joe D. Howerton, Deputy
District Director
Immigration and Naturalization Service
20 West Broadway
New York, N.Y. 10007

Re: LENNON, John Winston Ono
A17 597 321

Dear Mr. Howerton:

I am pleased to enclose herewith the affidavit of my client,
Mr. John Lennon, filed in response to the letter of the
District Director dated July 25, 1975, in support of
our request for the granting of non-priority status in
this case. Because of Mrs. Lennon's medical condition
and the necessity of obtaining statements from the
Lennons' accountant and Mrs. Lennon's obstetrician and
management consultant, the affidavit could not be submitted earlier. It is hoped, nevertheless, that a
determination as to non-priority status can be reached
prior to the pre-trial conference scheduled to take place
before Judge Richard Owen of the United States District
Court on September 4, 1975.

The affidavit sets forth in response to each numbered
question, the response of my client, and further sets
forth the humanitarian factors which, we submit, establish
clearly that adverse action on this application would be
unconscionable. As you know, the relevant Operations
Instruction, Section 103.1 (a) (1) provides that the
District Director "shall recommend consideration for
non-priority" ......"in every case where ...... adverse
action would be unconscionable because of the existence
of appealing humanitarian factors".

.../.

1776

Memo from Leon Wildes to Joe D. Howerton,
Deputy District Director, INS
(pages 276–279)

John Lennon
page two

Our litigation in <u>Lennon versus Richardson</u> et al. has
permitted us to review first hand all of the approved
non-priority cases in existence. This information,
to our best knowledge, has never been previously
available to the public or the Bar. My office has
analyzed the 1843 cases in which non-priority status
has been granted by the Immigration and Naturalization
Service. My analysis of these cases convinces me that
non-priority status should be granted in this case if
the humanitarian policies of the non-priority cases are
to be carried out.

Before proceeding to an analysis of the cases and an
analysis as to why it is submitted that the standard
established in these cases requires the granting of
non-priority status to Mr. Lennon, I would first review
the history of the Lennon case insofar as non-priority
status is concerned. Former District Director Sol Marks,
who originally considered the case, testified in pre-trial
proceedings that he never considered the question of whether
Mr. Lennon ought to have been granted non-priority status.
He testified that there would have been no need to grant
non-priority status early in the case because the Lennons
were seeking only additional time to continue the search
for Mrs. Lennon's child, Kyoko, and that he personally
would have granted such extensions of time were it not for
instructions which he received from Washington ordering
him not to do so. In answer to a question as to whether he
would have recommended non-priority status if Mrs. Lennon
were granted residence, he answered, without equivocation,
that he certainly would have done so.

> "Q: If thereafter Mrs. Lennon had been found
>   eligible to remain in the United States,
>   as she was, would that have been a case
>   for voluntary departure?
>
> A: It would have altered the circumstances.
>   If we then had a legally resident alien
>   and a citizen child, and Mr. Lennon whether

.../.

1777

John Lennon
page three

he was a distinguished person
or not, I certainly would have
submitted for non-priority
consideration." (Transcript of
deposition of Sol Marks, pages 68-69)

District Director Kiley, however, at a time when all of
the files in the Lennon case were with the United
States attorney and presumably not available for his
thorough review, in answer to a previous inquiry made
by my office, indicated that he would not recommend
for non-priority status in this case. It is unknown
what considerations led him to this conclusion, as he
did not to my knowledge have the file available at
the time, nor did he call upon Mr. Lennon to submit
oral or written evidence as to his qualifications
for such status. This is, to my knowledge, the first
time that the question is actually being considered
upon a full record. Mr. Marks, it will be noted, was
testifying based upon some 35 years experience with the
Immigration and Naturalization Service, and based upon
what he would have presumably done then had he remained
District Director.

An analysis of all of the non-priority cases follows.
Of the 1843 cases granted such status, 138 involved
aliens with previous drug convictions ranging from
simple possession of marijuana, the lightest offence,
to heavy trafficking in heroin and cocaine, the more
serious offences. Many involve multiple offenders.

Although there are many cases with highly individualized
circumstances, there are several discernable categories
with drug convictions who are characteristically placed
in non-priority status. Elderly aliens, particularly those
who have been in the United States for a long time and/or
would be separated from U.S. citizen or permanent resident
families, constitute one such category. Similarly treated
are the young, the mentally deficient, the ill or economically
dependent. The major consideration, common to all these
categories, is the hardship caused by the separation of the
family unit.

.../.

1778

John Lennon
page four

Although the cases usually contain factors beyond the
separation of a family unit, there are some cases in
which the separation appears to be the only humanitarian
factor involved. Case 9-8, a copy of which is attached,
is the case of a young man who was recommended for non-
priority status because expulsion "would separate subject
from his LPF wife and USC child. It would be a hardship
on all of them to be separated as they are a well-adjusted
family and devoted to each other.". The alien was
convicted of transporting marijuana when he was 24 years
old; Lennon was convicted of possessing marijuana when
he was 28 years old. Not unlike Lennon, the alien was
reported to be "a person of high calibre in spite of his
conviction for transporting marijuana. He is respected
by people that know him and his employers hold him in
high regard. He is a good husband and a good father.".
No other humanitarian factors appear in the record of this
case. It appears to be a case with fewer equities than
Lennon's and a conviction of equal seriousness.

On the other hand, non-priority status was granted in the
attached narcotics cases where the aliens were also
convicted of other offenses which were much more serious,
e.g. murder (case 24-14), where an alien was described as
"the largest supplier of marijuana and narcotics in the ....
area" and an admitted heroin addict "using approximately
18 grams of heroin a day" (case 9-9) convicted of selling
a nd possession of cocaine (case 5-19); and in case 12-3
where an alien was convicted of auto theft, contributing to
the deliquency of a minor, vagrancy (pimp), rape, burglary
second decree, disorderly conduct, robbery, suspected robbery,
narcotics and other offenses. This case is not only
significant because   non-priority status was granted to
a man with a long criminal record, but also because the
reason stated for granting such status applies in the
instant case: "Non-priority is considered in order to
avoid separation of the family. While it is not evident
that subject's wife and children are dependent upon him for
support, it appears that in the event of his deportation a
hardship would result to them, particularly the children
who are of tender years.".

.../.

1779

279

H 10022   CONGRESSIONAL RECORD — HOUSE   *October 9, 1975*

CONGRATULATIONS TO BOTH JOHN LENNON AND HIS ATTORNEY, LEON WILDES

(Mr. KOCH asked and was given permission to extend his remarks at this point in the RECORD and to include extraneous matter.)

Mr. KOCH. Mr. Speaker, the U.S. Court of Appeals for the Second Circuit issued a decision on Tuesday, October 7, barring the U.S. Immigration and Naturalization Service from deporting John Lennon for a 1968 conviction in Britain for the possession of marihuana found in his London apartment.

The court decision was based primarily on two reasons: First, that British law does not require a person to have "guilty" knowledge that marihuana is in his possession, and second, that John Lennon had been singled out and selectively prosecuted as evidenced by the discovery of certain documents and letters to government officials.

Mr. Lennon's attorney, Leon Wildes, is to be greatly commended for his diligence and persistence in seeing this case through to a successful conclusion as well as for his excellent legal skills in shepherding this case through the courts.

However, it is a great source of concern to me that most aliens in this same situation but who are unable to afford such excellent legal aid as John Lennon could, are still subject to deportation because of the the way the law is written.

I have introduced legislation, since 1973—H.R. 567 in this Congress—which would amend the Immigration and Nationality Act to allow the Attorney General, at his discretion, to waive the now automatic bar to immigration of aliens who have been convicted, at any time in their lives, of marihuana possession. This bill has been introduced in the Senate by Senator ALAN CRANSTON.

The wording in the law was decided upon in 1960 when marihuana was a felony under both Federal and State law. Now, every State in the union treats possession of minimal amounts of marihuana as misdemeanors or less. In six States, it is decriminalized and a civil fine imposed.

If Jack Ford, who has very courageously admitted to using marihuana, were a citizen of Britain and convicted of possession there and sought residence here, would it not be shameful if he were arbitrarily kept out of this country?

And, additional good news. Two Lennon gave birth to a baby boy today, name: Sean Ono Lennon.

The article from the New York Times on the court decision follows:

[From the *New York Times*, Oct. 8, 1975]

DEPORTATION OF LENNON BARRED BY COURT OF APPEALS

(By Arnold H. Lubasch)

John Lennon yesterday won a major court decision here barring United States immigration officials from deporting him for a marihuana conviction in Britain.

The conviction is not sufficient reason to deport the popular British rock musician from the United States, according to the decision, written by Chief Judge Irving R. Kaufman of the United States Court of Appeals for the Second Circuit.

In the 26-page decision, Judge Kaufman issued a strong warning that "the courts will not condone selective deportation based upon secret political grounds."

This alluded to Government documents that were submitted to the court, indication that the Nixon Administration started deportation proceedings against Mr. Lennon in 1972 for fear that the former Beatle would make appearances in the United States promoting opposition to the then President.

Judge Kaufman declared in the decision that the 1968 conviction of Mr. Lennon, which resulted in a fine for possession of marihuana found in his London apartment, failed to provide sufficient grounds to exclude Mr. Lennon from the United States.

DECISION IS 2 TO 1

In the 2 to 1 decision by the Court of Appeals, written with the consent of Judge Murray I. Gurfein and a dissent by Judge William H. Mulligan, Judge Kaufman ruled that the conviction did not make Mr. Lennon an "excludable alien" because the British law did not require him to have "guilty knowledge" that there was marihuana in his apartment.

Mr. Lennon, who said that tomorrow was his 35th birthday, has been living here with his wife, Yoko Ono, who is expected to have a baby next month.

"It's a great birthday gift from America for me, Yoko and the baby," Mr. Lennon said of the court decision.

Last month, the Immigration and Naturalization Service, citing Mrs. Lennon's pregnancy as "humanitarian grounds," said that it was temporarily suspending its efforts to deport Mr. Lennon, but that the deportation case would remain pending.

According to the Government documents, which Mr. Lennon's lawyer, Leon Wildes, obtained from the Government under court orders, Senator Strom Thurmond, Republican of South Carolina, wrote a "personal and confidential" letter to the then Attorney General, John N. Mitchell, on Feb. 4, 1972, suggesting that action against Mr. Lennon could avoid "many headaches."

Attached to the Thurmond letter was a memorandum from the files of the Senate Internal Security Subcommittee asserting that "a commune group" was preparing to go to California to disrupt the 1972 Republican National Convention and that "a confidential source has learned that the activities of this group are being financed by John Lennon."

A second memo from the same files contended that "radical New Left leaders" planned to use Mr. Lennon "as a drawing card to promote the success of rock festivals" to obtain funds for a "dump Nixon" program.

"If Lennon's visa is terminated," the memo added, "it would be a strategy counter-measure."

A subsequent memo from the Deputy Attorney General Richard G. Kleindienst to Raymond P. Farrell, then Immigration Commissioner, turned over the Thurmond letter and the memo that had accompanied it to the Immigration Service on Feb. 14, 1972.

Mr. Kleindienst asked in his memo to Mr. Farrell if there was "any basis" to bar Mr. Lennon from the United States.

Then, Sol Marks, the Immigration Service's New York district director, noted in a memo for his files on March 2, 1972, that an Immigration official in Washington had informed him by telephone to begin the deportation proceedings against Mr. Lennon.

Citing these documents, Mr. Lennon's lawyer, told the Court of Appeals that "there is substantial reason to believe that official governmental action was based principally on a desire to silence political opposition squarely protected by the First Amendment."

In his ruling yesterday, Judge Kaufman said that the decision to bar Mr. Lennon's deportation was based on the court's interpretation of the immigration law regarding foreign convictions, but added "a brief word on Lennon's contention that he was singled out for deportation because of his political activities and beliefs."

"We do not take his claim lightly," Judge Kaufman said, adding his warning against deportation for political reasons.

"If, in our 200 years of independence, our judge said, "we have in some measure realized our ideals, it is in large part because we have always found a place for those committed to the spirit of liberty and willing to help implement it.

"Lennon's four-year battle to remain in our country is testimony to his faith in that American dream."

Ed Koch's congratulations to Leon Wildes for his
successful representation of John Lennon

How a former Beatle helped shape immigration policy

By MICHAEL WILDES

FORMER BEATLE John Lennon left us a beautiful legacy of extraordinary music. He also left us an immigration legacy that, while less well known, could have an equally profound effect upon life in the United States as it relates to immigrants.

The recent steps announced by President Obama to expand the Deferred Action for Childhood Arrivals program and now to offer deferred action to certain parents of U.S. and permanent residents have their roots in the John Lennon case. We can visualize a smiling Lennon because it was the successful litigation and outcome in this case that enabled the government to accomplish this feat.

How did he accomplish this?

John Lennon and Yoko Ono were placed in deportation proceedings precipitously in 1972 when their request for an extension of their visitors' stay was summarily denied. The reason for instituting deportation was not because they had broken any American law, but simply because then-President Richard Nixon felt that the presence in the United States could adversely affect his chances for reelection.

Throughout the deportation proceedings, which lasted almost five years, from 1972 to 1976, immigration officials publically said they were treating the Lennons no differently than any other undocumented person and that the Immigration and Naturalization Service had no option other than to deport every illegal alien. Thousands of letters sent to the INS also received written responses to that effect.

Nothing was further from the truth. My father and I, who are both immigra-

tion lawyers, had learned of a number of completely deportable aliens who remained in the United States, and we set out to prove that the government had full discretion and authority to withhold deportation in appropriate cases.

The immigration judge refused to allow the INS staff familiar with such cases to be questioned, so a lawsuit was filed under the Freedom of Information Act to secure the data. In response to the lawsuit, we were furnished with 1,843 case files describing persons who, though fully deportable, had been permitted to remain indefinitely for one reason or another.

Lennon asked that we study the cases and publicize the findings, so that others who could not afford costly litigation might also benefit. We did so in heavily footnoted law review articles in which we analyzed the cases that had been granted "non-priority" status and the individuals who were allowed to remain. The INS gradually began to focus its energy on its most serious cases and, through its prosecutorial discretion, deferred action in meritorious cases similar to

those cited in his articles.

Our efforts, with Lennon's encouragement, have since benefited thousands of deportable non-citizens whose cases had similar humanitarian aspects. Lennon himself benefited from the program.

The U.S. attorney for the Southern District of New York suggested to the federal judge in Lennon's case that the INS would conduct a review of the case utilizing personnel who had not previously been assigned to it.

My dad, Leon, presented Lennon's application to a new official appointed to conduct consideration of Lennon's case, which resulted in its approval, and Lennon was actually granted "non-priority" status (now referred to as "deferred action"). Shortly thereafter, the U.S. Court of Appeals overturned Lennon's deportation order, and he was granted lawful permanent residence status on July 27, 1976.

As a result, the Department of Homeland Security, which replaced the INS, makes use of its prosecutorial discretion today to consider deferred-action cases. It recognizes that like all law enforcement agencies, it has finite resources and it is not possible to investigate and prosecute every immigration violation.

In its efforts to use its limited resources wisely, it is able to benefit deserving individuals. Lennon's contribution to the development of this program of prosecutorial discretion should be recognized as a legacy of immense value that he bequeathed to his adopted homeland.

Michael Wildes is managing partner with Wildes & Weinberg PC, New York City, and a former mayor of Englewood.

John Lennon and the author's father, Leon Wildes.

Index

Italic page references indicate reproductions of documents.